architectura + natura

LANDSCAPE

=LANDSCAPE

editor
Dirk Sijmons

Architectura + Natura 2002

CONTENTS

Holland revisited — 7

The programme guide — 11

An Amsterdam delicacy — 23

The Return of the Water Management Map — 29

The Skill and the Art of the Engineer — 43

Worked out and done with? — 55

New adventures ahead — 87

Green Heart? Green Metropolis! — 99

Blue surprise — 109

Suburbia — 117

Plans — 128

Rotterdam, holiday zone — 147

Designing with landscape antecedents — 155

Brabant: a possible continuation — 163

The Netherlands – a Kunstwerk once again! — 183

Literature — *215*

Illustration acknowledgments — *221*

List of Projects — *228*

HOLLAND REVISITED

The best place to visit Holland is Japan. Holland Village, in the outskirts of Nagasaki is a condensed scaled down version of the real thing. Or maybe it is the other way round and Holland Village in Japan is actually the original which makes its European counterpart nothing more than an oversized, inflated and (quite literally) watered down version lacking the purity and essence of its prototype. One way or the other and regardless scale, the vision of Holland as Theme-Park is irresistible. Could besides tulips, cheese, ecstasy and Big Brother the country as a whole become a marketable export product? The latest addition to Nagasaki Holland Village, called "Huis Ten Bosch", is an Eco-City with round the clock computer controlled energy conservation and waste recycling system. The town is with the help of Dutch engineers is built on land reclaimed from the sea complete with dykes and six km lengths of canals. Similar to Amsterdam in the old days its canals are flushed daily by using locks in combination with tidal range. In between replica's (or are they the originals?) of the Utrecht Dom tower, the Dutch royal family's residence and a bustling cheese market Japanese actually live in this virtual Dutch town with house prices ranging between one and five million pounds sterling.

Holland © as a product was recently re-branded by its policy makers and marketing strategists under the slogan "Polder-Model". The polder-model is based on a consensus policy of a mixture of Calvinistic constraint and free market frivolity. The origin of the "Polder-Model" can be traced to folk hero Hans Brinkers; who during a one night stand held first his finger and later his whole arm in a hole in the dike to stop the water that threatened to flood the country. The Dutch attitude towards consensus and tolerance is often attributed to such continuous fight against water, which after all demanded, and still demands, a unified front. The historian Simon Schama refers to "a communal identity retrieved from the primal flood and made watertight in conditions of peril" and points out that the period between 1550 and 1650 when the political identity of an independent Netherlands nation was being established coincided with a time of dramatic alteration of the Dutch landscape. This period, often referred to as the Golden Age, is now surpassed by the Second Age of economic boom.

Holland Village

The notion of the actual creation of land is the essence of Dutch landscape architecture. Whilst in the Anglo Saxon world landscape is first and foremost a visual representation and a mental construct wrapped into a wet blanket of subjectivity, for the Dutch landscape is about the physical and rational manipulation of an objectified reality. The Dutch landscape is an efficient live-work unit while the British landscape represents the ultimate escape capsule. No doubt this explains why British landscape architects can design gardens and cannot design landscapes while exactly the opposite holds true for their Dutch colleagues.

In recent years the Dutch landscape has become more extreme in contrast and juxtaposition between urban and nature development. Agriculture is on its retreat and replaced by either housing estates or nature reserves (or should we say housing reserves and nature estates?). The authors of the essays in this book have been instrumental in the debate and design of the reorganising of the Dutch landscape. Their greatest achievement is to provoke a U-turn in the Dutch attitude towards land reclamation by asking the simple but sublime question: what would happen if Hans Brinkers does no longer hold his finger in the dyke? After generation of reclaiming land from the sea and controlling natural processes into watertight compartments H+N+S landscape architects have been instrumental in the idea of flooding large trunks of the Dutch landscape. The work of H+N+S landscape Architects is of such exemplary importance because the practice operates on the cutting edge between the development of landscape theory and practice. Ideas and concepts developed by H+N+S such as "Framework Planning" based on a simultaneous differentiation in space and time of dynamic change and landscape continuity to allow economic flexibility and ecological sustainability, have had major influence on Dutch government policy regarding national and regional planning. The quality of H+N+S Landscape Architects is that the office seamlessly operates in between scales; linking detail design to regional strategy in an unprecedented manner.

Let's pray Holland will never be finished. Imagine the exodus of planners, policy makers, landscape architects, engineers & ecologists colonising all the far corners of the world cloning their beloved Holland Villages: New Amsterdam, New Almere, New Nieuw Vennep……

I suddenly got it; H+N+S stands for History Never Stops.

Eelco Hooftman   Edinburgh, August 2000

The Borssele polder

=LANDSCAPE

THE PROGRAMME GUIDE

Once outside the built-up area, a lot of people seem to imagine themselves in the countryside. This misunderstanding cannot simply be dismissed as proof of how far the modern city-dweller has become alienated from the surrounding agrarian land. There is more. It is even more astonishing in a country whose landscape is, down to the smallest detail, so thoroughly artificial. Foreigners see it immediately. The Portuguese tourist who, in the Vrij Nederland newspaper, recently described his stay as 'a voyage through a painting by Mondriaan' was clearly not a victim of the confusion of landscape and nature. So is this confusion an expression of the longing for 'nature' felt by a largely urban population? Or have we been brought up for so long to speak the words 'nature' and 'landscape' in a single breath that the one has become interchangeable with the other? Or perhaps the depiction of the relationship between man and nature, in the form landscape architects have given it over the centuries when laying out country estates, has lost so much of its expressiveness that these landscapes are now seen as 'real nature'? Whatever the answer is, it appears that an essential element has been lost in society in the connection between citizen and landscape. If we wish to carry on a good public debate on the landscape we have to learn once again to 'read' it as an expression of culture. 'Lire, c'est vivre plus' also applies to landscapes. Reading more will turn out to be exceptionally profitable: it will enable society to rediscover the pleasure of the manipulability of topography.[1]

Melancholy and motoring organisations

Almost twice as many people are members of nature organisations as of the Wegenwacht [motoring organisation]. Interest in the landscape is also increasing in the wake of this mass involvement in nature and environment. It is focused mainly on cultural history. The friendly annexation of the topic of 'landscape' by the environmental movement means that discussion about it assumes a rather digital character and gets stuck between building and preservation. You either keep your landscape or you impair it. There does not seem to be a middle way. The intellectual escape route from this dichotomy is melancholy. The startling success of Geert Mak's book *'Hoe God verdween uit Jorwerd'* [How God Vanished from Jorwerd] on the loss of rural society, proved that it was touching a nerve. A similar story can be told about the rapidly evaporating images of the historical man-made landscapes once so full of character. But melancholy is a fairly unproductive emotion when it comes to reflecting on the landscape. The natural and social processes that bring about changes in the landscape cannot be halted.

At the same time, melancholy is an understandable reaction. The colour photos on the cover of this book were taken in 1972. A lot has changed in the intervening 25 years. What has happened to the landscape in Bert Haanstra's 'Fanfare'? A great many valuable landscapes have been messed up, changed unrecognisably or mutilated in the name of progress. And the landscape is still being snapped up from under our noses by projects that look as if they have been dropped from aeroplanes, or being unfeelingly buried under a layer of levelling sand.

But in addition to this there is the misplaced feeling of melancholy in city-dwellers who prefer to see their dynamic existence played out against an unchanging landscape setting, and have not the slightest idea of the landscape's function as a production area. It is commonplace in the media to approach changes in the countryside from a melancholic angle and of course to make critical sounds about the latest wretched plans of the government, farmers' organisations or project developers. It has for a long time been progressive to be conservative regarding environmental changes. Everyone seems to derive rights from the existing situation and wants to pass on his memories unimpaired: this is the landscape seen as an everlasting lieu-de-memoire. From this point of view, the process of change can only be described in terms of 'damage', 'destruction' and 'decline'.

And yet this concern and the consequent conservancy approach is too narrow (and too confining) a basis for a discussion of the future. Shutting oneself up in a world of melancholy amounts, de facto, to surrendering to project developers out for quick profit, policy officials with frighteningly similar views, and the initiators of other schemes, all equipped with blinkers. The result of this sort of distanced attitude is a self-fulfilling prophesy, with the fact that one was right being repeatedly confirmed by one disastrous project after the other, and by a degenerating landscape.

So the point is to find a third way between the protection of towns, villages and landscapes based on a glamorisation of history and, on the other hand, an undifferentiated, directionless urge for creation and renewal. This is only possible by means of a restoration of confidence in one's own abilities. Landscape architecture can transcend this dichotomy by consciously taking up a position, by opting for cultural commitment and, most of all, by making appealing plans. Each task presents us with a two-part challenge: to add a worthwhile new layer to our historically stratified landscape and, in the process of change, to give substance, in a meaningful way, to the link with the past.[2] Now that the enormously expanded interest in architecture is also spreading to urban design, landscape architecture and planning, we are probably past the nadir of the crisis in environmental identity. There are all manner of signs that indicate that the third way is also starting to make headway in politics. A good barometer is provided by the interest environmental planning arouses among MPs. During the reconstruction it was the sought-after portfolio, in the eighties it was a subject for backbenchers, and now there are again people, like Duivesteijn at the intervention microphone, and the minister-president admits that the feeling of 'standing at the drawing board' is one of the most pleasant sides of his job. Our socialist-liberal team occasionally blunders into overly one-dimensional infrastructural planning. However, the policy document 'De Architectuur van de Ruimte' [The Architecture of the Environment] and the high-grade teams of designers appointed to supervise the major projects make it clear that even our public administration is gradually coming round to the idea that tomorrow's cultural history has to be made today.

Landscape step by step

If we wish to be serious about revitalising our cultural landscape we must first of all see to it that the supervision of the abovementioned major projects does not become bogged down in an attempt to 'fit them into the landscape'. The use of the term 'fitting in' usually indicates administrative impotence and unassimilated social guilt and it amounts to no more than paying lip-service to the landscape. It has been decided (by a small majority) to make a certain investment (Schiphol, VINEX, Betuwelijn, and so on) but in the execution we want to see or notice as little as possible of the new acquisition. This attitude of smoothing things over as much as possible often leads to poor environmental quality and to results that lack any style even before they start. It is usually more productive to examine the possibilities these projects have, as a new element, for enriching the existing landscape, or, as in the second Maasvlakte and other large-scale plans, of creating a new landscape.[3]

If you are convinced that the landscape is formed (and therefore also changed, adulterated and degenerated) by ad hoc decisions and numerous processes operating independently of each other, you cannot expect better times from one day to the next as a result of integrated planning, vertical policy coordination or any other magical government instrument. There is only one answer. The snail strategy. To launch each separate project with deliberation, give close administrative guidance to every process of change, embed it in an open process and have it supervised with care by designers. In short, work on a step by step improvement of the situation.[4]

Never built Netherlands
The route of the southern HST appears to have been determined primarily by planning considerations (such as clustering with existing infrastructural lines). It is true that the densely populated delta region is faced with complex problems when introducing new infrastructure. But even so one inevitably has the impression that this means opportunities have been missed. A route over the Oesterdam, with a view of the Oosterschelde, via Kreekraksluizen and Hellegatsplein would have provided a spectacular entrance. The juggling with vertical curves (over the first obstacle, then under the next) shows that they shied away from the consequences of a clear intervention. The line is 'fitted in' rather than its qualities as a new autonomous element being made use of.

Map-reading

It becomes immediately clear that there is sufficient work to be done when one looks at the 'Nieuwe Kaart van Nederland' [New Map of the Netherlands]. All the democratically approved projects have now been coloured in together on a topographical background, on a gigantic map published last year. The urban projects are red and the rural green. The number of green projects is almost as large as the number of red. The red projects occupy part of the landscape, the green change it fundamentally. But even this map only provides a limited view of the radical changes in store for our landscape over the next fifty years, let's say. All the creeping processes and things that have not, or not yet been converted into projects are not included. The solutions to environmental problems, the implementation of integrated water management, the completion of an overall ecological structure, and also, perhaps most of all, profound changes in agriculture and its market [5] are not on the map. These are examples of the rapidly developing 'programme of requirements' which will have a considerable effect on the rural areas. The first reaction to the map is one of disbelief: is all that hanging over our heads? Are these things all well geared to each other? Has anyone realised what the cumulative effect of all these changes will be? Is there actually anyone in charge of it all?

Instead of losing oneself in moral considerations, one might wonder how all these projects can be carried out to the highest possible standards. A number of strategic projects may serve as a lever to exact all manner of changes. If we put our rose-tinted spectacles on we can see all these plans as programmatic fuel for the creation of new landscapes. The optimum approach to each individual project would make a solid contribution to the improvement of our landscape.

But it is not sufficient. Devoted attention to every project still does not make a landscape. The best result of this would be that we fill the 'environmental planning' house with countless pieces of designer furniture, but without cohesive decoration. There is more than the separate projects. Something also has to be said about the whole, the landscape.

Prescription?

Anyone who stands up for collectivity or the public good in these times of rampant individualisation is treading on thin ice. We are no longer discussing ideals or ideological differences. The individual project already demands the utmost of administrative elasticity and is the maximum for which a majority can be won over, if not a consensus. Environmental planning is rivalled by a dry list of ICES projects. This seems to be just about the largest grain-size of collectivity in which our society can express itself at this moment in time. All one can do is design the pieces of a fragmented society. The fashioning of individual parts of the carpet metropolis and the patchwork landscape also fits in marvellously with miscellaneous postmodern philosophers whom designers like to quote. But this conclusion is not inevitable. If the result of the analysis shows a fragmented reality one does not necessarily have to lapse into the naturalistic error, even without resources, of also upgrading this result into a design solution. In environmental planning we can succumb to the temptations of postmodernism only once. The consequences are irreversible.

The other way round, one should not push regulatory control so far that it leads to a confining rigidity. The consequences of exaggerating the ambition of manipulability have been revealed too clearly for that. The issue is to find a balance between things that simply have to be planned because they are part of the inalienably collective domain, and giving space to social and natural processes which allow themselves neither to be predicted nor planned. There is every reason not to see the 'ineradicability' of uncertainties as a limitation, but to approach it positively as a challenge inherent in social dealings.[6] 'Planning oriented towards a surprise-free future turns out, surprisingly, to yield a society without a future', as Koningsveld drily concluded in his plea for fostering planning as a social experiment. This requires a government that also treats the main and side issues differently in its regulations – a balance, or rather a symbiosis between making and growing, between determining and leaving undetermined, between formal design interventions and infills. To make it easy, let's call this mix 'bringing about' landscape. There actually is a course to be set for the direction in which we wish to bring about landscape.

Of course the question remains whether, without a shared system of standards and values, and after the proclaimed 'end of ideology', motives can still be found for such a consummately collective product as the landscape, even when it 'only' involves bringing landscape into being. The answer may well be found by not looking for unity of thinking at all, or putting energy into a quest for new values, ideologies or other philosophical sources, but - bearing in mind the guiding role played by development agreements in the genesis of the landscape - by looking for motives that produce, rather, a unity of action. The only motives still capable of this naturally have to be sought in the conditions for the existence of the inhabited mega-structure called the Netherlands. They will therefore have more to do with utility than with high ideals or transcendent goals.

Multiplex

Bringing about landscapes can already be considerably helped along by environmental planning if it swaps its egalitarian principles of colourless 'neutral consideration' for the employment of a consistent, rigid hierarchy that can order its thinking and increase its decisiveness. It is in fact nothing other than making soberly explicit the balance of power in environmental planning and the logical order of priorities: first things first.[7]

Three layers can be distinguished in this model:
1. The foundation; the most important layer of environmental planning is that of the future of our water management. Since time immemorial, and today still, the regulation of land and water remains a primary condition for the existence of our country. Decisions made at this level therefore have priority. Answers have to be formulated to the consequences of the rising sea-level, the lowering of our river water and the essential rebuilding of the water

management system in the West Netherlands. This layer is so basic that it is often mistakenly overlooked.[8]

2. The next layer is that of infrastructural planning. This includes decisions on road, rail and water infrastructure and their points of intersection; decisions with tremendous guiding influence on all subsequent social-environmental processes.

3. It is only in the third layer that the location of housing, industrial sites, agriculture, cultural amenities, etc. are dealt with. Strangely enough it is usually right here that discussion of environmental planning begins, ignoring or relativising the more determinant first two layers. This turns the logical hierarchy upside down, which is the cause of many of the acute problems of environmental planning.

This objective perception reveals the network of relationships between public and private tasks and between the various inalienably governmental tasks. What is more, it does justice to the fact that the programme in the Netherlands has since time immemorial been determined by utility.

In our landscape virtually everything has a function, has had a function, or in any case has a demonstrable historical reason behind it. The elements of the landscape are parts of the 'blue network', from the prosthesis that made it possible for Holland to survive below sea level in the delta; or else they are part of the agricultural machine which makes exceptional cultivation and enormous yields possible in the fertile delta with its outstanding flat land and mechanisms for fine hydrological adjustments; or they are relics of the defence systems that used flooding to make parts of the country inaccessible. Functionality, a certain austerity and an anonymity of form determine its atmosphere, which is still aroused by centuries of Calvinist work with sweat on the face. In short, the Netherlands is a country of usefulness and necessity. We need not be ashamed of this. It is precisely the uncompromising pursuit of this functionality, which made the ruthlessly modern Netherlands of the seventeenth century into a tourist attraction, that still provides the quality of our most important landscapes.

However, the picture is enlivened by fact that the dominant forces of usefulness and necessity are never entirely monomaniacal. Miscellaneous 'gentler' goals, wishes and aspirations, were always able to hitch a ride with them too. In this respect too we can say there is a tradition, from landscape painters, though the care of monuments, to social ideals that could be grafted onto the hard housing programme.

A second source of variety is that at every level usefulness and necessity have different forms and meanings. For example, 'necessity' is hardest and most recurrent in the first layer, in this marshy country it is in fact a condition for existence, whereas in each subsequent layer necessity becomes more transient and dependent on circumstances.

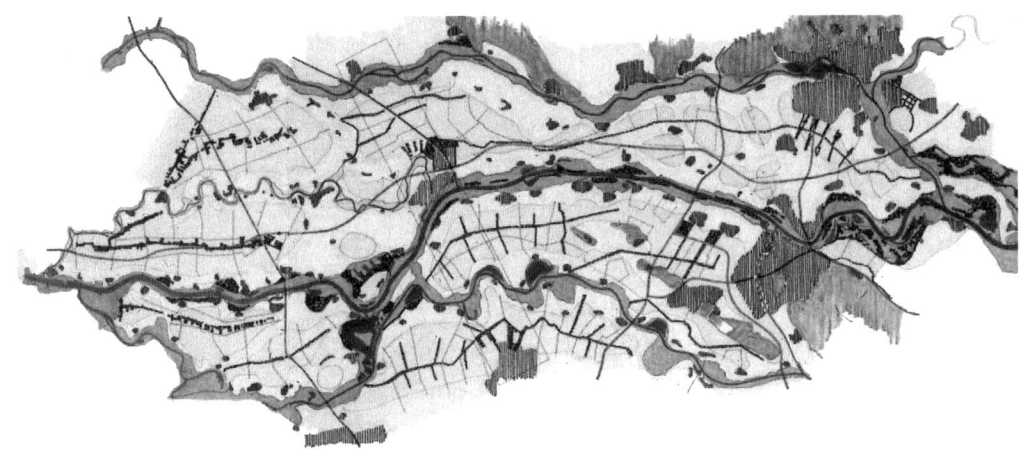

The casco concept

The 'Ooievaar' plan was the first experiment using the casco concept. The concentration of natural development in the river forelands leads to the formation of a cohesive framework of such a size that prospects of self-regulating natural processes arise and exceptional forms of recreation are made possible. The basin areas are arranged for agrarian use, where the businesses can also genuinely remain standing in the future. Flexibility is built in by the dimensions and a double water system (high and low level) by which means the farmers can regulate each plot hydrologically to suit its specific use. Natural elements inside the dykes, which are now drying out, are linked to the high water system so that a framework is formed on a smaller scale too.

Control of the third layer

It is in the third layer that the struggle for the scanty space rages. The most voracious user of space is the city. In rural areas more complex processes occur amongst the functions. The picture is formed by intensification, renovation and the repeated adaptation to the demands of new uses in agriculture and horticulture, and the consequence is an almost uninterrupted process of transformation. The parts of the landscape that need a long time to develop cannot withstand this environmental dynamic.

Nature, forestry and drinking water extraction are examples that need long to very long development times. They can be designated as 'low dynamic functions'. Trees need time to grow, moorland systems hundreds of years to develop, and pure ground water is the result of a slow percolation of rainwater through the soil, which may require thousands of years. The time factor cannot be simulated, however technically advanced we may become.

Agriculture, recreation, the construction of industrial sites, etc. are determined by market forces with a time-scale geared to economic depreciation terms. We call these 'high dynamic' functions.

In order to ensure that enduring qualities are created or preserved when a new layer in the landscape is 'brought about', it is essential to employ a number of rules, as simple as possible, that can manage the major differences between the various functions in the countryside. In the eighties the 'casco concept' for landscape planning was developed in order to tackle this tangle of problems. This approach represents a systematic decoupling of functions that frustrate each other's process dynamics. The low dynamic functions are combined and clustered in a framework. The high dynamic functions are allotted spaces that give them the freedom of action essential to them.

Long (and very long)-term security for such functions as nature and drinking water supplies[9] is found by seeking out inherently 'safe' places in the system for their framework. Good candidates for this are hydrologically isolated areas that cannot be impaired by polluted water. Apart from this, the strategic application of land engineering to layers one and two of the environmental planning edifice will yield important building blocks for the framework.

Environmental flexibility is provided in the space available for the high-dynamic functions such as agriculture. Measurement, division and water systems are instruments by which to achieve these flexible possibilities for development. Flexibility is of vital importance because, as has already been said, economic development can only be predicted to a limited extent.

City land and urban landscape

The other producer of environmental dynamics on level three is the city. The Netherlands has always been a landscape of cities. In the fifteenth century the countryside was already pinched in by small trading cities and since then has in fact been entirely within the urban sphere of influence. In the seventeenth century there was already a notable correspondence between the composition of the urban and rural populations. Nowadays, satellite photos show, south of an imaginary line from Alkmaar to Venlo, that the Netherlands consists overall of an urban domain in which the West Holland conurbation almost joins up with the granular city of the Brabant urban centres, which in its turn merges seamlessly into the Belgian conurbation of scattered building and illuminated motorways. The Ruhr area is not far away either. The delta metropolis of the

North-West European low countries is almost a reality.[10] In this urban domain agriculture develops into a knowledge and capital-intensive urban variant, and the question is what position nature can occupy[11] and what demands the future recreator will make on the countryside.[12]

North-East of this line it still gets dark at night. But new urbanisation is also going on in this relatively thinly populated part of the country. Set free by such communications media as modem and fax, countless free agents in the liberal professions and also a lot of old people are settling here. An influx of people whom we might easily call the fourth wave of suburbanisation.[13] This follows the first wave in the seventeenth century, when the canal barge brought such places as 's-Graveland and Vecht within reach of Amsterdam's merchants, the

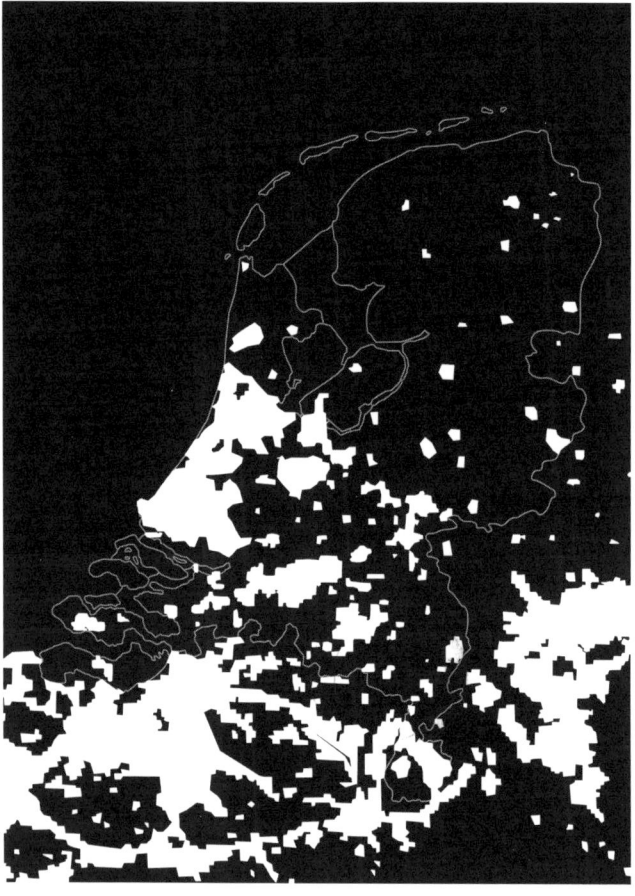

Where is it still dark at night? In a cartographic exercise, we did once try to look for the places in that dark part of the Netherlands which one might call agrarian core areas. We superimposed this light-dark map with one of the places where it is still quiet, analysed the outlines left over where the country is still without drains, checked this against the presence of dealers of John Deere tractors (the Rolls-Royce of the countryside) and the tours by the country music band Normaal, and did a concordance analysis with the presence of a surfeit of satellite dishes. However, a crossing of this subset with the distribution of season ticket holders at the Amsterdam Opera brought this illusion to an end. This map took no account whatsoever of the so-called agrarian reservations we had just discovered. The whole of the Netherlands is in any case socially and culturally urbanised.

second in the nineteenth century when the railway created the first commuter towns in the inner dune periphery and on the Utrecht hills, and the third when the car sharply increased mobility and accelerated widespread urbanisation. The fourth wave relies on minute glass-fibre cables that make people and functions footloose and fancy-free. Urban expansion in loose wrappers and the occupation of the countryside by spreading suburbanisation makes urbanisation into a landscape architecture issue too.

What = landscape?

Now we have just about made everything, even urbanisation, into a landscape architecture issue, the approach taken by this book will gradually become clear. =Landscape is intended to be a programme guide to the 21st-century landscape, in which we shall show how the most diverse programmes can contribute to a living man-made landscape. The book is composed of plans, essays, lectures and articles by H+N+S Landscape Architects (H+N+S = Landscape) over the last few years.

1. A cultural policy programme with this aim was set out in the 'Nederland weer Kunstwerk!' scenario.

2. Eric Luiten's article: 'Designing with landscape antecedents' develops this topic further.

3. A landscape design view of infrastructure and landscape is developed in the essay 'The skill and the art of engineering'.

4. This incremental approach is developed in 'Brabant, a possible continuation'.

5. 'Worked out and done with?' an essay on the relationship between Agriculture and Environmental Planning provides a look at the possible consequences for agriculture and the design commissions ensuing from it.

6. The role played by uncertainties and the acceptance of chance are dealt with in 'Into new adventures', an essay on the accountant-like dullness of types of natural goal.

7. This stratification is explained in: D.F. Sijmons, Vliegtuigstrepen in een wolkenlucht. In: F. Feddes (ed.), Oorden van onthouding, vormgeven aan de natuur in een verstedelijkend Nederland, Nai uitgevers, Rotterdam, 1998.

8. The organisational task for this basic layer is dealt with in the essay 'The return of the water management map'.

9. 'An Amsterdam delicacy' tells how drinking water extraction can produce landscapes.

10. 'Green Heart? Green Metropolis?' develops a view of the desired configurations between red and green in continuing urbanisation.

11. See also 'IJburg, vermaert voor ieders oogen' (not included in the English version).

12. An estimate of the needs for future recreation is included in 'Rotterdam holiday country'.

13. The essay 'Suburbia' deals with the task this presents.

AN AMSTERDAM DELICACY

Whoever, by way of pastime, enjoys identifying metropolises (at last a hobby for Rem Koolhaas!) can practise by studying photographs of skylines and famous buildings, or maps of main structures and locations. But for these eccentric metropolis-spotters, the surest clue to the identity of a city are the urban details of the exterior space: telephone boxes, traffic lights, post-boxes, lamp-posts and, last but not least, switch boxes and transformer kiosks.

Although nowadays some of these objects are ordered from catalogues, and there is a certain degree of internationalization, every city has its own combination, often with specially made elements which are immediately recognizable to the practised spotter. I shall resist the temptation to present a chronological and typological classification of the stunning products of Amsterdam's public design of urban details and street furniture.

But whoever should hit upon the idea of producing an identification handbook (for Woodsmen in Highly Urbanized Areas) would in the chart's main key undoubtedly, as first bifurcation, ask the question:

a. your urban detail has a clear three-dimensionality and stands, hangs or lies in or on the urban space;

b. your urban detail is seemingly two-dimensional and lies horizontally on the surface level or projects slightly above it.

We shall leave 'a' for another occasion and focus in this essay on 'b', the Class of covers of drains, of manholes, of mains shafts and of sewers'. If there is an architecture parlante, then there will be a soft whispering, and yet these modest urban details have great power of expression. They are the visible manifestation of virtually everything that has to do with the metabolism of the city: intermediaries between the upper world and the lower world.

The simple but beautifully designed cast-iron covers are ornamented with symbols, numbers and cryptic inscriptions such as 'Vecht links' and 'Duin rechts'. As a child, for some time I believed that these were medals awarded to road sweepers in recognition of their work. Most of the medals in the city had evidently been awarded to a certain W (maybe the Trespassers W from Winnie-the-Pooh?). Within the category of covers, let us focus on the family of water mains covers. My personal favourite is also the smallest of its kind: the cast-iron cover

The origin of the water can be seen on the well covers. 'Vecht' means water from the Bethune polder in the Vecht area, 'Duin' means water from the Waterleiding dunes. In the centre, the water that comes out of the drinking water pipes is a blend of the two.

measuring 12 by 12 centimetres which is embellished with a capital 'W' and marks the position of a mains-tap in the city's water mains system. A beautiful, flat cover which in busy streets has often been polished by the shoes of passing pedestrians.

Water supply at the urban level is taken for granted nowadays, but in the past, good-quality water in seaports was always a problem. Few people realize that up until relatively recently Amsterdam was situated on the coast and that at ebb-tide, Amsterdam wormers and cocklers used to take their sleighs to the mud flats near Diemerzeedijk (to the east of the city). In this saline and brackish environment, the river Amstel was of course a source of fresh water, but the latter was unsafe because of the tanneries and tar yards situated upstream. In dry periods, drinking water was shipped in. Virtually all of the canalside houses in Amsterdam were adapted to the economical use of rainwater; to this end, for example, they were equipped with water basements and glazed roof tiles. Nevertheless, this water was often undrinkable because of

Until only recently Amsterdam was on the coast. Here are two Amsterdam cockle fishers at low tide on the mud flats near the Diemer seawall, in about 1930.

bacterial contamination, and in effect this is how Dutch beer came into being. Nowadays, a glass of beer with breakfast is perhaps considered a bit unusual, but brewing beer is of course a way of processing water in order to preserve it.

When Amsterdammers leave their city's sphere of influence, they envelope themselves in an aura of metropolitan overconfidence, or are seized by a strong sense of oppression. Both emotions are due tot the strong attachment Amsterdammers feel for their city, and to their proverbial chauvinism. Newcomers to the city, who have only recently exchanged Paramaribo (Surinam) or some remote corner of the Netherlands for Amsterdam, display similar behaviour. This takes place within such a short space of time that there must be some agent producing this change of attitude. My theory, which has yet to be contradicted, is that his phenomenon has everything to do with the addictive properties of Amsterdam's drinking-water. This water is of a very high quality, delicious, and available to everyone. The city council provides it free of charge to every thirsty passer-by, via the beautiful cast-iron drinking fountains along the public highway. The distinctive taste (neutral, refreshing, yet slightly creamy and full-bodied) is due to a combination of types of water. The secret lies in mixing water from two different sources.

One quarter of this mixture is drawn form the 25 million cubic metres of water obtained annually from the Bethune polder. A large amount of seepage water rises in this small polder (situated four metres below sea level) from a deep groundwater stream which flows from the neighbouring Utrecht ridge. This water has been on its way for hundreds of years and has picked up all manner of minerals and trace elements along its subterranean course. As regards ionic composition (and thus taste) it has a pronounced lithotrophic character.

The remaining three quarters is dune water. Beneath the coastal dunes – literally floating on the deeper saline groundwater – is a large 'bubble' of fresh water. This is rainwater which has seeped down through the sand layer and is free of bacteria because of the low temperature at this great depth. This source has been used to produce Amsterdam's drinking-water since 1854. Because catchment began to exceed the annual precipitation surplus, since 1957 purified river water has been infiltrated in the dunes. The total amount of water with a more atmotrophic character thus obtained amounts to some 70 million cubic metres. If this combination had not come into being more or less by accident, we would, like the Scottish, be able to speak of a successful 'blend' of various 'malts'. The flavour is so distinctive that the really advanced metropolis-spotter would immediately be able to identify Amsterdam tap water in a blind taste test.

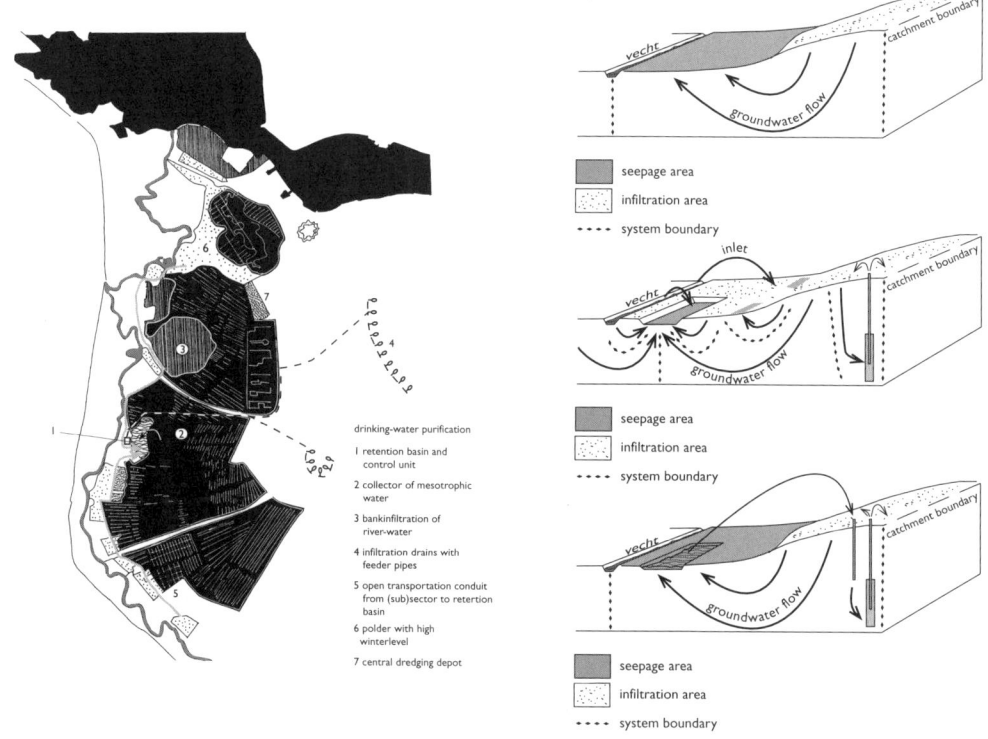

The Vecht ponds: an alliance between the extraction of drinking water, recreation and nature.

In this plan, the roles played by use, organisation and management are reversed. The manager - in this case the Amstel and Gooiland Water Purification Company - not only adopts a more service-oriented position, but also makes demands of the organisation and use. On the basis of the objectives of 'integrated water management', this plan examines the effect of the return to an appropriate hydrological balance on other functions. A strategic alliance between nature, recreation and the provision of drinking water appears to enable the landscape to change into a sustainable 'drinking water machine' with very impressive natural potential. Work is being done on seasonal retention, modifications in the use of the present extraction points on the Utrecht Ridge and the extraction of water later on the system when it has already had its beneficial effect on nature. A slight increase in the price of drinking water has enabled the Municipal Drinking Water Company in Amsterdam to purchase the land needed and the area can now be enriched with a natural recreational area of a size and allure to match the Randstad.

What measures need to be taken in order to safeguard this flow of precious liquid in the future (even if demand rises sharply), if at the same time consideration has to be given to reducing the detrimental ecological effects (drying up of sources, for example) of water catchment? In the first place, there are plans to obtain a larger proportion of Amsterdam's production in the dunes. This would involve the use of a new technique, the so-called deep-infiltration technique, whereby the river water no longer filters from ground level in the arenaceous dune floor, but is introduced in deep fall pipes at a depth of 25 metres. The advantage of this method is that the characteristic dune vegetation does not absorb nutriments which are present in large quantities in the river water.

There are also plans for the other source of water in the Utrecht ridge. Under consideration at the moment is the possibility of discontinuing groundwater catchment here. Catchment would be resumed only when the water has done its beneficial work for nature in the form of seepage. It ought to be possible to store water obtained in the wet season in the ground profile or in specially

The taste of water	
Good taste	Uden
	Hoevelaken
	Amsterdam
	Amersfoort
	Naarden
	Voorschoten
	Fertila
	Aqua Viva
	Etten-Leur
Reasonable taste	Chaudfontaine
	Ty Nant
	Spontin
	Spa Reine
Moderate taste	Evian
	Bar-le-Duc
	Barendrecht
	Mont Roucous
	Den Haag

The result of a blind test carried out by the Consumers' Association

constructed surface basins. Large tracts of the area will as a result be less suitable for agriculture, but the plus-point of this solution is that it is sustainable; sustainable in the sense that the amount of water collected does not exceed that which falls in the entire catchment basin in precipitation surplus. A requirement is that the water companies purchase land and that large parts of the Vecht lake district become nature reserves.

The cost of these plans could be covered by a rise in the price of water of approximately 30 cents per cubic metre. And the inhabitants of Amsterdam, the city of Utrecht and the region in between (Het Gooi) would have an enormous nature reserve and recreation area providing them with water for bathing, showering, washing the car, washing-up, etcetera. It means that – together with the reserve function the IJmeer and Markermeer (large lakes to the east and north-east of Amsterdam) are to fulfil for the production of drinking-water for the entire Western Netherlands – in the future, Amsterdam will be surrounded by large areas with a function for drinking-water production. And then the connection between the minuscule urban element of the water mains cover and the largest 'detail' becomes clear: the urban configuration – the location and the city form which determine whether inhabitants of the city feel confined or not.

Because of the diffuse distribution of building development and the complex interrelationships between the component cities and towns, the Amsterdam agglomeration (which forms the northern wing of the Randstad, the urban agglomeration of Western Holland) is in danger of filling up and becoming one large nondescript urbanized area. There is a pressing need therefore for a strategic link between drinking-water catchment, nature conservation and the recreational requirements of city dwellers.

The commitment to these three social concerns could result in the new and old catchment areas becoming the most important open areas in the carpet metropolis which is now unrolling. New wilderness would be created near Amsterdam, which because of their informal and public character would be 'wildernesses to lose oneself in', and which, because of their size and allure, could serve as a counterpoint to the well-regulated urban household agenda.

The anticipated sharp rise in the price of drinking water on the world market will ensure that these investments are recovered. If the price of water around the year 2030 approximates that of crude oil (as the United Nations forecasts), than that delicious Amsterdam delicacy will not only be more addictive, but also more expensive that that other speciality for which the city is famous, the soft drugs.

Dirk Sijmons (in: Maarten Kloos, ed: Amsterdam in detail, ARCAM pocket no 10, Amsterdam ARCAM, 1996)

THE RETURN OF THE WATER MANAGEMENT MAP

Poets and foreigners are sometimes astonished: how can the Netherlands possibly exist? 'It is not certain whether these regions belong to the land or the sea', wrote the Roman visitor Pliny almost two thousand years ago, and he is in essence still right. Due to centuries of human effort even the lower-lying areas also belong unmistakably to the land, and the sea, river, ground water and other waters have been forced back into controllable areas, though this organisation is never entirely secure. It has often been said that the Netherlands is artificial through and through. But it is also a gigantic water machine. Artificial Netherlands is or it is not. That depends entirely on the operation of the water machine, a machine that can never rest.

The Netherlands as a water machine

Anyone who spends every day amidst the astonishing will not be astonished every day. Anyone who lives in the Netherlands may for a long time overlook the importance of the water machine; just as the occupier of a house does not think about his foundations or the exact location of his electricity cables every day. This all changes as soon as something goes wrong with the machine, for whatever reason. At that moment the self-evident condition of existence is no longer so evident and it is time to give it deliberate consideration.

It is a cliché to say that the Netherlands is a country of water, and a cliché has to be given new sparkle every so often.

This means that the attention the Dutch people, administrators, planners, designers and everyone else has devoted to their position between land and water has undergone periodical swings throughout history. The system of water management – its principles, its design, its execution – has repeatedly been adapted. When it is working as it should, attention can be focused on something else, such as the restructuring of agriculture, expansion or densification of the cities, the exploitation or development of nature, or the construction of infrastructure. But as soon as the system becomes maladjusted, the country's intimate relationship with water is news once again. Work is then done on a new adaptation, either matter-of-factly or with pride, in panic or with deliberation. I would like to argue that there is every reason to do so even now.

Globally speaking, there are three sorts of cause for shortcomings in the water machine. First there are the more or less wilful acts of 'nature'. Disastrous floods have in the past often led to large-scale structural changes in the water system: one terrible night in 1953 gave the impulse for a mammoth project that was to take forty years to complete. Secondly, an intensification of human activity can also disrupt the water system. One can again compare this to the foundations or electricity in a house: they can take some rough treatment, but they cannot be endlessly overburdened. The third sort is vaguer and more subjective: it all works well the way it does, and it's alright the way it is, but are we still content or happy with it? Could it be better, or more beautiful? This is a question of the way we experience it, and of cultural values.

All three sorts are up for discussion at the moment. It's true that the dykes have now all been raised to Delta height, but in times to come answers will have to be found to a less explosive but in the long-term certainly no less drastic advance of the water, in the form of the rising sea level combined with sinking land. At the same time the changes in urban development, agriculture, nature conservancy and infrastructure in recent and coming decades are so great that the existing water system cannot simply absorb them. These same changes also lead to a cultural malaise against which a renewed orientation towards the water system may be a possible antidote. If 'living at the waterside' on an individual scale is very highly valued, why should the monumental life on the waterside, which is the whole of the Netherlands, not be rediscovered as a whole too?

More than sufficient reason to consider the water machine not as a self-evident basis for environmental planning and design assignments, but as an assignment in itself. More than sufficient reason to consider the water machine not just as a problem, but also as a source of inspiration when solving other problems, a source of inspiration as it in fact always has been, and not just a threat. More than enough reason to rediscover the water management map.

The rediscovery of the water management map

The existence and importance of the water management map was not discovered all at once. Among landscape planners and architects the map certainly only very gradually crept in. With hindsight, I would say the late seventies were the turning point. Until that time the policy and administration of the Netherlands was divided along party lines, it's true, but it was organised on clear lines. In rural areas the primacy of initiating change was clearly in agriculture. The postwar objective of securing the production of affordable primary foodstuffs for the country's own population remained undiminished.

Using their own set of instruments, the urban planners developed new expansions of the existing urban area at the expense of landscape, preferably not too valuable ones. And whether it was city or countryside, it was mainly topographical maps that planners and designers used as their 'underlay'. The attempt was made to base the environmental plans on the existing landscape structure, so that the new landscape would look as much as possible like the old. Water management considerations played a secondary, subordinate role in all this. In the rural areas, for example, the organisers from the Ministry of Agriculture marked out the course, after which the water managers lowered the water levels and improved the drainage of areas previously too wet.

By the end of the seventies a new set of adjustments was necessary, even for areas that had been worked not so long before. Some landscape planners now began to scent danger. How long can one continue to work on an approach in which new wants always had to be included, in the patterns of the old man-made landscapes that had developed in the course of history? What is left of

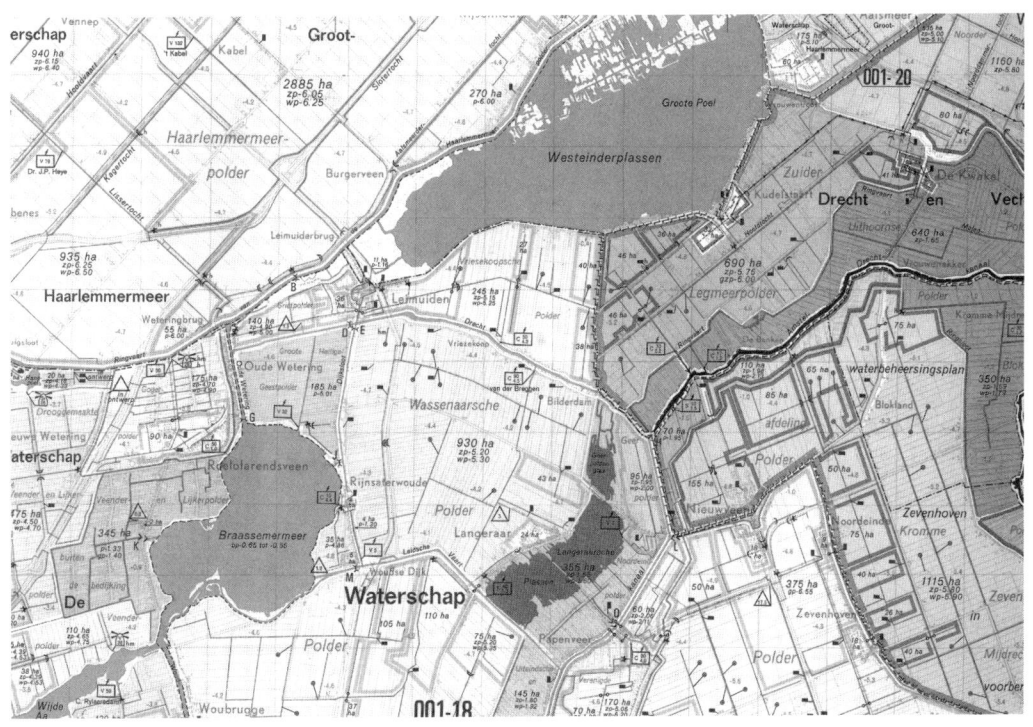

Section of the Water Management Map covering the surroundings of Westeinderplassen / Braassemermeer. The Netherlands as a water machine, composed of polders, marshes, lakes and waterways. Connection and isolation by mills, pumping stations, sluices, dams and culverts. Each unit has its own water level; low in the winter and high in the summer.

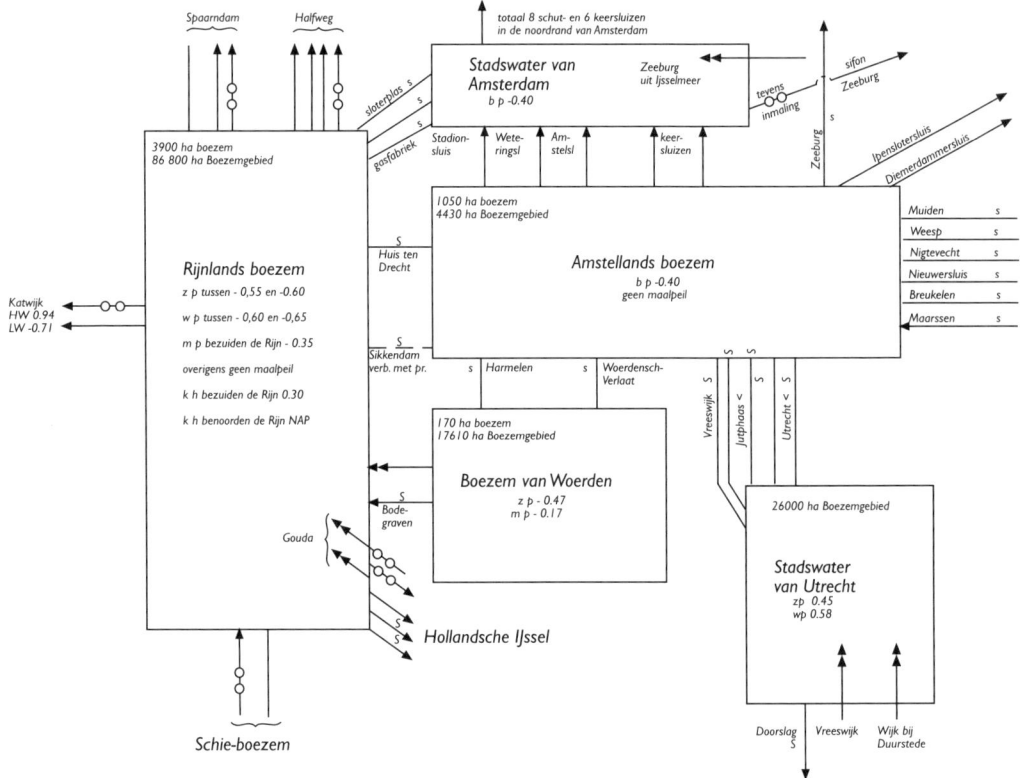

Flow-diagram of the South Holland and Utrecht water machine.

these patterns? And are topographical maps sufficient as a guide in the design process, or should they be supplemented by other instruments? To ask the question was to provide the answer, and the search began.

Anyone who digs in the Netherlands will sooner or later come across water. That was true here too. Since then the realisation has grown among landscape planners and architects that tinkering with the structure of the landscape also means tinkering with the water system. This system of surface water and ground water has been described and mapped in many ways, such as the water management map, the electronic diagram of the Netherlands water machine. To a layman this sort of diagram looks like an insoluble puzzle. To a professional it is an indispensable aid to running the machine. For a long time landscape planners were laymen in the closed technical world of the water manager. But now their interest had been aroused, a modest number of them began to learn the language of the water machine and a start could be made in the essential dialogue on the way the water machine could be remodelled in a responsible way.

Imbalance in the water system

The water management system is overburdened, is starting to do unusual things and so has to be remodelled, reconsidered and redesigned. Why?

First of all because the relationship between land and water is gradually creeping out of balance: the water level is rising and the land is sinking. By the year 2050 the sea level is expected to have risen by twenty-five centimetres, ten centimetres of which is due to the autonomous rise in sea level and fifteen centimetres due to climatic changes as a result of the greenhouse effect. The relative rise is even greater for the Netherlands, since the land is also sinking. Under the influence of geological processes, but mainly as a consequence of the exploitation of the peat areas for agriculture, the ground level in the West Netherlands has over recent centuries sunk substantially, to several metres below the present sea level. This process is continuing. Depending on the soil type, in the polder areas they are counting on a depression of between zero and sixty centimetres by 2050.

The rising sea level does not necessarily mean that the sea is the greatest danger. This comes from the other direction – from the rivers. As a result of the rise in sea level the rivers will find it harder to flow into the sea and will therefore find a way out somewhere else in the delta. This effect will be reinforced even more by the same climate changes, since in the six months of winter they will lead to more precipitation and therefore a greater influx of river water. More water is coming into our country, it is hard for it to flow away, and the result is higher water levels along the rivers, the increasing risk of floods and therefore the necessity of drastic measures to supplement the recent raising of the dykes.

The imbalance between land and water will put pressure on the polders too. If the water level in the surrounding polder drainage pools remains the same, the drop in the soil level may lead to the instability of their banks, thereby again increasing the danger of flooding. The increased precipitation resulting from climate changes will in addition give the water management system more water to deal with. In this way it is expected that the drainage capacity of the polder areas will have to increase by ten to forty percent. A few weeks ago there was a photo in the Volkskrant newspaper showing the only steam pumping station still working. It had to be put into operation to help drain off the huge amounts of water. Is this the writing on the wall?

While the water is rising and the land sinking, we have in our use of land become more and more dependent on the possibility of lowering the water level. In the eyes of most of its inhabitants the Netherlands is a very wet, water-rich country. This image is probably one of the most persistent misunderstandings which we maintain amongst ourselves. Man-made landscapes with plenty of water and marsh were in abundance until halfway through the last century. In the winter and early spring large parts of the river and peat meadow areas were flooded and the grasslands and low-lying parts of the sandy areas in the East Netherlands were hardly accessible until July as a result of high water levels.

The introduction of steam pumping stations, an increase in the scale of water management and new drainage techniques made it possible to drain the grasslands to such an extent that they could be worked all year round and could already be grazed in early spring. The land consolidation that started in the fifties led to the landscape becoming so thoroughly drained that from the seventies there was hardly any area whose use was limited by water levels too high in the spring. Agriculture and stock breeding have in the meantime become entirely dependent on these water management facilities.

This water system enables a huge increase in agrarian productivity, but it also has an almost bizarre side-effect: the Netherlands are starting to dry out. The ground water levels in the higher sandy areas have dropped by several metres over the last century. This means there is less and less visible water in the landscape. In the summer, more and more river water also has to be let into the polder areas to compensate for the water shortage, although its quality is by no means as good as the areas' own rainwater.

Urbanisation and the construction of infrastructure have a comparable effect. They go hand in hand with an increase in the paved land surface, which means that the rainwater always runs away more quickly and no longer has the chance to soak into the ground. In this way there is less water from precipitation available for filling up ground water reserves, which means that less drinking water can be drawn from this reliable source.

Towards a new balance

The water is rising, the land is sinking and drying out. In the winter season good precipitation water is thoughtlessly drained off, which means that in the summer, in agriculture, for drinking water and for water level management in natural areas, we are becoming increasing dependent on external sources of water of uncertain quality. There is a shrinking area of surface water and at the same time a growing need for water storage. All these processes point in the same direction. The relationship between land and water is gradually becoming alarming. Dutch society is manoeuvring itself into a corner. If we stick to the present system, ever more Herculean labours will be needed to correct the balance. And that will also leave less and less elbow space for all the other things desired in land organisation.

If we want to retain and expand flexibility, we shall have to do some solid work on our relationship with the water. The increasing imbalance must be reversed and we have to find a new balance between land and water, a new system, in the best Dutch tradition. We must fundamentally review our water management on the basis of current views of integrated and sustainable water control.

This implies that we have to give water more and better space. We can retroactively revalue the former marshy areas to offer relief in wet periods and as reservoirs of good quality precipitation water in dry periods. In the winter we must not drain off good quality precipitation water so quickly and thoughtlessly into the sea. We have to curb the speed of drainage and use the rainwater to build up reserves so that in the summer we are less dependent on uncertain external sources.

In order to keep open the possibilities of the Dutch delta for future users, we shall in the time to come have to expand the storage capacity of the Dutch water system by ten to forty percent. This can be done in the form of new marshy areas or in other ways. It will be clear that a revitalised and more substantial water system will in any case have consequences for the landscape and landscape planning.

Four scenarios for future water management

I would like to explain, on the basis of four scenarios, how an increase in the water storage capacity could take concrete form. Imagine a handkerchief with the usual four corners. Each of the scenarios pulls at one of the four corners so that the handkerchief is taut. Somewhere in that area of tension lies the future of the Dutch water machine.

Several scenario studies have been done recently in order to obtain a view of the possibilities for future environmental developments. It is striking that a large proportion of their content is determined by attitudes towards two fundamental questions: the relationship between the structure of the environmental surroundings and the individual user-functions and sector concerns, and the question of the level at which the most important policy decisions have to be taken, the 'top' or the 'basis'. Both questions are also relevant to the way of 'dealing with water'.

As far as the first is concerned, the future of the water system depends in part on developments in land-use functions. The above makes it clear, and the introduction also refers to it, that the Netherlands' hydraulic future should actually be first on the agenda, before decisions are made at the level of infrastructure and user functions. As in the renovation of a house, the repair of the foundations has priority over new kitchen cabinets. In this perspective the water system is not a partial concern but a basic structuring condition. But in practice, this is not always guaranteed in decision-making and planning. Decisions on new housing and industrial areas, railways and motorways are often taken first, and only then is it examined how the water system can be adapted to them.

For this reason I have worked out two scenarios in which the review of the water system plays a guiding role, and two in which it follows other developments. In numbers two and four the motto is 'water rules'. Here, the water system provides the conditions for the developmental potential of the ground-use functions. In playing this guiding role it takes advantage of natural processes. In scenarios one and three it is 'functions rule'. The user-functions determine the preconditions for the water system and there is great confidence in the continuing development of technical aids to controlling nature.

The second question is important too. The future of the water system is partly determined by the scale of the organisation, by the question of 'top' or 'basis' and thus also by the division of roles between the various authorities and private bodies. Are the guiding decisions taken centrally or not, from above or from below?

This too remains an open question, whose possible answers are incorporated into the scenarios. In scenarios three and four the 'top down' approach is developed, under the motto 'a single system'. In these cases water management is primarily directed by national and possibly international authorities. Coherence-oriented guidance is a key concept in this organisational form. Scenarios one and two take an approach using units, subunits and fragmentation. They are dominated by the local and possibly regional authorities and this leads to a fragmented water management policy in which the Netherlands breaks up into a large number of units.

On the basis of these two issues the four scenarios can be put into the following matrix:

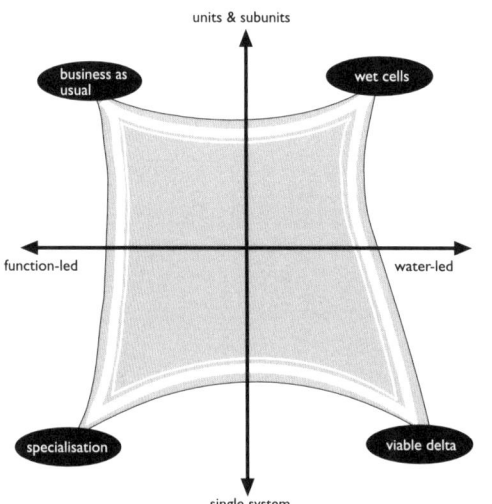

Four water scenarios for the Netherlands, seen as the corners of a matrix.

Each scenario is characterised by a metaphor and developed on the basis of a short sketch of its specific social, environmental and water management strategy.

Ground subsidence pumping stations in Groningen. The extraction of gas from the Groningen gas fields leads to local subsidence. Five pumping stations with sluices have been built in order to maintain the water level.

Scenario 1: business as usual

The Netherlands is the plaything of the free market. The space is there to be used. There is continuing and increased suburbanisation. All this is expressed in numerous adaptations of functions in the various sectors, usually small-scale and scattered in relation to the size of the terrain. The user functions are entwined and mixed with one another, with something for everyone. The area's role as a system is secondary to this. In decision-making the emphasis is on the local level.

Water management follows the changes and wishes of land use. Adaptations to water management always have to be sought within the present system's levels regime. In the West Netherlands it is certainly unthinkable that water levels should be tinkered with, because it has immediate consequences for the wooden pile foundations of the houses. In order to keep the system controllable in spite of this, increasingly advanced technical means are employed to keep its head above water. Water management is primarily focused on draining the excess precipitation in the winter half of the year, which means that ever-larger amounts of river water will be needed to supplement the shortfalls in the summer.

Scenario 2: Water units

The Netherlands is made up of many regions with their own characteristics and their own independent water management. Recycling and sustainability are concepts that occupy a major place in this. Respect for nature and the cultural heritage take priority. The communities, regionally organised, dictate

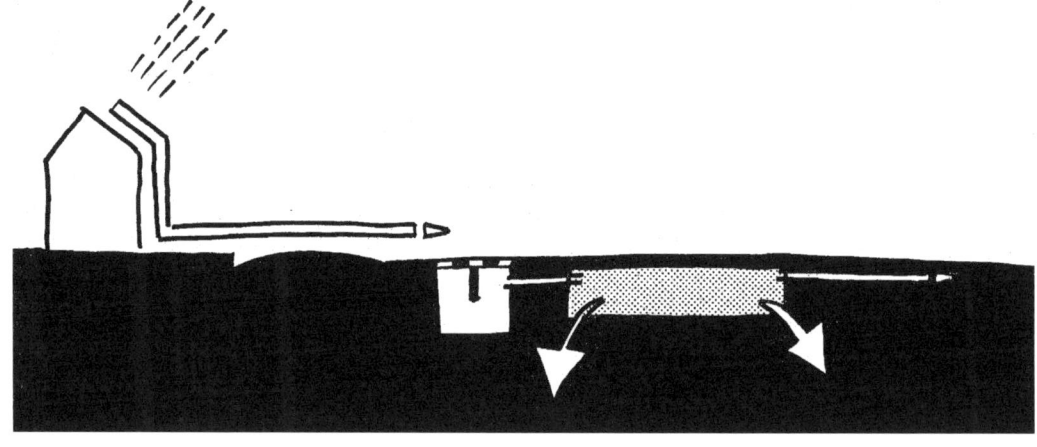

The 'Leidsche Rhine' water system. A design for a sustainable urban water system whereby the pure water is retained in the ground and in the open water of the city itself.

the collective arrangements. There are strict regulations to save vulnerable areas and enable them to function under the influence of natural processes. Within each region there is a pronounced mixing of functions and at the same time a decrease in the most intensive forms of land use.

In water management in the regions the recycling concept leads to the will to close off the water balance within the areas much as possible, so that no water foreign to the area has to be let in during dry periods. In order to achieve this, much more water has to be retained during the winter than at present, which means substantially more land being used for the hydraulic system. The path followed in order to combine both quality and quantity management within a single organisational unit is continued vigorously and expanded with management tasks for other public amenities. The water manager becomes an environmental manager.

Scenario 3: specialisation

The hierarchy of social functions and the organisation and management derived from it are laid down by the state authorities. The market may help to execute this allocation of functions. The authorities and the market realise that, on a global scale, fresh water is the major economic factor of the twenty-first century, comparable to the role played by fossil fuels in the twentieth. The position of Dutch-style delta regions as economic focus areas is thereby only reinforced.

Economic growth leads to continuing urbanisation in the form of compact cities. In the rural areas large-scale utility functions are allotted space on the basis of their international orientation. This leads to a sharp compartmentalisation and segregation of functions. For every function there is a place in the system that is best suited to it.

The water system is geared entirely to this extremely varied group that requires water and will therefore be environmentally highly differentiated. This means that the highly technologically developed agriculture will be well served by water management. In addition to optimum drainage there is a fine adjustment for the supply of fresh and very pure 'process water'. The water system is very much technologically oriented.

Scenario 4: inhabitable delta

The Netherlands is here seen as part of the delta of a river system that includes a substantial part of Western Europe. The characteristics of this system (both natural and man-made) can be used in the sense that they create space for human activities. Major changes to the system whereby new limiting conditions are created should serve in the first place to strengthen the

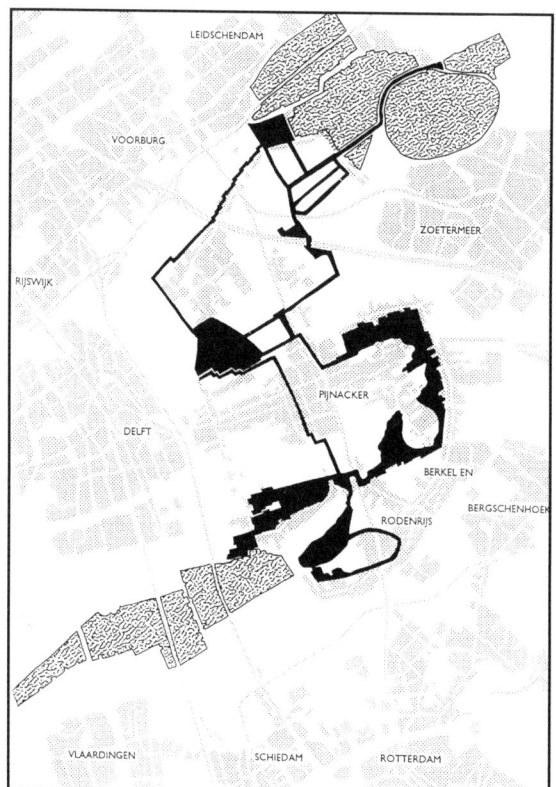

Design for a new intermediate drainage pool in the southern wing of the West Holland conurbation. In order to make good water management provisions for advancing urbanisation, a new water system has been designed that can buffer surface water and add recreational and ecological qualities.

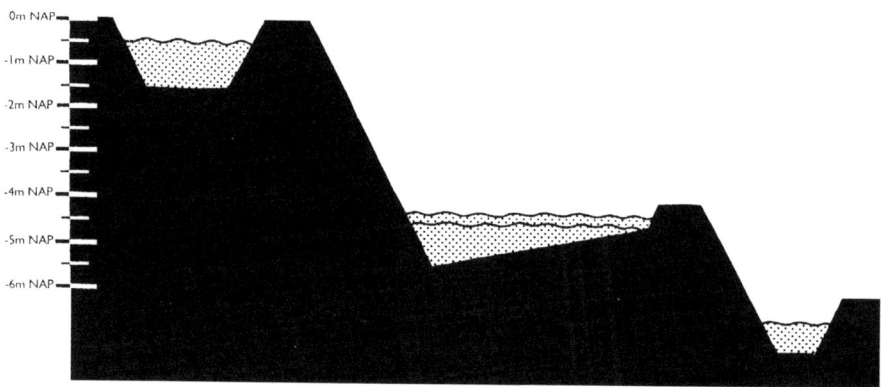

maintenance-free operation of that system, and its robustness, flexibility and durability; not to be able to accommodate the ups and downs of concrete user-functions and sector concerns.

Organisation, management and use for concrete user-functions are possible as long as there is no tampering with the operation, robustness, flexibility and durability of the water system. There is a selectively controlling authority that

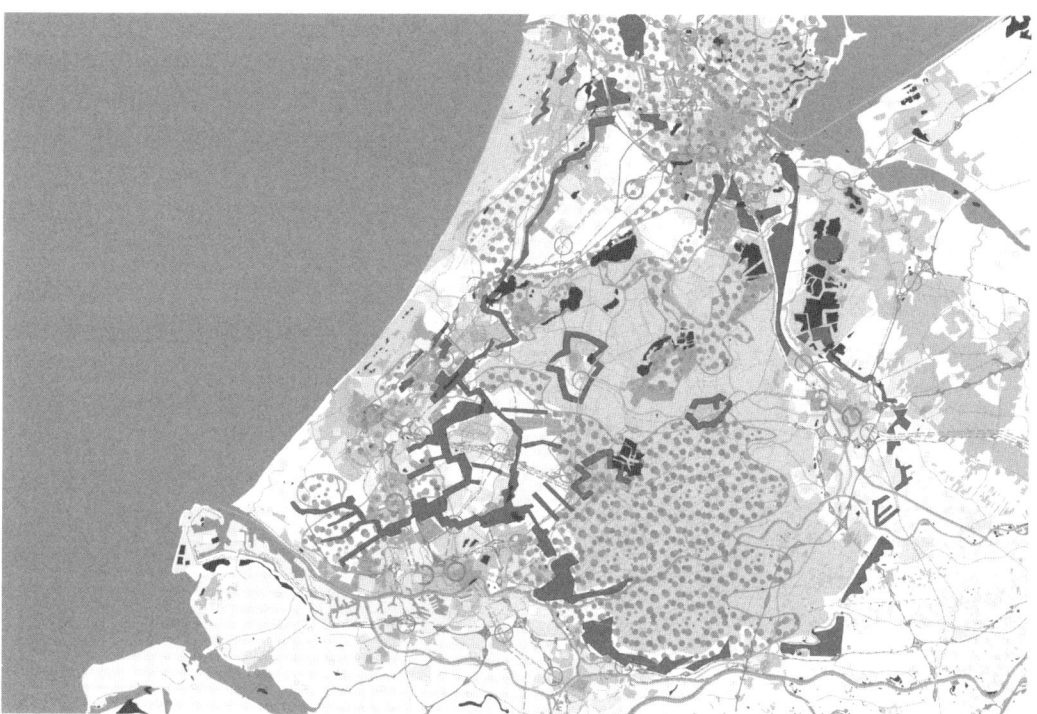

When one links the notion of an intermediate polder drainage pool to the task of storing water, and projects this onto the Delta metropolis area, it is practical to look for 40,000 hectares in which a fluctuation of fifty centimetres in the water level has to be acceptable. Thinking in terms of spatial structures, one can reason in two directions: the Network Model and the Ring Model. The network model argues for a broad range of developmental possibilities for the Delta metropolis as a whole. In the ring model the point is that the whole of this retention capacity is as it were linked to the ring of cities and that the idea of fostering the Green Heart is translated into terms of water.

facilitates the market. Water demands and receives a great deal of space and land-use functions make way for the creation of the new water system. Large-scale marsh areas are created as a water buffer zone. At the same time they provide an enormous expansion of the area for nature and recreation.

Epilogue

Whichever of the four scenarios provides the pattern for the concrete shape of the Netherlands in the future, it seems that in any case a number of changes in water management in the first decades of this new century will lead to major modifications in the Dutch landscape. Water will be more visible and will assume a dominant structuring role. This requires further integration of environmental and water planning, in which elements such as the water situation map can play an important part.

But it is rather ironical that the Department of Public Works, which publishes the water management map, decided in the early nineteen-nineties not to issue any more new series of maps. Considering the planning task ahead, that is already an incomprehensible decision, since it is an indispensable resource for the future of the Dutch water machine. The rapid reversal of this decision should be the first step towards this future. More than this, it is time for an updated edition of the map, incorporating the latest insights into the functioning of the Dutch water machine. This new version could display the relationship with the ground water system, on the basis of the functioning of the surface water system, and attention might be focused on a number of important aspects of water quality.

The water management map is, at an elementary level, the 'mental map' of the Netherlands. It is thus much more than just a technical aid: it guides us in the future state of the Netherlands, the unavoidable low country near the sea.

Utrecht, 12th January 1998
Lodewijk van Nieuwenhuijze, assisted by Fred Feddes

THE SKILL AND THE ART OF THE ENGINEER

I have been passing it almost everyday for years and yet I still notice it. The point where the railway line from Utrecht to Amsterdam and the Amsterdam-Rhine canal slowly diverge after running in parallel for kilometres. The high-tension cables continue to accompany the railway line for a short distance but then follow the canal. The train passenger from Utrecht to Amsterdam is just getting used to the view of a sturdy row of poplars along the canal when, shortly beyond Breukelen, they gradually but inevitably go their own way. You can keep the fixed row of trees in view for a long way across the pastures. Smaller and smaller until they finally disappear on the horizon together with the canal and the pylons.

Of course it depends on my mood how sensitive I am to the drama of this spectacle. But even without attaching any symbolism to it, this choreography, with the railway line and the canal in the leading parts and the high-tension cables in a creditable supporting role, is still worth musing on. After all, does the naturalness with which these long lines lie there not strikingly contradict current views on fitting infrastructure into the landscape? The railway line is simply set on a low embankment, slightly above the level of the pastures, with a ditch on each side. Fortunately there is no vegetation along it. It is only at the stations that the Dutch railways have traditionally had a more outspoken allure and expressiveness. One cannot actually call the route of the railway compact because it only follows the trunk road and the canal for a while and then makes its way across the polders with long, widely-distanced uprights. The other leading actor, the canal, is also a line that ultimately appears not to concern itself with anything else. This self-assured image is well supported by its monumental vegetation. The Traffic Route Division of the State Forestry Service planted trees as uniformly as possible along the whole route of the canal from Wijk bij Duurstede to Amsterdam. Poplars ready for felling have been replaced by new ones planted in exactly the same way.

The tension between technical services and the landscape

Is it really so simple to create harmony between infrastructure and the landscape? Do we only have to apply the technical requirements without concern, with a monumental gesture here and there to give the project greater charm? No, it is often not so simple. In most cases one piece is missing so that the puzzle cannot be completed.

The straightforward logic of the technical intervention, with the accompanying charm of honesty and directness, is always in a relationship of lesser or greater tension with the vulnerability of the landscape in which the new intervention is to take place. In order to resolve this tension (because the contrast cannot be reconciled) one needs an invention that enables everything to fall into place. And there's the rub. Only the complete identification and consideration of this tension can lead to a satisfactory approach to the problem, so that subsequently the laws of 'hard logic' can as far as possible be applied to the design of the new technical element and its location in the landscape. One might say that engineering skill is not enough, it has to be engineering art – involving the inventive resolution of the tension inherent in the task. This can be pointedly illustrated by two examples: the reinforcement of the river dykes in the finely-meshed river landscape, and the location of wind turbines in the flat open area of the coast of Friesland.

Reinforcement of dykes

Since the Middle Ages the system of dykes along the Dutch rivers has at set times been heightened and strengthened, always little by little and with the least possible movement of soil. However, despite the fact that they have been constructed by many different hands, they offer the same appearance everywhere. The characteristics of old dykes are the narrow top and the steep, usually concave slopes. This means that as you ride along the top you feel as if you are floating above the landscape. On the outer side this landscape is dominated by the river, usually flowing peacefully at its summer level but at high water rising threateningly to fill the full breadth at the winter level. The force of the flowing water has in the course of time led to most landscape patterns in the river foreland growing or being carved out parallel to the river (and therefore parallel to the dyke too). The inner side of the dyke looks out over a completely different scene. Here it is characteristic that the landscape is attached to the dyke at right angles. Houses, windbreaks and woods often literally run right up to the dyke. The curved course of the dykes means that the eye of the observer on its top is led first one way then the other, in a gradual and pleasant rhythm reminiscent of the smooth transitions of parks arranged in the English landscape style.

The reinforcement of the dykes that has been going on since the seventies is achieved not so much by heightening as broadening. The new supporting banks on the inside, intended to increase the stability of the main bulk, and the 'seepage channel' under the dyke extend it and displace the landscape that has

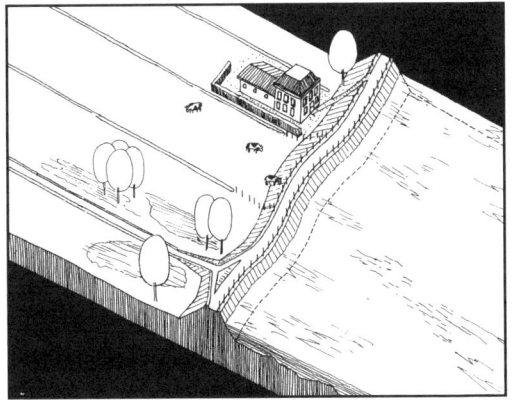
Typical old dyke.

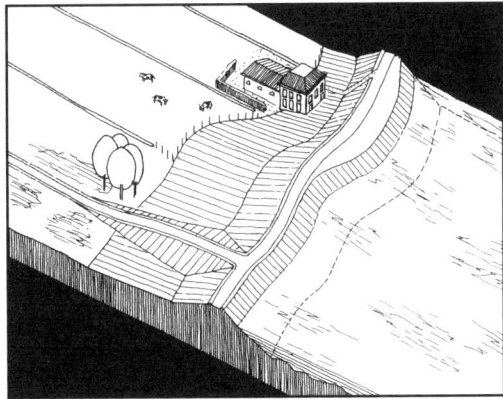
Strengthening the dyke leads to discontinuity.

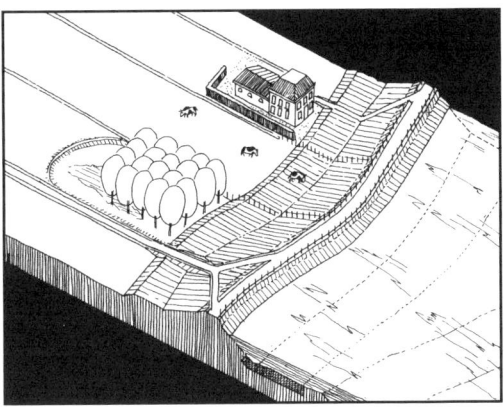
Proposed solution.

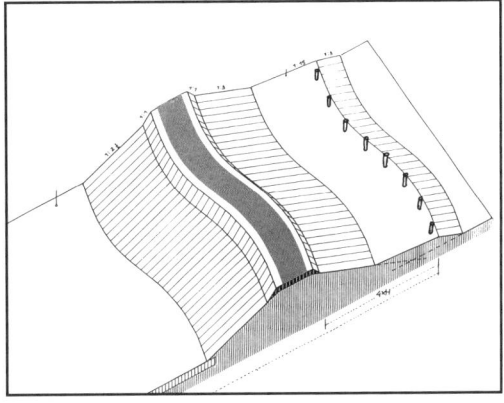
Articulation of the cross-section by a 'nipped top' and a raised base.

grown right up to it. What is more, the slopes are gentler. Instead of steep slopes of one in two or even one in one and a half, they are now one in three, not only for firmness' sake but also for the ease of mowing. And then the difference from the old dykes becomes apparent. From the top you do not experience a one in three slope as a steep wall that seems to disappear beyond the outer bend. Even in a low winter sun one no longer sees an obvious shadow side. The dyke has changed from a striking line in the landscape into a ponderous, colossal body. The campaigns against the strengthening of the dykes, an attempt to 'save the river landscape from the Ministry of Public Works' bulldozers', are primarily fighting against the erasure of the characteristic elements of the landscape. They include arguments for taking the new dyke in a bend round a dyke-house; saving a piece of steep slope with valuable vegetation and broadening the top of the dyke at this point; to save a small wood inside the dyke or a beach outside it. The somewhat lumbering engineering that characterised the first set of dyke reinforcement plans was forced to squat down and make compromises and here and there make itself appear more attractive. It leads to toe-curling examples of landscape adaptation because the pride and logic have gone out of the project: the continuity of the long conspicuous line has been lost. The tension has not been well resolved. The occasional saving of landscape elements is praiseworthy but cannot bring back the charm of the old river landscape. The real pain lies elsewhere. The problem has to be stated more fundamentally. Only the modelling of the awkward profile of the new dyke itself offers any consolation, though of course in compliance with technical specifications and with an eye to the demands the water boards make regarding its management. A way out is provided by the women's magazine advice that stripes in the length and dark colours also have a slimming effect on the fuller figure. Transposed to our problem of the clumsy looking profile of the dyke, this primarily means the shaping of the top by

The option of making the top of the dyke very narrow and letting the slope run up steeply gives one the experience of floating above the landscape.

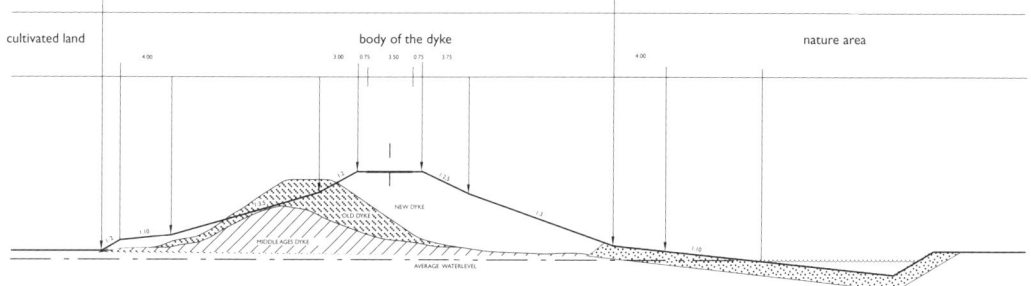

The section of the dyke designed for part of the River Waal, in which the section technically required has been both actually and optically narrowed. On the land side of the dyke the mowing path has been raised slightly; on the water side this path changes into a wet dyke-base.

drawing in the uppermost part of the slope and making it steeper. Looking along the dyke, this change of angle creates a long stripe that interrupts the broad dyke. And looking from the top you again have the feeling of floating above the landscape. The end of the dyke is also a stripe like this: a raised mowing path with a sharply delineated border on the inner side and a depression in the outer ledge of the dyke. In so doing it is important that spatial boundaries and formal user-boundaries (between the water board's property and the adjacent private land) should as far as possible coincide. Fencing at random points along the dyke detract from the desired effect. So when this transition is clearly marked the rest of the bank on the inside of the dyke can be smoothed away as inconspicuously as possible, gradually sloping down to ground level and preferably again being used as a garden, grounds or for agriculture. And as far as saving landscape elements is concerned: if the newly-designed dyke profile is applied with the greatest possible continuity, its present course can if necessary be deviated from. Careful design of the new bends and uprights is an essential part of the job. The intriguing and yet natural variety in the route on the dyke may then return in a 'gradual and pleasant rhythm'.

Wind Energy

The second example concerns wind energy and a landscape whose vulnerability lies in its emptiness: the marine clay polders along the coast of Friesland. You can see so far across the flat open country that anything high such as a wind turbine can be seen from kilometres away. This is not so bad in itself. A windmill can be attractive and can also make the vastness of the land measurable. But a closely grouped set of windmills of different sizes and

1000 MW in a line along the coast, from the Hook of Holland to Lauwersmeer.

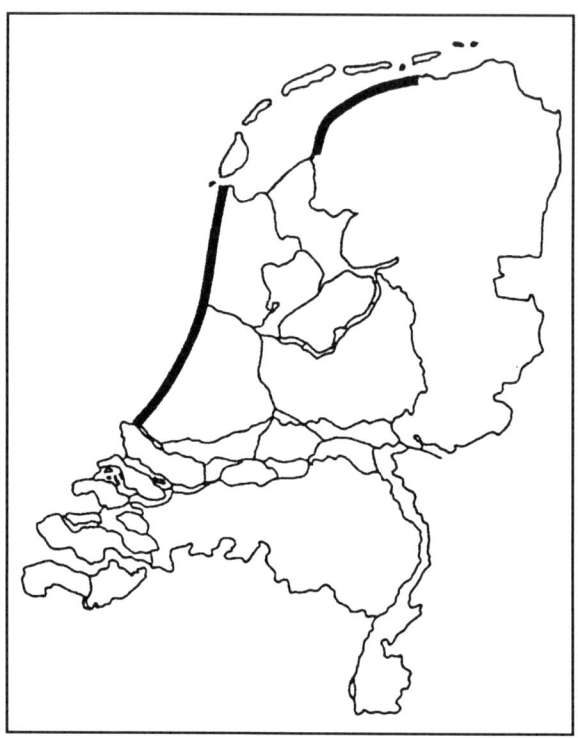

heights, and are also visible, soon violate the serene straight line of the horizon. Furthermore, the coastal area is a part of the richly varied habitat of the birds of the mud flats. Many of the 'permanent inhabitants', such as geese and wigeons, fly over the dyke of the mud flats to forage inland. In bad weather migratory birds follow the line of the dyke. Since it is precisely at this point that they are forced to fly low, the chances of colliding with the sail of a windmill are high.

And yet it is a phenomenon we cannot avoid. In a windy country like the Netherlands, electricity sourced from wind is a sustainable and clean form of energy. State policy is that in 2000 wind turbines should yield five percent of the total energy consumed. That amounts to 1000 megawatts. To achieve this, an unbroken line of turbines along the whole coast of Holland and Friesland would be needed. This is because it is also inevitable that the turbines have to be located in the windiest areas.

In the example of the turbines in the empty country of the Friesland coast, it seems at first sight logical to limit the spoliation of the horizon by locating as few windmills as possible. A few very big ones with enormous capacity, as a remedy against the spectre of an uninterrupted line of turning sails along the whole coast. Technical progress actually makes this solution possible. Ever-larger mills are being developed, some even as tall as eighty metres. The main

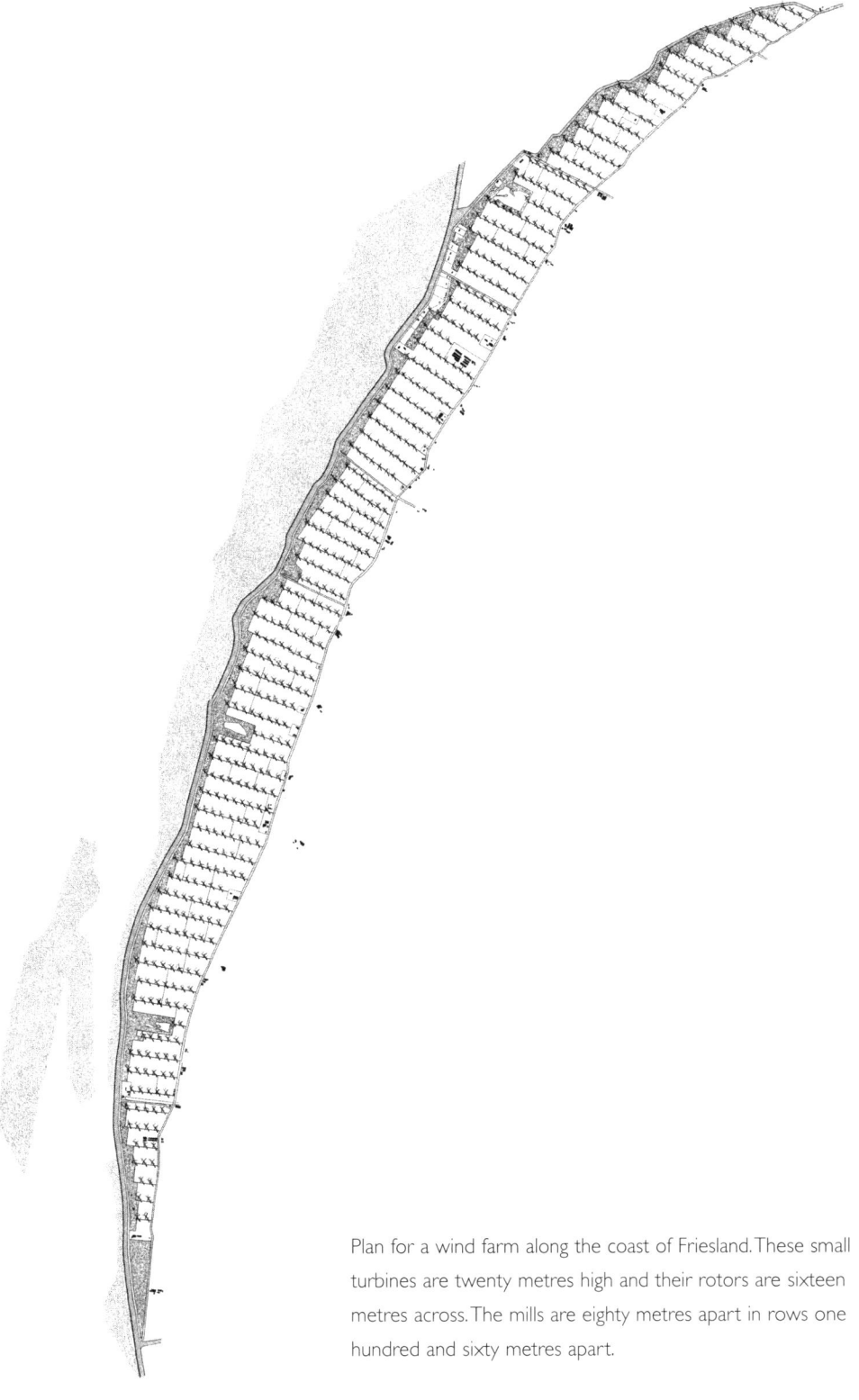

Plan for a wind farm along the coast of Friesland. These small turbines are twenty metres high and their rotors are sixteen metres across. The mills are eighty metres apart in rows one hundred and sixty metres apart.

A section through the planned wind-polder on a line at right-angles to the dyke.

reason these mills yield more is that at greater heights the wind blows harder and more consistently than just above the ground. However, larger mills have to be located further from each other. When we take the area covered by the mills as our starting point, we see that the same amount of power can be produced by smaller mills. This insight all at once gives us the freedom to solve the problem in the opposite direction. Imagine that it was precisely small turbines we were going to use, a great many at the same time. The mills would then visually become part of the landscape and be less trouble to birds. Instead of limiting the number of mills as far as possible, we put as many as possible close to each other: a windmill plantation, almost like a form of agricultural production fitted into the pattern of the polders. Their fixed rhythm and large numbers will give the wind-polder a beauty of its own. In the end there could be areas along the Dutch coast where there are no windmills at all and other parts where they are located so regularly and close together that they themselves become a landscape.

On shattered fortune

There is another factor in the construction of the so-called 'linear infrastructure' (mainly railways and roads) which the artless train passenger or car driver does not see but may well suspect: the increasing fragmentation of nature in the Netherlands. The series of maps of the main road network from 1930 to 1990 show how the scale of the continuous areas of land within this network has diminished. There is the looming spectre of nature in the Netherlands falling apart into unusable scraps as a result of the construction of even more hard, intensively used lines.

Ecological linking zones, corridors, wildlife tunnels and adapted culverts are all very familiar weapons in the battle against the barrier effect. The many technical amenities to allow animals to cross barriers are infectious samples of the engineer's art (or is it engineering skill?). A combination of measures is needed to hold back the fragmentation of the Dutch landscape. Making connections between separate natural areas is not the most effective instrument. The functional enlargement of the surface area of continuous natural areas within the mesh of the infrastructural network offers a much

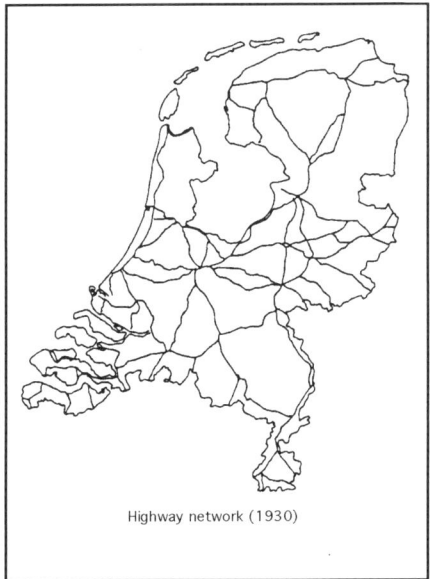
Highway network (1930)

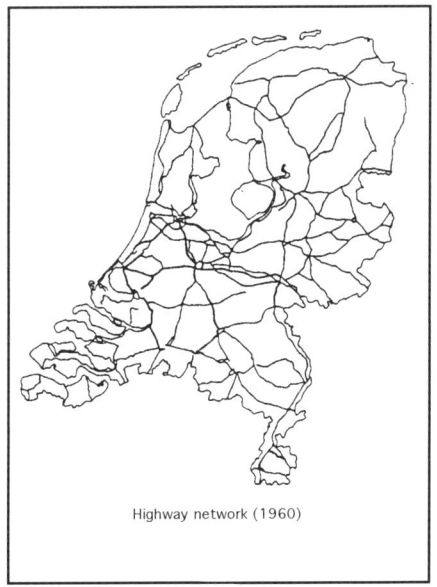
Highway network (1960)

Highway network (1989)

The densification of the road network makes the mesh for continuous natural areas ever-smaller.

higher yield. This increase in surface area combined with habitat improvements reinforces the existing cores of the natural area, making them into units which are as far as possible self-sufficient. In so doing, there is nothing discreditable about reintroducing species into an area where they are no longer found as a result of, for example, being cut off from it by barriers. For that matter, a railway line or road not only forms a barrier, but along its length its extensive managed margins also make it an ecologically connective line.

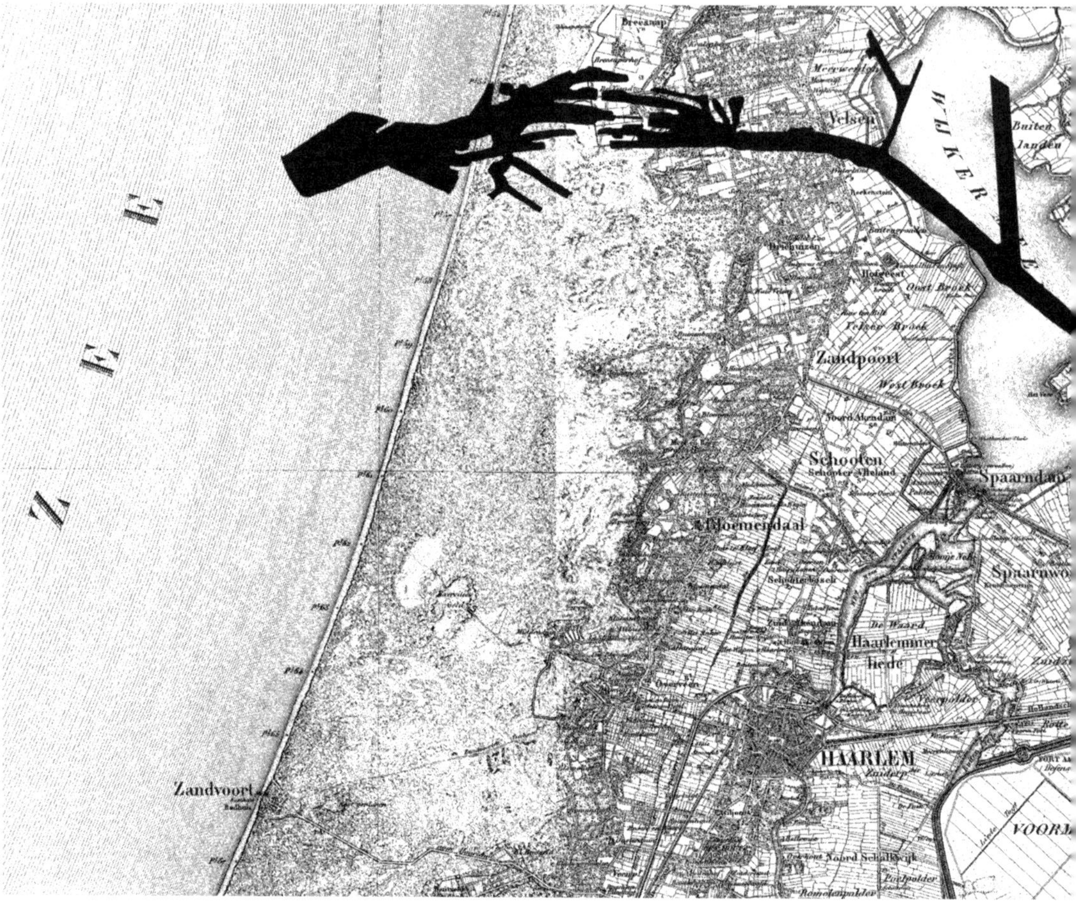

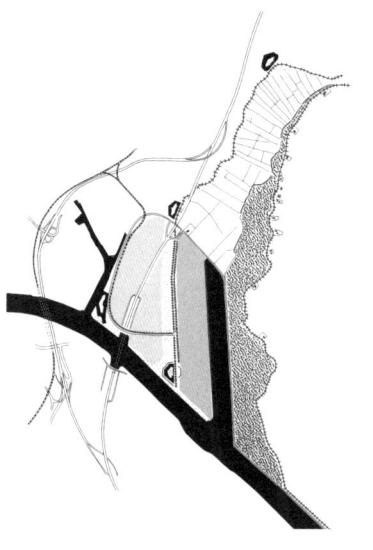

A sea-port in the Wijkermeer Polder.

Map of a planned asymmetrical port.

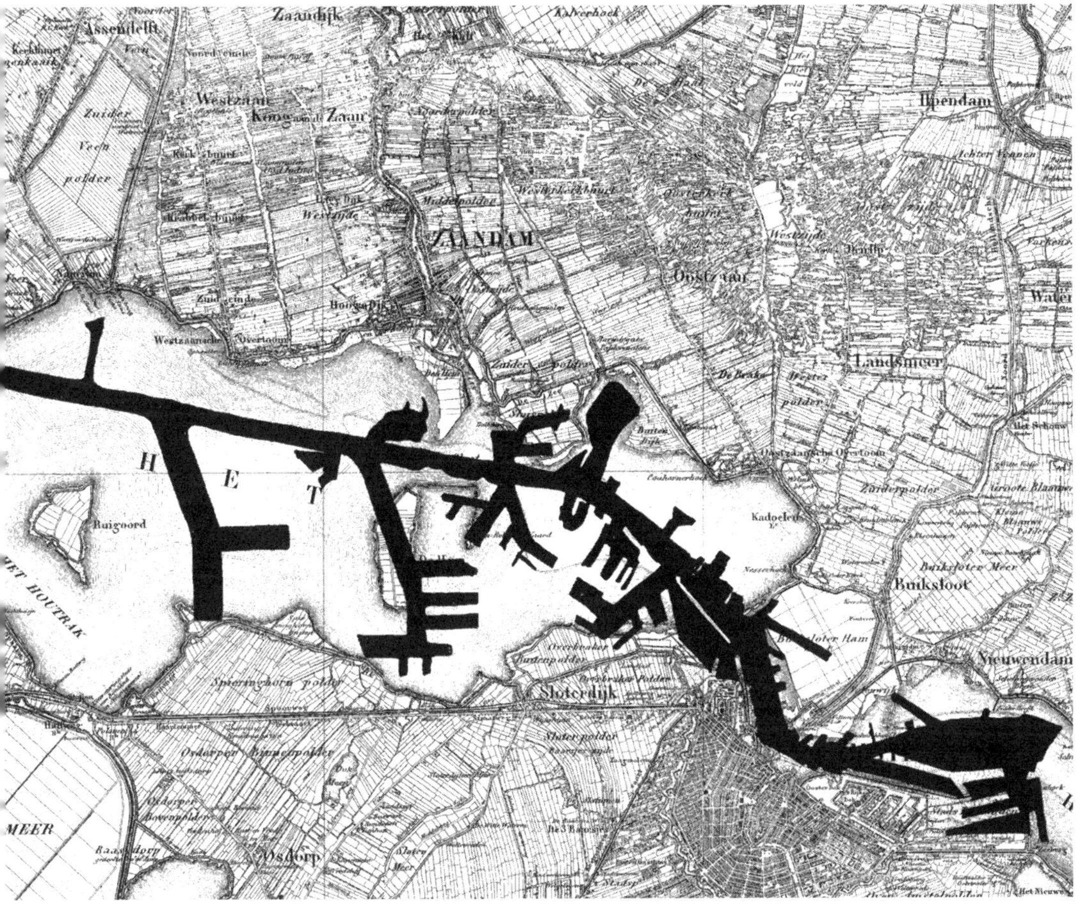

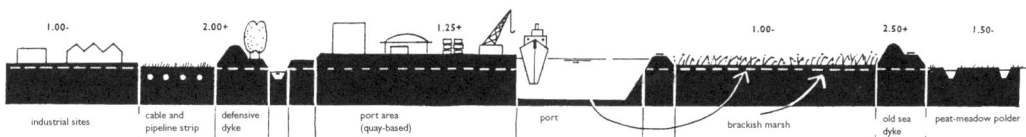

Cross-section from defence dyke to sea dyke.

A seaport in the Wijkermeer Polder fits into the series of ports excavated between Amsterdam and IJmuiden in the drained areas of the impoldered IJ. Seen on a local scale, there are countless patterns and elements that would not easily bear the location of a port: the forts and defence dyke of the Stelling van Amsterdam, the age-old Assendelverdijk and the transition from Beverwijk to the open polder land. The simplest solution to this dilemma is to dig a port on an asymmetrical model. The raised quay area would then be on the inside, just as the protected land was before. Brackish seepage from the deep port nourishes the marshy area which gives back the former sea-dyke its wet outer land.

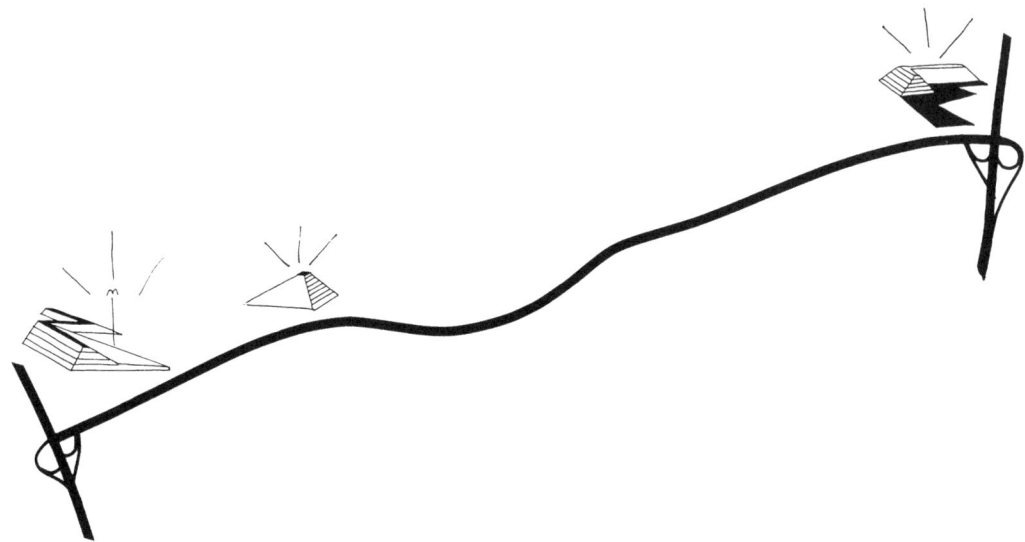

All three intersections (Zaartpark, Molenleij and Turfvaart) on a very limited area along the southern ring-road of Breda mark the presence of the city and at the same time provide access into the city for the course of a stream. Both aspects appear as exuberantly as possible in the design. This choice leads to dramatic height differences which are executed as conspicuous sculptures. The rough and sturdy forms and the uniformity of treatment of the three places are suited to the scale of the motorway.

I am rarely aware of it, but when I am in the train, looking mainly at the spectacular spatial effect of these long lines, I am in fact in the middle of the longest (and narrowest) natural area in the Netherlands.

Yttje Feddes, Berdie Olthof
Simultaneously with the publication of this book, this article also appeared under the same title in the Landscape issue of the magazine 'Kennis en Methode' (22), 1998, no. 1.

WORKED OUT AND DONE WITH?

Agriculture has dictated the planning and organisation of rural areas for many years. And now, at a time when discussions regarding the future organisation of the Netherlands are coming to a head, this very same agriculture is conspicuously absent. The agricultural sector has neither programme nor environmental strategy. Indeed, it is more like a residual item that is only of interest to other types of environmental use, whether it be in the form of urban development, infrastructure or natural development, as a supplier of land.

Does environmental planning and organisation have nothing more to offer agriculture now that the external production conditions are well-nigh at their most optimal? And conversely, has agriculture nothing more to offer environmental planning than simply the question of the degree and rate at which land is being taken away from cultivation?

We are standing on the threshold of a radical transformation of the agricultural sector and the field of agriculture. And yet Dutch agriculture does no more than discuss future opportunities internally, and then sit back and wait. There is much that needs to be done.

A double misunderstanding

Mesmerized by all the dynamics, the frenzy, and the ringing of mobile telephones, we try to convince each other that we are living in a post-industrial society as well as in an information society. But seen from Dr. Porter's viewpoint, the Netherlands presents a very different picture. In 1992 Porter was commissioned by the OESO to develop a method for investigating the competitive power of national economies. We see that the familiar index numbers derived from the Gross National Product have lost a great deal of their volume due to the operations of international enterprises and fluctuations on the currency market. Porter's method is simple but revealing. He cuts the economy up into smaller consistent sectors and compares their market share with the total volume in these sectors on the world market. Seen from Dr. Porter's viewpoint, in 1986 the Netherlands looked very different to what we might expect.

Surprisingly, Dutch economic assets are to be found in agriculture and the associated food industry. However, this agricultural delight is marred by natural gas occupying eighth place. For those interested in Philips, electric

Still an agricultural country: the strongest economic sectors in the Netherlands measured according to their share on the world market.

1	Cut flowers	63.9 %
2	Birds' eggs in shell	61.1%
3	Pigs	56.6%
4	Flower bulbs, living plants	56.4%
5	Fresh cream	53.1%
6	Cocoa	48.6%
7	Fresh tomatoes	43.4%
8	Natural gas	40.1%
9	Fresh potatoes	35.5%
10	Cocoa butter	32.4%

lights and televisions only managed to get into fourteenth place (30.6%). Holland's Japan therefore, is not in Eindhoven, but out in the country.

This brings us to the second misunderstanding. The Netherlands no longer has a truly rural area, such as we still see in France or Spain. From the fifteenth century onwards the Dutch countryside has become bound to an urban society that is scattered over a mass of larger and smaller commercial towns. Of course there is a difference between the lifestyle in towns and that in the provinces, but this has nothing to do with the economic difference between town and country. The Dutch countryside has become completely urbanised both socially and culturally.

Not gaining land to use for agriculture but getting land back from agriculture

One would think that with all its prime locations, agriculture would in some way influence Dutch town and country planners' almost inflationary production of images of the twenty-first century. Nothing could be further from the truth. Let us consider the Working Document 'the Netherlands in 2030'. Comments on the agricultural sector are bogged down in minor references and requisite reports in the keys to the charts. Agriculture is conspicuously absent in the Planning Department's futuristic panoramas. Apparently all the green areas on 'the New Map of the Netherlands' indicate recreational and EHS projects. There are hardly any agricultural projects at all.

In a relatively short space of time the position of the biggest land user (as far as surface area is concerned) in the field of environmental planning in the Netherlands has changed dramatically. Here is a brief summary.

After the Second World War, agriculture played a key role in the reconstruction of the Netherlands. A spectacular increase in productivity resulted in low food prices. This made it possible to freeze wages over a long period of time, which was very helpful to industrial development in the Netherlands. Agricultural policy was a food policy that was aimed at a certain degree of autarchy. The enormous effect of agriculture on the form and organisation of rural areas was not even discussed. Environmental planning was at the service of agriculture, and through the medium of land consolidation as well as education, information and research (the OVO-triangle), the role played by the minister of agriculture was comparable to that of the Japanese MITI.

About twenty years ago, and heralded by the first wave of environmentalism and the N'70 manifestation which for a year focused attention on the position of the natural world, the excellent relationship between environmental planning and agriculture started to show the first signs of wear. Land consolidation and its effect on the natural environment came under attack. During the seventies and early eighties, warnings from private researchers regarding the consequences of intensive cattle farming were argued away by solid counter-expertise from Wageningen. The three 'green papers' on National Parks, National Landscape Parks and Relationships, all underline the increased self-confidence of nature conservancy. The criticism did have some effect.

A purely rural landscape such as one still sees in France no longer exists in the Netherlands.

In order to allow other social objectives to come into their own, the land consolidation act was replaced by the more versatile land development act. Resistance to the Relationships Paper and the National Landscape Parks (Winterswijk: "we are farmers, not park keepers") clearly shows that institutional compromises were badly received by supporters. The most convincing sign that the tide had turned was possibly the last minute cancellation of the building of the Markerwaard. More than anything else, it was the lack of a good agricultural objective that prevented the completion of the engineer Lely's work.

During the last decade the relationship between environmental planning and agriculture has been dominated mainly by changes in European agricultural policy and the consequences of the GATT agreements. The change from product subsidies to income support has eased the pain of the new direction taken by agriculture. However it is abundantly clear that this support cannot last forever. Sooner or later the discipline of the world market will take its toll. This will result in series of displacements between different production sectors that are very difficult to predict, as well as a possible reduction of the agricultural acreage. Consequently, for the first time agricultural organisations are opting for the stimulation of certain production sectors when reviewing the zoning of the National Area for the VINEX. These choices are confirmed in four 'courses', each dependent on different environmental conditions.

At present, the relationship between agriculture and environment tends to be almost completely overshadowed by fertilizer, BSE and swine fever. The only interest shown in agriculture seems to concern its role as a supplier of hectares of land that can be taken out of cultivation. Other sectors are particularly involved in the question of how to sell the skin before the bear is caught. As a rule rational forecasts do not take into account the toughness and great appeal of farming as a way of life, even though a part of its economic basis has fallen away. Planners are elated with the treasures they think they have captured. This is understandable in a country where everything has always had to be worked out down to the last square metre, and where they are now apparently about to simply acquire a paradise of hundreds of thousands of hectares of land to be used in any way they like. In a period of two decades we have moved from a time in which even the last Zuider Zee polder was apportioned to agriculture, to a situation in which land is being reclaimed from agriculture in order to satisfy all other land-users. Even more alarming is that as yet no aspirations have been listed on the twenty-first century's environmental agenda. Things are equally lax in the field of planning. Besides being ominously renamed the Rural Areas Department, the Department of Land Development, once so proud, has seen its agricultural activities dwindle, and those for the new clients (the natural environment), barely increase.

Worked out & done with?

What is the matter? Has environmental planning and organisation nothing more to offer now that external production conditions are more or less at their most favourable? Admittedly, additional investments in fine-tuning the external production factors even further, will put us in the levelling part of the S-curve. Every guilder invested will produce far fewer spectacular effects than in the heyday of land consolidation. The real reason behind the deafening silence is the uncertain prospects of Dutch agri-business. This uncertainty appears to have a paralysing effect on thinking about the relationship between environmental planning and agriculture.

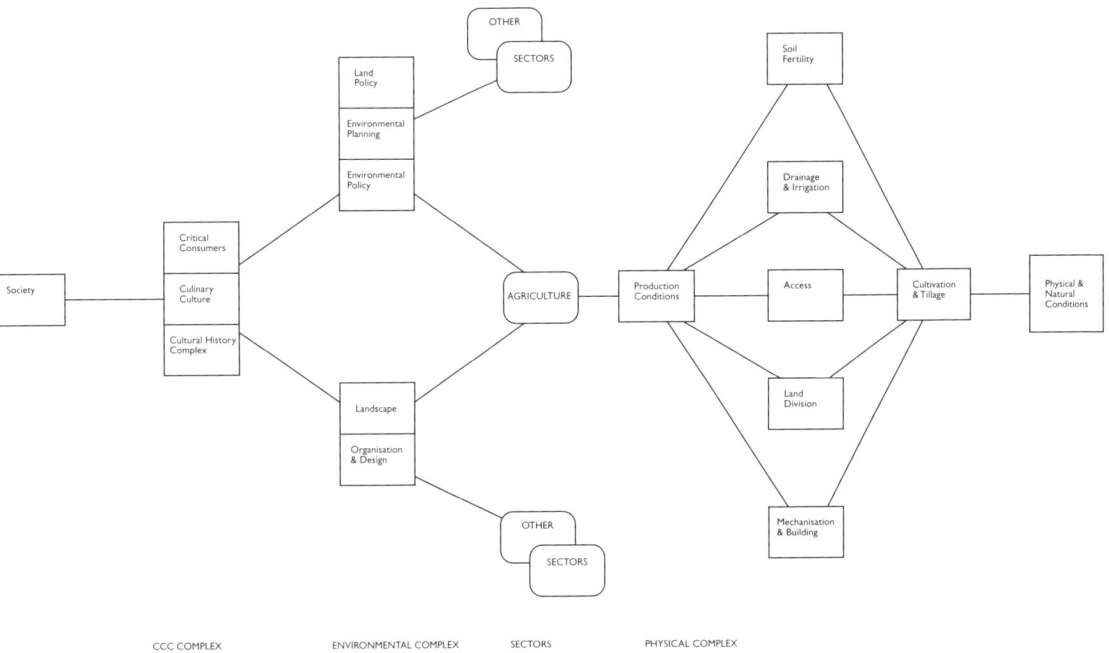

The relation between 'agriculture' and 'environment' shown in its constituent parts.

ENVIRONMENT AND AGRICULTURE

What is the relationship between agriculture and environment? In view of the terminology to be used in the rest of this essay, it would be useful to divide up the different constituent elements and to describe the relationship between each. These are described in the outline below.

Agriculture is situated in the middle. On the left is the social complex with which it has a web of relationships, and on the right is a physical complex to which agriculture owes its means of support. In the social complex we distinguish three clusters of which agriculture has to take particular account: the 'critical consumer' (environment- and animal-friendly production), the 'culinary culture' (cosmetic and culinary quality) and the 'cultural history complex' (landscape and the natural expression of agriculture). The relationship is sometimes relatively direct, as in the case of consumers, and sometimes a number of fields of policy in which the government protects certain social interests play an intermediary and regulating role: land policy, environmental planning and environmental policy. The mutual understanding between agriculture and otherusers of the environment occurs partly via environmental planning, and at a later stage in the policy cycle, via the organisation and design of the landscape. The physical complex is situated at the other end of the spectrum with which agriculture is associated. All the aspects that collectively determine the production conditions for each farmer are discernible here. There are relationships between all the constituent elements that influence the position of agriculture. In principle, all of these are ropes that can be 'pulled' in order to change the context of Dutch agricultural production.

A profile in environmental terms

An environmental description of Dutch agriculture is often interpreted quantitatively: the average size of the company, the size of the property, the yield per hectare, etc. For our purposes however, a qualitative profile that looks for similarities and differences in physical situations and in the consumption of land by agriculture is far more interesting.

We tend to almost forget it, but we should realise that we are all living and working in a delta area that is flat, fertile and has a temperate climate. This situation distinguishes Dutch agriculture from many other agricultural regions elsewhere in Europe and the world. For many of our foreign colleagues, the plots of land that need to be flat because of their use are miracles of flatness. Nevertheless, there are also physical differences in Holland: the difference between Holocene and Pleistocene and between sand, clay and peat.

Reclamation has mostly been a combined enterprise that has yielded quite a number of differences (in soil, drainage, seasonal conditions, location and access) at both meso and micro levels. Cultural and technical efforts during the past century have more or less eliminated any remaining differences. And it is precisely these efforts, which were mainly aimed at maximising agriculture, that have created problems for the natural environment. Besides the on-going fine tuning of the drainage system, a situation has now arisen that demands a certain collectiveness per region or per polder. This uniformity has created the conditions for a low-cost price bulk product of fairly good quality.

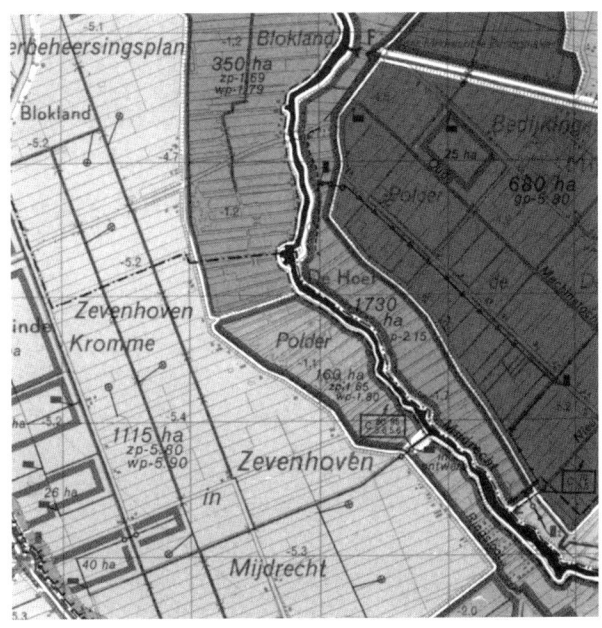

Enforced collectivity: the water management map clearly reveals that the utilised landscape in the lower Netherlands is divided into compartments. Decisions concerning ground water levels ensure that all compartments have the same hydrological conditions.

But (and this is a big but) this situation also sets strict conditions for the future. This enforced collectivity can act as a springboard for certain cooperative forms of innovation, but it can also be a great handicap to individual experiments at company level, to deviant courses as well as to avenues of exploration.

Current agricultural debate does not focus enough attention on this point. The present environmental situation is highly restrictive and offers a certain dragging resistance to change. Agriculture and production landscape have developed in concert and will not easily allow themselves to be separated. The innovation that is an extension of this historical development can benefit from the momentum that has been gathering. The innovation that seeks to move in a different direction will encounter more difficulty. The main issue is to discover the freedom in present environmental preconditions and how, wherever it proves necessary for facilitating new company styles, we can break the chain of enforced collectivity. Of course, we shall not be entirely successful in this, but there are undoubtedly possibilities for somewhat reducing the 'grain size' of this enforced collective advance and introducing new agricultural differences.

AGRICULTURE OUT OF THE TRAP

The crisis in which Dutch agriculture finds itself is the result of developments that have taken place over the last few decades and which cannot simply be undone. The clock cannot be put back. But nor can things continue as they are. Agriculture has reached an impasse. The stagnation of increasing demand coupled with a great increase in production (overproduction), is putting the selling price under pressure. On the other hand, as a result of the EC levy on imports, the farmer has to pay unvaryingly high prices for his raw materials. Indeed, the land price is one of the highest in the world. As far the present level of mechanisation is concerned, the input of capital has reached its limit. In short, unless there is a change in policy, the agricultural sector will have to undergo a 'detached reorganisation' unlike anything that has been seen before. The 'survivors', or those who are left after reorganisation has taken place, will only be able to last if there are further labour redundancies, increased productivity and specialisation.

However, the darkest hour comes just before the dawn. There is evidence of certain new trends, which although initially appearing to limit the freedom of movement of farmers even further, paradoxically offer sufficient perspective with regard to other developments within the agricultural sector.

The international field

In the first place, the tariff walls behind which Europe has managed to ensconce itself so successfully and for so long are gradually being levelled out as a result of new world trade agreements (GATT). The European agricultural market is being liberalised. Future price-setting processes will be more subject to fluctuations on the world market. Dutch agriculture is largely dependent on imports from third world countries for its raw materials such as tapioca cattle feed. Imported raw materials are now still relatively expensive because the European Community sets a threshold price for them that is considerably higher than the world market price. As compensation, its own raw materials such as maize are relatively expensive, also as a result of high land prices. The GATT agreements will eventually result in a decrease in the price of raw materials as well as in the price of export products. It is important to distinguish here between two groups of agricultural products: products that are brought directly and often fresh to the consumer, and products that are sold to processing companies. The first group is not, or is barely, subject to rules or price protection in line with European agricultural policy. The second group concerns mainly bulk products that are subject to tougher EC intervention. Often intended for export, in future these products will be faced with lower unit profits and with the fluctuations in the world market price. At the same time the sale of this group of products is highly dependent on transport costs and consumer appreciation for the way in which the processing industry converts the bulk into high-quality final products. It is also true that in the future both products will depend very much on the 'whims' of the consumer, and that production will have to be as sustainable as possible in order to meet national and European environmental requirements.

Secondly, competition within the EC will increase as a result of the 'internal' market expanding to the east, and the gradual shift of the policy that guarantees and directs selling prices to the income support of individual farmers (MacSharry). The European market is moving from a seller's market to a buyer's market.

Thirdly, the consumer wants more variety and makes high demands with regard to the quality and taste of the product.

In addition to this, we should ask ourselves how long and at what price, we can continue exploiting third world countries for the production of low-cost raw materials for cattle feed and fertilizer. One assumes that countries producing raw materials will gradually produce more food for their own markets instead of exporting raw materials at knock-down prices.

Finally, consumers, politicians and management are becoming increasingly inflexible about the way the agricultural sector treats animals, as well as the way in which this affects the environment.

The question now is how an agricultural entrepreneur is to survive, given high and rising production costs, and selling prices that are relatively low and falling, given consumer demand for a supply that is more varied and of an improved quality, and given the higher costs involved in animal- and environment-friendly production. Do the trends and new needs mentioned above possibly offer a starting point for a way out of the dire situation in which Dutch agriculture now finds itself?

I see three possible courses for the renewal of Dutch agriculture. The strategies are not precisely geared to specific branches of industries or sectors. In practice it will boil down to looking for the ideal mixture, for a certain combination of these three lines of renewal, which may differ from company to company and from branch to branch:

Technology and planning

Using the very latest scientific knowledge there is an attempt to find the ideal balance between economy and ecology by way of optimisation. Characteristics are specialised products, a high investment level, increased efficiency, continuous monitoring of production and sales, a high level of technological know-how, and rigid planning. Companies that are oriented towards bulk production will be inclined to innovate along this line. It is especially big companies that can afford such a strategy.[1]

Flexibility and market

The motto here is: being flexible enough to take advantage of the shift from the seller's market to the buyer's market. Medium-sized companies in particular are eagerly searching for new ways for the consumer to benefit from the fruits of their labour. 'Extended rural economy', 'Rural innovation'; a lot is happening. There is far too much to list, or even condense into one atlas.

The companies on this line come from all over and have very different company styles, and are very much on the lookout for opportunities to open up new markets with new activities. They have put their hopes on developments on the agricultural work floor and based them on the belief that a more direct link with the consumer may produce good results.[2]

Sustainability and environment

The limits of agricultural ingenuity are determined by environmental preconditions. It is something every company has to deal with, and as a consequence more sustainable production methods have to be found.

True sustainability can only be found in the ecological agriculture of a company with mixed business intentions. Constructions have to be found in which consumers are provided with information on the quality of the available products, as well as the special production methods and conditions involved (which are geared to natural conditions and the protection of the environment), so that the consumer will also be prepared to pay for extra quality. Success depends on the use of proper distribution channels for product information as well as the products themselves. What it comes down to is 'safeguarding' the 'stofstroom in the column' in such a way so as to ensure that quality marks will help the consumer to recognise both quality and ecological production methods.[3]

The question now is how dependent are the options on environmental conditions? To what extent can the government use the environment to encourage and support this process of renewal? Before even starting to answer this question, practical rules and instruments will have to be found in order to guide future processes in the right direction.

COMPLEX PROBLEMS: SIMPLE RULES

The agricultural sector is a firm supporter of individual freedom of enterprise. The Dutch farmer very much likes to be master of his own land. For decades now collective rules have been effected in a tense relationship between farmers, agricultural organisations and the government. The agricultural sector is by nature inclined to oppose measures that affect its own operational management. Measures that focus on the quantity, the quality and the price of agricultural products are generally accepted more easily. With the passing of time, everything that concerns the output of the agricultural sector has been subjected to more and more regulation. This has occurred either on the initiative of the government or the EC, or on that of collective institutions such as agricultural organisations.

Options for manipulation

In the past government agricultural policy focused mainly on creating equal chances for all farmers, whether it involved farming on sandy soil or on heavy marine clay. The government adopted general measures in an attempt, as far as possible, to put the external production conditions of different farms on an equal footing. However, when production volumes began to exceed demand, agricultural policy began to focus more on price regulation and assigning quotas for the production volume, as well as gradually replacing its price guarantees with income support.

A deep-rooted need for freedom possibly explains the aversion of every true farmer, market gardener or fisherman to rules in the field of environmental planning and the environment. And indeed, the Rules that restrict the agricultural entrepreneur's freedom to decide for himself which means of production to use (land, water, air, fertilizer, etc), always begin with a capital R.

So far, agriculture has mainly concerned itself with the question of how to avoid environmental planners' mania for organisation. Government attempts to pursue an environmental policy more or less suffered the same fate until it became clear that such a policy was inevitable. It was only then that agrarian organisations took up the initiative to reorganise these matters themselves.

Obviously the fundamentally negative attitude of farmers makes it a singularly unattractive task for the authorities (and especially politicians) to deal with questions concerning the tense relationship existing between agriculture and environmental planning and between agriculture and environment.

The solution to the environment problem of agriculture lies in the formulation of a number of simple but effective rules, designed to gradually improve the situation. This cautious approach is based on an absolute belief in the fertile interaction between making and growing.

In the first place we must have a set of uncomplicated rules so that citizens, businesses and society's midfield, or in other words all sections of society, are encouraged to come up with socially desirable solutions. Such as a series of regulating levies in Environmental Planning to encourage the economical and multiple use of space (for the elaboration of this idea see Brabant, a possible next step). Should undesirable but not inadmissible functions wish to establish themselves in a particular place, they will only be allowed to do so after paying a considerable amount in tax. Levies such as these then go into a fund that can be used to finance useful projects for the function concerned.

In this way the core areas (areas available for use) can simply be marked for the bulk production of stock breeding, agriculture and market gardening (and possibly also fisheries). Similarly, on the other side of the spectrum, the EHS and recreation space can be realised in the same way. This could well become the procedural regulatory basis for what is known in planning terms as the casco concept. An approach like this can be combined wherever necessary with contingents that are negotiable or not. For agriculture this system of regulating levies should clearly be used to tax surplus mineral consumption. In short this is a package that makes it possible to encourage space-saving measures.

The use of sustainable measures to combat fundamental environmental problems (partly caused by agriculture itself) will undoubtedly result in an increase in the physical differences in various regions and types of landscape. The specific characteristics of the area concerned would determine the selection of policy instruments. This would be the case in operations with large-scale implications, such as solving the problem of dehydration in sandy areas by reducing the extraction of groundwater resulting in certain basins becoming wetter, or creating water retention in peat areas by reintroducing summer polders. In view of man's huge technical efforts to eliminate physical differences during the last few decades, this could be regarded as being very strange. Sustainable solutions to environmental problems give rise to areas which, agriculturally speaking, are less than perfect. New differences are created. In large landscape renovations such as this, the challenge for agriculture now is to adapt to these new physical conditions. In these new zones new forms of agriculture could produce special products, and through this interaction, give rise to an appearance that is surprisingly natural. You could say that this is a true linking of agriculture and useful nature without endless government funding. In connection with this, land policy could become more important as an instrument.

The period of product price support and the present era of income support (MacSharry), could be followed by encouraging specific forms of agricultural land use. In order to create new differences, the government could buy land and then – legally – give the usufruct and control of it 'for nothing' to farmers as a supplement to primary operational management. Of course it does involve

The larger watercourses in Waterland are linked so as to supply a peat reclamation area (left) with clean surface water. The resulting denitrification and dephosphatisation of the Markermeer water, so rich in nourishment, takes place by way of an extended supply route and the use of a marshland zone. This gives rise to new agricultural contrasts: the marshy meadows flanking the watercourses are suitable for extensive grazing by beef cattle.

a considerable investment on the part of the government, but then at least there is something tangible as compensation.

What can we finally expect from the classical discipline of land organisation? Further improvement of external production conditions will not really do much to increase the yield. When it comes to fine-tuning however, a mild form of land organisation could be effective in bringing about a gradual optimising of the external conditions that are geared to the individual farmer who changes his activities.

A particularly good example here are the perimeters of agricultural areas: areas where city and agriculture meet, the infrastructure, nature reserves and recreational areas, as well as contact zones with the exploiters, the consumers and (fellow) users of agricultural activities. If we look beyond the inconvenience and threat that lurk in these zones, we will discover future common areas that have the potential to allow new and unexpected dimensions of agricultural entrepreneurship to develop.

MOVING TOWARDS A NEW KEY

Making predictions in the field of agriculture is a tricky business. Looking back on four attempts to make reliable predictions for the ministry's structure document, Piet Slot, the man who played an important role in the policy of the Ministry of Agriculture from the war until well into the eighties, frankly admitted to an audience of town and country planners that he had been completely wrong each time. Each attempt had been hampered by unforeseen factors, and developments had taken an unexpected turn. A combination of technical innovations, changing political attitudes and unpredicted changes in the economic situation often played havoc with the predictions. The lesson that has consequently been learned in landscape planning is that in planning, built-in flexibility is of vital importance to agriculture. Without committing ourselves we attempt to predict environmental development in the various agricultural sectors. An exercise like this is nevertheless necessary in order to identify the most vital points for the future agenda of agricultural research.

We proceed with care, taking the existing environmental situation with all its opportunities and limitations (such as enforced collectivity) as a starting point. Important factors here are regional differences, the specific characteristics of production sectors, and the idea that the most important investments (and disinvestments) will always be made at company level. If the government chooses to supervise the environmental transformation processes generally and the manipulative means outlined earlier are applied, then we may have new key units. We can also make a broad outline of what they require of their

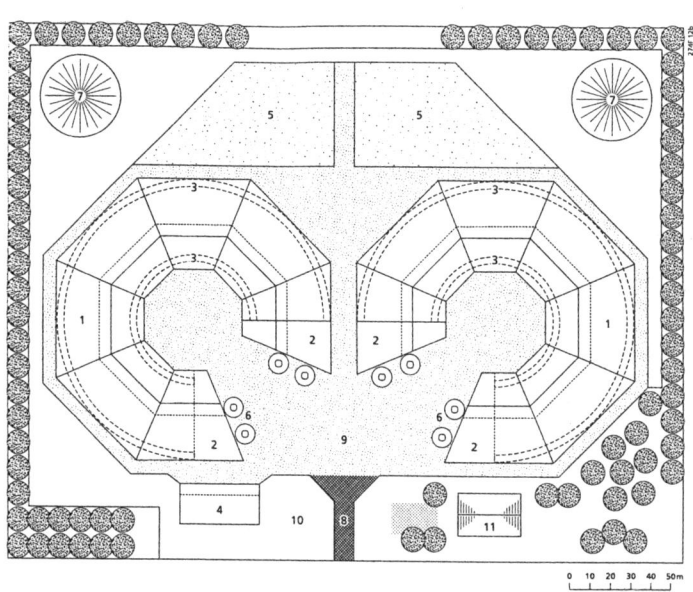

Would-be industrial buildings for the summer shed-feeding system for about one thousand cows.

environmental conditions. Our (not patently obvious) basic assumption here is that agriculture that belongs to an existing or non-existent sector extends unbroken over larger areas. Naturally, amongst the various key units we not only come across newcomers and runners-up, but also a number of those that are familiar. Some key units will need a bit of prodding from government planning or institutional finance, whilst others manage on their own. Occasionally there is evidence of one production sector displacing another. This is followed by the presentation of nine 'candidate' key units. The list could of course be extended. There is a brief description of each key unit, followed by an inventory of the spatial/environmental conditions for each one. In order to be able to distinguish them from one another, and to emphasise the future central role of marketing, we have given them names that have been taken from the firmament of the STAR.

Bertha 90210

This key unit refers to the core sectors of cattle breeding and diary farming, both of which are land-bound. They are probably situated in river areas, in parts of the Dutch peat grasslands, in sandy regions (in the route of the middle course of the stream valleys) and of course in Friesland. Bertha 90210 comprises every conceivable variant of future dairy farming, such as those that were investigated in the Koeien and Koersen (Cows and Courses) report.

The most striking variant is that of a 'dairy-industrial complex'. There is a good chance of raw fodder extraction, diary, breeding and manure processing developing into separate specializations within this variant. Wherever possible, this new key unit displaces agriculture from the edges of the peat district and the edges of the marine clay regions. In its most industrialised form, the complex extends over a gigantic area. The system of summer stable feeding and milking is introduced on demand in large stables with up to a thousand cows. The familiar Dutch landscape with grazing cows will be a thing of the past wherever this form of diary farming catches on. If one starts off with land-bound raw fodder extraction this could require up to five hundred hectares in terms of acreage, and if the sale of manure is also organised so that it is land-bound, then we are talking of about seven hundred hectares.

However, the Koeien en Koersen report also outlines less extreme variants: the hard-working one-man business with thirty-five hectares and five cows, or the grassland farmer with about eighty cows on eighty hectares. In these cases land-bound dairy farming is clearly a central activity from which, besides the sale of milk, other sources of income must be tapped. It is especially those farmers who feel a sympathy for 'technology and planning' that have a chance of progressing further in the direction of the large-scale variant.

The question is whether large areas such as these can be realised in the form of unbroken 'blocks', or whether a perfectly organised transport system and good communication will make it possible to 'fragment' a part of the acreage and spread it over a greater distance. This development can only succeed if the government is actively involved. However, this future image of diary farming clearly jeopardises the quality of life in rural areas. Many farmers will have to stand aside. And what will happen to the buildings and the land that fall vacant?

Will we have to do without such scenes?

Martine Bijl, Hak vegetables and Hak fruit

Business is booming in the cultivation of tuber vegetables. For convenience' sake this also includes the harvesting of high-quality sowing seeds. The prospects for agricultural crops however are a little less rosy, and only seed-potatoes and sugar beets appear to have any future at all. It is mainly due to a differentiated consumer demand that vegetable farmers can look to the future with any confidence. Indeed, vegetable farming is expected to gradually dominate traditional farming areas, such as marine clay areas and the polders of the IJsselmeer. Farmers who change to the cultivation of tuber vegetables will have to undergo a considerable mental adjustment, which should prove to be interesting material for agricultural sociologists. While arable farming requires the use of machinery on a gigantic scale at peak times, vegetable farming requires a combination of machines and manual workers at peak times. In order to cultivate tuber vegetables on land formerly used for arable purposes, certain adjustments will have to be made to the soil and in the field of hydrology.

Frau Antje

One of the leaders in the field of Dutch agriculture in the twenty-first century will be cultivation that is knowledge and capital intensive. This key unit is responsible for the coordination of tree cultivation, perennial plants, bulb cultivation, cut flowers, half-standard cultivation (revival of fruit cultivation), high quality raw materials (sowing seeds and plants), vegetable firstlings as well as intensive cattle farming. Bulbs are an example of the cultivation of raw material below the surface of the soil. Tree cultivation will take place more and

Our biggest large-scale arable farming pales into insignificance beside industrial-scale farming as seen in Picardy and Montana.

Is the industrial scale of the Ijsselmeer polders an indication of the scale of future bulb cultivation?

more in containers. Even now there is frequently very little 'solid ground to stand on' in cultivation under glass.

And wherever cultivation does take place in the ground, we shall have to search for ecologically sound ways to disinfect the soil and reduce the use of pesticides to a minimum. Temporarily flooding the bulb fields is in fact the only environmentally friendly way to combat nematodes and other pests in the soil.

Under the motto of 'cooling costs more than heating', there is still a future for cultivation under glass in the Netherlands. But only if it is optimised with regard to the environment and is situated on sites where residual heat from

 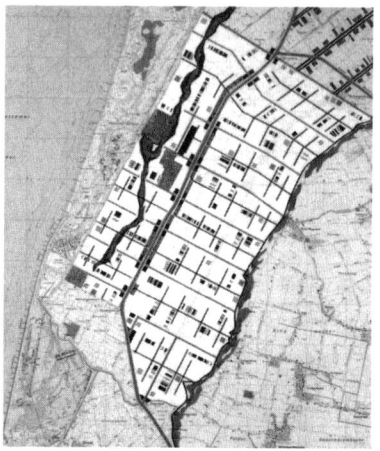

An aerial view of the 'travelling bulb stall'. At the top of the province of North Holland a spray-system for turning the soil over is used to convert a large area of land into ground that is suitable for bulb growing, in a sector that is anxiously looking for a clean substrate. A reduction in the use of pesticides and land-disinfection practices is imperative if the sector is to survive. Sand is removed from the substratum by suction and then sprayed over peaty soil. This has far-reaching effects on the natural environment and, by diffusion, on the landscape too.

The region where spray-turning has become widely used could be utilized entirely for the bulb-growing industry. An adjustment to the water system would facilitate both draining off dirty water and hyrological fine-tuning, thereby making it possible to flood each plot by seepage pressure. This is the only environmentally friendly way to disinfect the soil.

nuclear power stations, total energy, CO_2 production and an optimal linkage between energy consumers with their daytime peak (the city) can produce perfect examples of industrial ecology. This sector partly takes on the form of a small and medium-sized multinational company by establishing branches elsewhere in Europe and in other climactic zones, in order to provide the market with firstlings each season.

Knowledge-intensive vegetable cultivation cannot survive without good transport routes and modern distribution centres for the supply and sale of their products. A certain spatial concentration is necessary to produce a sufficient number of keen experts and cheerful enthusiasts. After all, it is they who must maintain the level of advanced knowledge on which this sector depends. This cultivation is at its strongest if it is situated in the proximity of urban conglomerates. In order to cope with strong fluctuations in demand, it depends on the urban labour market and a labour reserve. An interesting phenomenon occurs when urbanisation ousts glass cultivation areas: enforced relocation to the new outer city area is so generously reimbursed that part of it can be used to finance technological innovation. As far as the environment is

The creation of new projects could ensure that problems which cannot be solved at company level are dealt with: environment, the supply and retention of water with a low sodium content for recirculatory cultivation, energy, and last but not least, problems concerning the quality of the landscape (Huissen site).

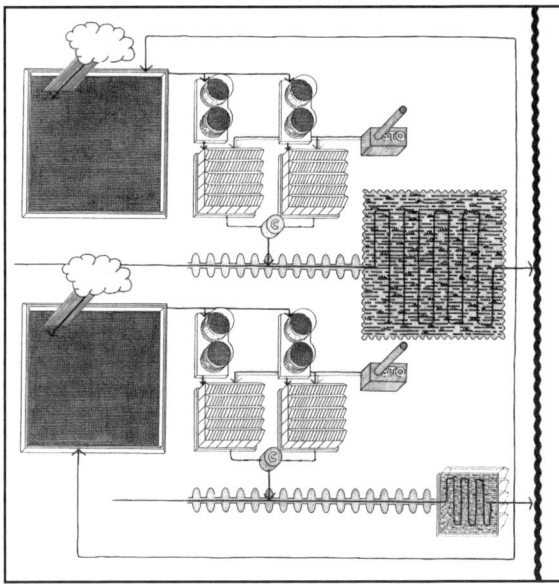

The umbrella approach, meaning complying with environmental standards for the project as a whole, is necessary to solve environmental problems for cultivation where there are no known techniques that are soil-free. Temporary heliophyte filters that are later occupied by new glass once the production of all the industries in one strip is 'clean'. Herein lies a financial incentive: for the moment, the interest that has to be paid on the land bought collectively for the swamp filter is still putting pressure on the exploitation of the project (Huissen plan).

concerned, much depends on whether umbrella arrangements (drawing up the environmental balance for a group of companies) can be made. This sector is technologically so highly specialised, that any expansion or new establishment can only be prepared and executed by specialised project developers.

The intensive livestock breeding of chickens, ducks and pigs is on the decrease. Cutbacks have resulted in the dominance of large companies that are almost entirely self-sufficient. Raising, breeding, fattening and slaughtering (and possibly even the processing of meat) takes place in large integrated companies. For veterinary reasons, company clusters are separated from one another by a type of firebreak. No pig farms are allowed in these zones, but one can expect to find other functions such as units of the ecological plan. Raw fodder extraction and the processing of manure continue to form the Achilles' heel of this sector and impose limitations on the amount of livestock.

Intensive algae cultivation

An underexposed opportunity for agricultural production lies in tying together technological, infrastructural and agricultural complexes in Dutch urban areas. The type of vegetable production that falls under this category not only benefits from foodstuff technology, which is very strongly represented in the Netherlands, but also from its relation to the pharmaceutical and petrochemical industries. Whereas the agrification of land-bound cultivation in the moderate zone has a relatively modest future (cannabis, chicory, marigolds, Jerusalem artichoke), good opportunities for the biomass production (through lower plant orders, micro-organisms and fungi) are logically the result of the strength of the Dutch economy. The manufacture of amino acids by fermentation on an industrial basis is also very promising.

This key unit also represents a variety of developments that extend from raw fodder production and industrially cultivated algae and seaweed to the use of agricultural products as an input for industrial processing. The dozens of industrial applications of potato flour as a raw material proves the viability of this type of development. New fronts have been opened for the technological contribution to agriculture. The genetic manipulation of plants and micro-organisms that affect growth are expected to greatly influence food production. In the bio technology complex in Leiden (!), the new technology being tested in companies such as Mogen and Genetech ranges from making several varieties of potato virus resistant, to the manufacture of pharmaceutical products through the metabolism of genetically manipulated animals. Developments in the field of after-harvest techniques continue to be very impressive.

The demand for products that belong to this key unit is expected to increase considerably. In any case, the petrochemical industry will have to focus on replacing fossil raw materials, which are gradually becoming scarce and costly, with alternative organic materials. The actual amount of land occupied by this key unit is not large and is coupled to present industrial and agro-technological centres. The links with other key units – land-bound or otherwise – are many. All in all, one could say that there is an agro-technical development with agriculture in the strictest sense forming a vital link in the total process. These production chains will mainly be supported by 'modern growers', and companies will emerge that are no longer traditional family businesses. The

Fermentation tanks for the conversion of sugar into amino acids in Hofu, Japan.

role of the government will lie mainly in appropriate industrial policy. The proper functioning of the investigative infrastructure is of vital importance to this key unit.

Monsieur Michelin

In the foreword of the Dutch translation of their epic cookery book, the Troisgros brothers, all of whom are three-star chefs from Roanne and famous because they serve only the very best products from their region, offer us the following encouraging words: "Hollanders, we congratulate you on your

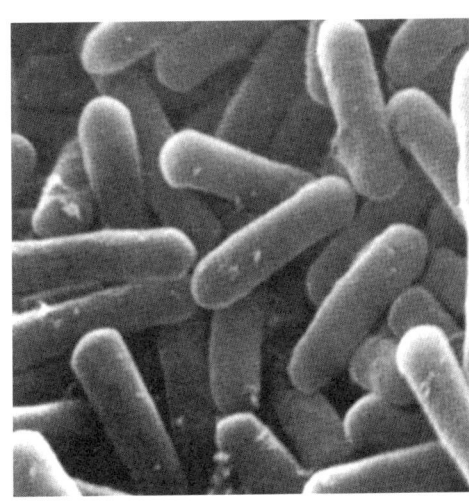

The use of lower orders of plant, seaweed, algae, fungi and micro-organisms for the production of biomass or additives will be used increasingly in food production chains, the pharmaceutical industry and to meet the petrochemical industry's demand for organic material. Bacillus Bevis, a bacteria that produces antibiotics.

spinach". Following three decades of basic culinary education, the Netherlands now appears to be ready for the next step: a culinary cultural offensive in which the focus of attention on the delights of home produce is linked to a reinstatment of the seasons. There are people who get a kick out of eating ostrich steaks, cumquats and raspberries at Christmas. Nevertheless, there is a small but interesting group of pioneer consumers who have created a market for regional specialities. With its differentiated landscape, the Netherlands offers wonderful opportunities for the production of different kinds of milk (blending for cheese making). Every type of land and the effects of impoverished soil and extensive grazing will yield a different type of meat (you are what you eat). The briny world is also a force to be reckoned with (sea kale, salicornia, sea aster, seaweed). The type of agriculture that this involves requires a certain measure of skill. Agrarian skill and a knowledge of the history of special cultivation and varieties is essential for the invention and rediscovery of regional delicacies and forgotten specialities. Amongst the hundreds of different kinds of apples and three hundred different kinds of pears that were common less than a hundred years ago, there are a number of very special qualities that deserve to be given a second chance. This key unit also includes

Systematic harvesting of the system also offers interesting prospects. For example, the more marshy parts of the Netherlands have a wonderful biomass production of the scaly ink mushroom. The small-scale sale and distribution of this product requires resourcefulness because it is highly perishable.

harvesting from outside the system, via hunting, erosion, culling in nature reserves (heckrunderen and red deer), and even the gathering of plants, mushrooms and forest fruits.

This key unit is to be found throughout the Netherlands: often in agricultural parts of the EHS with centres in lime-rich areas, along the coastal strip and the land bordering on the dunes, in the wet areas of the river region and in peat grassland areas. Monsieur Michelin is not only to be found in urban areas. The special agricultural conditions are more important than being situated near the market. The mycelium on which the key unit thrives is created by close cooperation between restaurants (possibly via a specialised distributive trade), cooperatives and enthusiastic area coordinators. The ecological plan and decreasing land prices in marginalised agricultural areas are favourable to the development of this key unit. Moreover, as suggested earlier on, Michelin can benefit from the stimulation of new agricultural differences. The main role of government is to subsidise area coordinators and establish a system of inspection and stamps for the products.

Mrs Farmer, née d'Urban

This key unit covers the trend of deprofessionalising parts of the rural areas. This development mostly takes place autonomously and has very little significance economically speaking. It is a way of life for economic survivors (Friese Wouden [Friesland Woods]) but also for those who have money and free time. Farmers who have a part-time job, hobby-like use, dog kennels, bee-keeping, stud farming and – a trend that has blown over from Germany – groups of city-dwellers who take over entire farms and continue to farm as an association. The Dutch variant of this category comprises small-scale arable farming and standard orchards. In short, advanced suburban rural life as is described in a magazine of the same name. The two extremes will gradually move closer to one another. It will become more difficult to distinguish between those who have a job on the side and leisure time farmers with an urban background. A more definite form of 'camping on the farm' produces a combined cultivation of dachas (simple holiday cottages with very few conveniences), and the use of agricultural land in surroundings with an

A Brabant variant of the Poule de Brest has taken top restaurants in the Netherlands and Belgium by storm. Agrarian entrepreneurs: an historian, a solicitor and two municipal officials from Den Dungen.

attractive landscape. Obviously, the fashionable second house for those who are well-educated, have an average income, and are opposed to the 'caravan culture', will seek out the man-made landscape as its setting. Here we see the gleam of an interesting future for those industries that are on the lookout for additional sources of income. This key unit is not only to be found in regions that are under the influence of urbanisation and in increasingly marginalised agricultural areas, but also in residual small-scale landscapes in the increasingly suburban northern and eastern parts of the country. All in all, these developments will deprive classical agriculture of a large area of land. Government regulation is mainly focused on segregation: stimulation in areas where this is seen as a positive development, and protecting fundamental agricultural areas from this 'disturbance' on the other.

Ko the Gamekeeper

Like many inventions, this too is based on coincidence. Quite coincidentally, in an important research project in the Shell laboratories for producing oil from biomass by boiling fibres under high pressure and then compressing and firing them, it turned out that if wood was subjected to all this torture, not only did it sweat out the black gold but it also appeared to have become

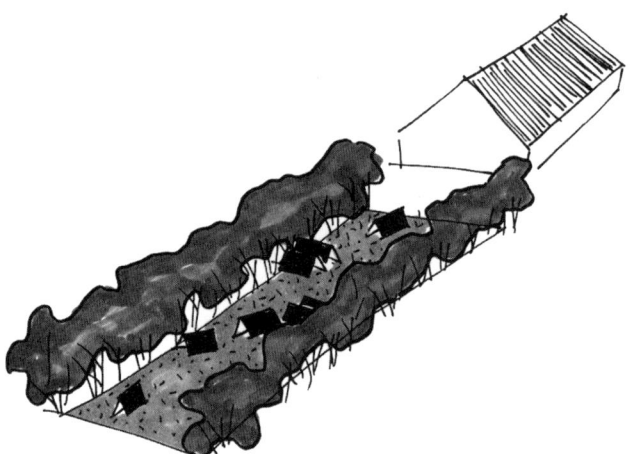

The highly popular 'camping on the farm' will be succeeded by the building of simple holiday farm cottages with very few conveniences (dachas). These can be built without too much red tape when it comes to obtaining building permits.

preserved without losing those properties that make it so suitable for building construction. Softwood species such as poplar and willow move up from category five to category two, and amazingly, species like beech and robinia into category one, which up to now has been a category occupied only by tropical hard wood. If we add to this the fact that with the exception of oil, wood shows the largest trade deficit in the European Community and that all the countries of the EC have committed themselves to closing this gap during

The fruit industry involving standard trees will become increasingly popular with associations formed by townspeople (and villagers), that will take over and run entire agrarian industries.

the next fifty years, then you will understand why increased (agrarian) wood cultivation is a fully-fledged key unit. The main issue not only involves wood suitable for building construction, but also the production of fibres for the paper industry. This can be realised through forestry, but poplar pulp is not the only raw material that can be used for this. The cultivation of cannabis can also produce the long fibres that are needed, and many farmers will welcome this extension of the development plan. This key unit will not only be evident in increasingly marginalised agricultural areas where the 'fast growing forestry' plan has caught on spectacularly well, but could prove to be interesting in the lower reaches of streams in need of water in the sandy regions of Brabant and Gelderland. Indeed, the highest yields are being realised with poplars under

The curing of softwood offers opportunities for replacing tropical hardwood in the building construction market.

similar conditions just across the Belgian border. Consequently, this key unit will also be boosted by the large-scale function changes in sandy regions that are necessary to organise the drinking water and industrial water supply along more permanent lines: stopping or adjusting the collection of groundwater restores the wet component to sandy areas. In other regions too, this key unit may occupy large areas of ground in the joins that separate different landscapes. In the meantime the government should make an important contribution by providing guarantees for use (in casco terms this involves a framework function), and continuing subsidies. This situation is one in which there is a transition to a market where domestically preserved wood has acquired a greater share, through consumer pressure and decreasing supplies from the rain forests.

Captain Iglo

With a backlog of about ten thousand years, the fishing industry will, by its own doing, also become sedentary and leave the hunter-gatherer stage. The farming of fish, crustaceans and shellfish will also become far more lucrative in our part of the world, because reduction of supply by overfishing (or the government's imposition of balanced fishing) must be balanced against the increasing demand by consumers whose diets include less or no meat at all. Parts of the estuaries and the seaward delta will be used for this. Situated

The curing of softwood offers opportunities for replacing tropical hardwood in the building construction market.
The cultivation of poplars on damp sandy soil offers enormous possibilities. Might this be Brabant after being made wet by a change in water extraction? Lommel, Belgium.

further out to sea, commercial farms coupled to new breakwater islands are also possible. Moreover, freshwater fish such as European catfish, trout and bass will increasingly be farmed. Intensive livestock farming will in part become intensive fish farming. There will also be links in which shrimp remains provide raw fodder production for pigs (or other fish). Of course there will still be offshore fishing, but on a smaller scale. Factory trawlers will be banned from substantial areas of the oceans and ecologically irresponsible fishing methods prohibited. This key unit may benefit from dynamic coastal supervision as well as natural and civil measures to counter the effects of the rising sea level. This will add the periphery and the places that are suitable for farming to the costal strip. With regard to supply, a distinction will be made between the fish farmer, often an ex-farmer who delivers cultivated products, and the fishmonger, who could be compared to a poulterer. The role of the government lies in the demarcation of rights of use for marine farming. Its most important task however, is to protect and restore depleted populations wherever possible. There should also be marine nature reserves where fishing is prohibited and which extend over large unbroken areas of the North Sea. The creation of wind turbine parks as a zoning measure can be used as a way of enforcing compliance.

A range of postmodern agricultural resources

Five of the eight key units require fairly strict government intervention in the environment. If we balance the time factor against the available finances, this

Compliance with the ban on fishing in Marine Reservations can be enforced through the use of wind turbine parks as a zoning measure. The turbine masts are also important because ten percent of the total biomass in the North Sea is tied to hard substrate, mainly shipwrecks.

means that there will also be an extensive 'residual category' around 2030. The environmental apparatus is characterised by slow procedures and slow implementation periods. Even if we assume that new land agents, project developers and financiers all do their share, dealing with all the areas that are likely candidates for one of these four keys will be very time-consuming.

Consequently, most of the land will have a somewhat chequered appearance in that it will comprise a mixture of mega-companies and small businesses, ranging from a basic farming set up to park farmers in urban agriculture, from automated rows of modern tuber cultivation to allotment gardens, and from container cultivation to agricultural areas filled with dachas. Precisely how colourful the patchwork quilt will be and where we shall encounter the range of resources depends on three factors. In the first place, where do government and agricultural organisations allow developments to take their course (or is it the slow environmental apparatus that hampers the timely seizure of an area for a certain, more explicit development)? Secondly, there is the vital experimental drive that rural renewal produces, and finally, the important differences in the Dutch landscape concerning the freedom to make individual decisions at company level. For example, landscapes with wind-borne sand deposits offer more flexibility than peat districts and the polders.

Looking ahead, we foresee an environmental development in agriculture that regionalises, or one that will make better use than ever before of the specific and relatively unique situation that has developed. The rich diversity of opportunities for cultivation our landscape offers, combined with a highly educated and highly skilled group of farmers, embedded in a smoothly running infrastructure for supply and transport, nourished by a home market that is prosperous and operates more and more critically, coupled to an agro and foodstuffs technological complex, annexed to the solution of environmental problems which initially appear to be insurmountable but prove to be a competitive advantage, and improved by an efficient research system, are all elements which when combined, guarantee an agricultural situation that other centres in Europe would find difficult to equal. Even if it were only possible to partly renew some of the classical land-bound sectors such as diary farming, and the tuber vegetable cultivation did not expand as expected, the image of an agriculture that is extremely vital both now and in the future would remain unchanged.

The proposed potential key units are of course not entities that have clearly defined boundaries. There are myriad overlaps and relationships. Some of them can be put to use or systematically directed so as to achieve a type of industrial ecology on a regional level in which residual products from one sector can be used as input for another sector.

Postmodern images of combi-cultivations will also appear on a micro-scale. Small-scale agriculture in combination with fruit trees, Denmark.

The collection does not include any separate unit that is labelled as 'biological' or 'ecological' agriculture. All key units have an 'ecological' variant wherever there is optimisation of the minimal use of fertilizers and pesticides, and where cycles are created. In some key units these variants are far removed from the current company plan (such as in Frau Anjes bulb-growing) whilst in others the ecology variant is situated very close (Monsieur Michelin). In the end it is the consumer who will determine what the relationship between 'ecological' and 'current' will be within the unit. Obviously the introduction of genetic manipulation in the food chain will shift the cutting edge of the consumer question from 'ecological' versus 'common practice' to 'natural' versus 'manipulated'. Consequently, the market is divided into three parts because Monsieur Michelin and 'ecological' agriculture supply an exclusive production for the most demanding consumers. Through the regulation proposed earlier on, the loss of minerals within the unit will basically be minimised. Sustainability has not therefore not been woven into this essay as a separate theme.

Nor has the term 'integrated agriculture' so far been used. This is because as an open-ended arrangement it will presumably become increasingly expensive and will be relatively short-lived. Indeed, performance-related payments will have to continually increase in order to close the gap between rising profits in 'ordinary' businesses and those in integrated business companies. The 'natural return' is frequently moderate. The 'property heirs' to integrated agriculture are Monsieur Michelin and the wide-scale use of new agricultural differences. Combined with the purchase of these sub-optimal agricultural areas by the government so that they can be used by selected business companies for a nominal amount, this will form an alternative to performance-related pay. Because these 'new differences' have evolved from the solution of regional problems, it will be possible to finance them using other government resources. Both elements have an interesting natural form of expression. Consequently, what is now known as integrated agriculture has acquired a more solid foundation.

In conclusion, I would like to make a few general comments on the environmental quality of rural areas. Withdrawn or proactive, there is one government obligation that must not be disregarded and which applies to almost all key units. The processes of change must be guided in such a way as to create new high-quality man-made landscapes. Contrary to a widespread misunderstanding, landscape is not something that is created by the (individual) farmer. Not only does it demand a great deal of design research, comparable to the recently published 'Koeien en Koersen' report, but also the passionate commitment of planners and landscape architects in the more systematic adjustments of the landscape.

Dirk Sijmons & Dick Hamhuis
This text is an abridged version of an essay of the same title, which was commissioned by the Nationale Raad voor het Landbouwkunde (National Council of Agricultural Research) and published in September 1997 in the NRLO series of explorations into the future 'Veranderende relaties tussen landbouw en Maatschappij op weg naar 2015' (Changing relationships between agriculture and Society up to 2015). A popular version was published in February 1998 in the jubilee edition of the WLTO, published by Roodbont in Zutphen.

---

1. This line of renewal requires powerful top-down supervision at regional, national and European levels. References for this perspective are taken from publications by C.T. de Wit, R. Rabbinge and the Albrecht/De Zeeuw commission.

2. Bottom-up supervision at a regional and national level is necessary here. References for this perspective are to be found in the work by J.D. van der Ploeg. An example is the Waterlandse Corporatie (Jan Boom).

3. This line of renewal requires top-down environmental regulations and bottom-up supervision of the entire column on national and European levels. References are to be found in the work of Goewie.

NEW ADVENTURES AHEAD

Far and away the largest project in the environmental planning portfolio covers an area of about 50,000 hectares. To put it into perspective: in this area all the VINEX urban expansions, the fifth runway at Schiphol, the second area of low-lying land next to the River Maas, the high-speed train line and the Betuwe line can all have a game of indoor football. And yet many people have still never heard of the Ecologische Hoofdstructuur (EHS) [Overall Ecological Structure Plan]. The EHS is an ambitious government plan to halt the decline of nature by substantially increasing the share taken by natural areas in our landscape in the space of fifty years and by strengthening the position of existing natural areas. This project should take shape by developing new natural sites in favourable locations and by creating connective zones between the natural areas in order to ease the migration and spread of plants and animals. This is by no means an unnecessary luxury in a fragmented landscape where many isolated populations are threatened with slow extinction.

Primal nature or farmer's nature

Debate in society about this mega-project has until now been limited to local flare-ups of resistance by farmers who find the return of land to nature difficult to swallow emotionally, and a more abstract discussion among biologists about the underlying views of nature. The line of thought of the adherents of natural development was soon jeered at with undisguised mockery as being the pursuit of 'primal nature', and such rhetorical questions as 'do they want us to go back to Betawe?' have become common. Since the question of effectiveness (how much chlorophyll do I get for every guilder spent?) is gradually but clearly going the way of the natural developers [1], we can reply to these 'fans of interweaving' equally condescendingly by referring to 'farmers' nature', meaning what they see as marginal tinkering with nest-protectors, ditch-side management and field weeds. Environmental philosophers point to the socially-based differences in the underlying views of nature [2], but they are also divided into several 'schools' that batter each other with learned arguments invoking ecological science. In the early eighties the environmental hygienists joined the discussion and pointed out the significance of nature (even when impoverished) as an indicator of healthy management in agriculture. The traditional nature conservancy groups surround the debate with their testy grumbling that 'for anyone who has not witnessed the decline of nature almost any nature seems good enough'. The 'yes it is - no it isn't' yo-yoing that has now dominated the professional debate on natural development for about ten years tends to displace the much more interesting question of how one can work on natural development and what role design would play in it. This was the reason for the Stichting LOCUS to put the topic of 'Designing natural development' on the agenda of its fourth annual design seminar. Various teams of landscape architects and ecologists were given three days to get their teeth into a choice of assignments including one on the Maas where it runs close to the border, the 'Delta bastion' east of 's-Hertogenbosch and a seaward extension of the Maas flats. The intention of the design seminar was an exploration of the possibility of creative dialogue between the two main actors in the development of the EHS. There now follow my reflections on the outcome.

Does form really follow function?

One of the design teams submitted an intriguing piece of work in the form of a matrix (Jansen en van den Boomen, 1993). They compared several possible directions for natural development in the area of the Maas near the border to the two positions the landscape designer can take up: 'arcadian' and 'autonomous'. If I interpret the matrix correctly, it appears they come to the conclusion that the architectural angle is largely irrelevant: plants and animals do not after all care much about the designed form in which they live. This conclusion, which lacks any sign of post-modernism, sounds as if the last ecologist or landscape designer to leave the seminar is turning off the light. The search for the conditions for fruitful collaboration comes to an abrupt end. In taking this attitude the two professions are slipping apart from each other like water off a duck's back. But is it really so simple? At the risk of being seen as a frustrated designer who has just been condemned to the role of make-up artist, I would like to consider this attitude more closely. Processes are of course troublesome to those who have been trained with the adage 'form follows function'. It is mainly the spatial determinists in landscape design (who are for that matter becoming increasingly rare), who stubbornly continue to believe in the possibility of solving virtually every problem by spatial means, that have a great deal of trouble with the fact that natural processes continue in their changes in an almost annoying way.

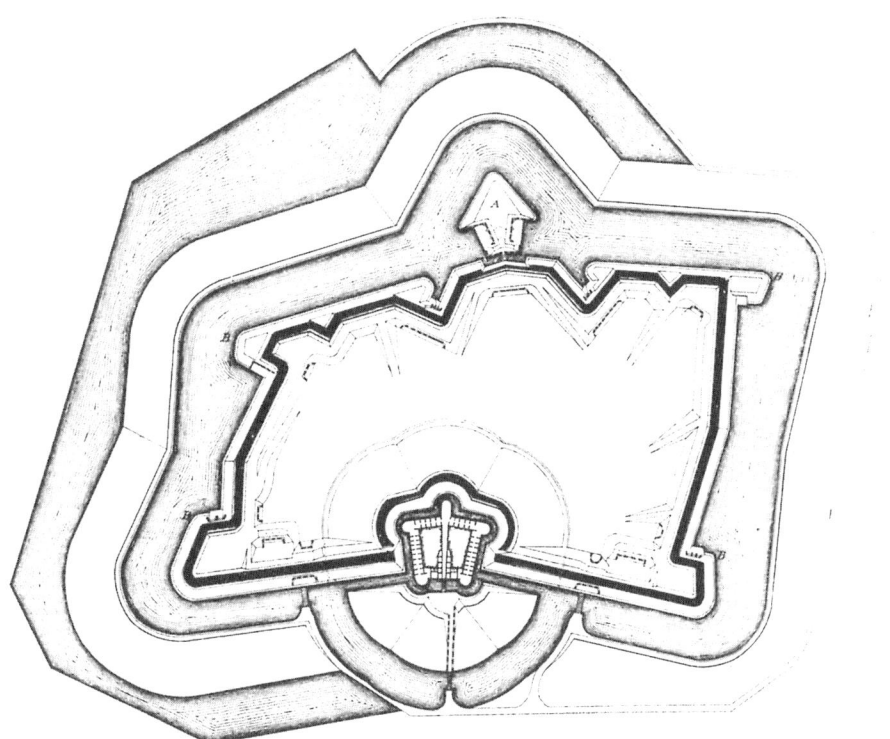

A nineteenth-century fluke: Fort Rijnauwen
Excavation of the material for the ramparts upturned the stratification of the soil. Sand came to lie on top of a layer of clay. In the course of time water erosion has steepened this gradient. The shape of the fort and its moat means that every possible degree of exposure to sun and wind and transitions from wet to dry are found here. A drowsy military existence and similar management has resulted in a habitat exceptionally rich in species. This construction can be considered a refuge for the majority of the species of plants, insects and fungi of the river region.

The first problem with the view that the landscape designer has little concern with the field of natural development is that no other object of design seems so much to demand the reversal of the usual adage into 'function follows form' as does nature. Plants and animals turn out to react more sensitively to their housing conditions than the most demanding of househunters. For those who wish to see it, our country is full of fine examples of nature following human deeds. Hundreds of examples of 'answers' to questions never consciously asked. The ecological communities of Zeeland on artificial rocky coasts as an answer to the use of riprap in a sandy estuary. Grassland birds as an answer to our specific agricultural exploitation of the low-lying peat areas. The formation of the Oostvaarderplassen in that part of Flevoland that was the last to be drained.

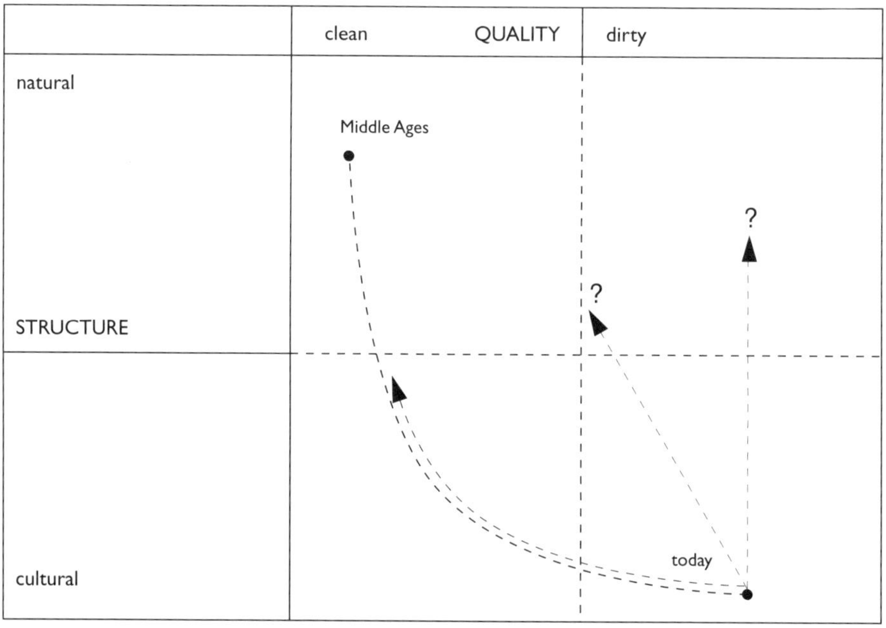

	clean QUALITY dirty
natural	
STRUCTURE	
cultural	

Paths of degradation and redevelopment.
Many ecosystems have been greatly changed and degraded. This simplified chart shows the path of degradation. An anthropogenic structure has been superimposed on the natural structure. It is mainly after the invention of fertiliser that the line shifted from the low nourishment to high nourishment area. The question of the course of natural development is indicated by the various dotted lines. Is there any future in scrambling back up the line we came down or are there other possibilities?

The nomadic ecological communities of the reclaimed land always present somewhere in proximity of a city, and even the couple of wall creepers on the main building of the University of Amsterdam. These are all examples of the resilience of the main contractor we have 'engaged' for the job of development: nature itself.

Choosing is for humans

Ten years ago, these signs of life in a nature declared to be moribund inspired ecologists and landscape architects to formulate ideas on natural development. The logical conclusion that 'answers' could also be induced into the desired direction opened up a challenging perspective. The newly developed natural technology turned out to provide elegant solutions not only for natural development but also for miscellaneous other projects. In this respect it appears increasingly to have developed into an 'advanced cultivation technique'.

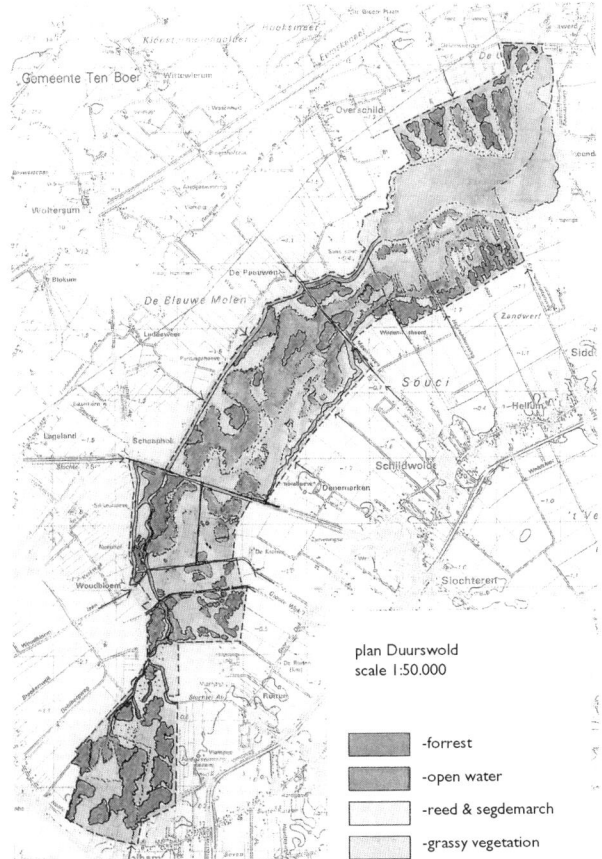

plan Duurswold
scale 1:50.000

- forrest
- open water
- reed & segdemarch
- grassy vegetation

Biologists' design language
One of the largest natural development projects conceived under the EHS is between the Hunzedal and the Schildmeer in Groningen. A metre of the top-soil was removed here and there to create a better situation from which to start, and this material was piled up to create height differences. The eco-technicians that did it know very well what nature wants. The existing contours are being reinforced (new gradients!) and in its creators' eyes the twisting, turning scene is more the product of a scientific process than of a design. However, the result is a monstrosity that turns its back on the existing landscape. This is an example of an ecocratic plan in which only the objectives of one single sector have played a part. The government seems not to be aware of the cultural component of its role of handing out assignments in this area of policy.

The realisation that there are possible choices has toppled the seventies' attitude that ex cathedra value-free judgements could be made on what was 'bad' and what 'beneficial' for nature. After all, choosing is for humans. Is it only ecological or also cultural arguments that affect the choice? Or, to take it a step further, can ecological arguments actually be separated from cultural values and standards? Or yet another step further: does this country get the nature it deserves? This professional debate rapidly expands into a social polemic, as witnessed by the blazing row over the conservation or surrender to the sea of Rottumerplaat, or more recently, the depopulation of Tiengemeten island. So it is partly a question of point of view in ecology too. The architect and the ecologist can look each other in the eye again. It is precisely this broadening of the issue that forms an important element in the collaboration between landscape ecologists and landscape architects. A combination of the primarily retrospective scientific work and the designer's prospective discipline provides opportunities to involve the cultural component in the debate on natural development.

One might take the attitude that no design work is needed for natural areas and that you just have to let nature take its own course. But because there is no causal sequence between programme and the one right solution, and because it is mainly artificial interventions that are needed in order to set the process of natural development in motion and guide it, design decisions are always an issue. Without collaboration with landscape architects, ecologists are condemned to a sort of biologists' design language. Nature has to squirm, after all! In his turn, the landscape designer who ventures into natural development projects without the support of ecologists will not get very far, having alienated his most important 'construction advisor'.

Man and nature
An extreme example to clarify the difference between an historical reference and a vision.
A realistic detail from what is probably the oldest prehistorical reference landscape that is relevant to the relationship between man and nature. The leopard Dinofelis, which was until recently assumed to be a predator specialising in hominids and apemen, with his prey. It is also probable that 'our' predator became extinct as a result of organised hunting by hominids. This historical reference makes it clear that this first (?) cultural act may well have been the most far-reaching. Since then we have been a species of animal that is 'on holiday' on this planet. The reintroduction of the Dinofelis is only possible at a conceptual level.

Does new nature also produce new landscapes?

The collective project is an adventurous quest for new forms for things that have until now not had any formal expression, or, perhaps more accurately, it is a quest for the possibilities of liberating forms from processes. These are forms which I am firmly convinced will avoid the dozy dichotomy between 'autonomy' and 'Arcadian' in the abovementioned matrix. The question of which elements still have to have their form defined in areas where natural processes are once again set free also requires interdisciplinary consideration. The most important question in this collaboration is perhaps the definition of the role of natural development at landscape level, in which the complex relationships with other types of land use have to be shaped. In the present cases the design process will point in the direction of new alliances which, it is true, will not achieve the natural objectives entirely but may well be able to provide the essential social consensus for these far-reaching changes. In short, the most complex problem lies perhaps not in the new natural areas themselves, but in their embedment in a living cultural landscape.[3] So in the end it comes down to representing the present-day position of man with regard to nature. There is too little attention paid to this problem in the rather introverted implementation of nature policy. It cannot be that the nature conservancy movement, as a newly-created 'do and fix' sector, itself suffers from the same sector-linked blindness they have always accused others of. A sizeable programme like the EHS puts at least part of the responsibility for the future of the landscape into the hands of nature policy.

Feasibility and natural target-types

What are the real obstacles to collaboration? The problems are concentrated mainly at the programme level. The social debate on the direction to be taken by nature conservancy and natural development (primal nature versus farmers' nature) has, one might say, been internalised within the EHS project with striking rapidity. The protagonists of virtually every orientation have all been given something. The polder model makes all views of nature equally legitimate. Everyone is right. The differences of outlook are safely tucked away in the conclusive typology of the natural target-types that make the policy controllable in a modern way and provides it with goals and visions (Bal, 1995). My objection applies not so much to the formation of a consensus (even if it is only an agreement to disagree) by way of this typically Dutch official filtering of semi-scientific typologies, as to the absolute and unshakeable belief that everything we might like is actually feasible. I am not referring to the problem of 'creating' systems that need an extremely long development period, such as living high moorland. I am thinking much more of the mechanistic certainty that systems congruent with predetermined goals will arise out of existing (and unique) initial situations. In order to explain this objection I am permitting myself a short diversion.

Reference images:
punishment for improper use

In recent years a powerful tool has been developed to make it possible to discuss the question of the direction taken by natural development: the use of reference systems. Whereas architects know this resource best in the form of reference images - 'the catalogue' of previously tried and tested solutions and completed projects to which one can refer in one's design - in the hands of ecologists this instrument is given a slightly different import. The original purpose of working with reference systems was to learn something about the characteristics (such as the potential) of the system in question (Baerselman,

Man and nature 2

We can give an equally striking example to illustrate the difference between a prospective vision and a projected image of the future. In a laboratory for artificial intelligence experiments are carried out using small insect-like robots that can do simple tasks like responding to instructions (collecting all the trashed plastic cups in the lab!) or which have to show reactions to stimuli (sound) and translate them into actions. They are intended for the exploration of planets by unmanned space vehicles. By crossing research into Artificial Intelligence with research into the construction of micro-tools, the development of new 'animal species' with a specific task or niche becomes a plausible (projected) image for the future. The question remains whether this can be called a vision. The same applies to the development of the genetic manipulation of plants and animals.

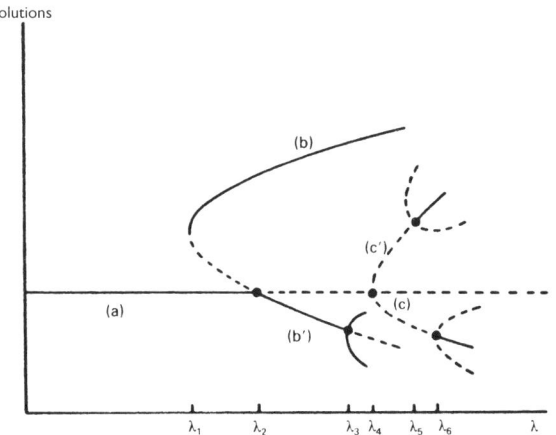

Where to?

Fork diagram. 'Steady state' solutions as a function of fork parameter $\lambda < \lambda_1$ then there is only one stationary state per value of l; the set of these states is the branch a. If $\lambda = \lambda_1$ then two other sets of states are possible (the branches b and b'). The b' states are unstable but become stable as soon as $\lambda=\lambda_2$, while the states in branch a then become unstable. If $\lambda=\lambda_3$ the branch b' becomes unstable again and two other stable branches appear. When $\lambda=\lambda_4$ the unstable branch a reaches a new forking point where two new unstable branches are possible, which remain so until l$\lambda=\lambda_5$ and $\lambda=\lambda_6$.

1990). However, a distinction was made between prehistorical or historical references and geographical reference landscapes. We can learn a lot for projects from historical references. They show us, for example, how to reconstruct from the soil ecological developments that can tell us something about the course of evolution over a long period of various ecosystems. What is especially instructive in the present situation is the study of the period of the major migrations (about 400 AD), when, as a result of social instability, large areas of cultivated agricultural land was abandoned and underwent a return to woodland (Joosten, 1992). This process can teach us all sorts of things in a Europe where hundreds of thousands of hectares of agricultural land are being abandoned. The process of leaving land to lie fallow and the departure of farmers from entire regions is occurring once again, because after the GATT agreements European agriculture has to compete on the world market. Geographical reference landscapes are more tangible. They are ecosystems that are still functioning well elsewhere and are comparable to what we want to develop here. They are able to provide information on driving natural processes and make it possible to identify so-called key species in a system.

Unfortunately a process is occurring in which the reference systems, a way of learning, are being confused with the objective: they are transformed into visions. This confusion also plays a part in the accusation that people who make use of prehistoric reference images aspire to a primal form of nature. Landscape designers can only make an indirect contribution to this discussion by pointing out the countless examples in which in this profession the least appealing results arose in cases where the products of analysis were elevated to design solutions without mediation. A situation arises in which all that now happens is the reproduction of images (from elsewhere or from the past).

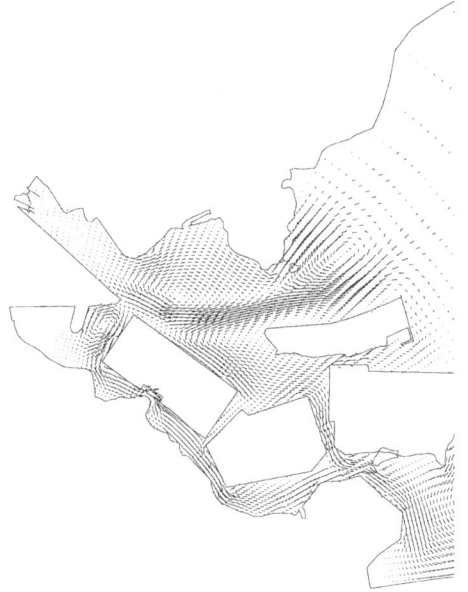

The arrangement of islands of the Amsterdam city-extension IJburg, has been optimised with the help of the Waterways Laboratory so that the speed of the water current when the wind is blowing landward or seaward sees to it that the ground on which a hard top layer of shells has been deposited is periodically cleared of silt that has drifted down onto it, thereby creating an ideal environment for triangular mussels, which in their turn are the staple diet of seabirds.

New adventures ahead

What is more important is that there is also reason for scientific doubt about the certainty with which natural target-types are posited. In ecology, the solid theoretical anchors of the clear stages of succession in the direction of well-defined climactic ecological communities are starting to drag. New and cautious hypotheses are leading in the direction of system descriptions that allot a more important role to processes of chance in which developments can take place in essentially different directions as a result of bifurcations from a specific initial situation (Prigogine, 1983; Kauffman, 1993). In this approach, stability in the traditional sense is only a temporary feature of the system. In this way of thinking the memory of the system plays a major part (the initial situation) but a complete return to an earlier state of the system is not possible. So it seems as if the way back along the path we followed from the figure shown at the beginning of this chapter has been cut off for theoretical reasons. It is natural – there are laws. Sometimes it is as if nature were running to a

Architectural definition and processes of chance: Westpolder.
The Province of North Brabant commissioned research into soil clearance as an instrument for natural development. Examples were set up in an infiltration area, a stream valley and in a potential seepage area: the Westpolder near Breda. Land beyond the removed seepage was annexed by surface soil clearance. The strips cleared keep to the original orientations of the plots, creating ponds oriented differently from the prevailing wind direction. The initial situation shown here forms the basic grid on which various natural processes have an effect in the course of time, with extremely varying results. Erosion and sedimentation will determine events in the ponds with the longest surface. Wind and wave action will cause local collapses in the intervening fields between the ponds perpendicular to the prevailing wind direction. Under the influence of these processes the grid will display and seriously modify various expressions of seepage-dependent nature. Only the three axes from which soil is cleared are formally defined: these new 'development axes' will be planted with vegetation. Apart from this chance will play the leading role (see page 142/143).

timetable. When the initial situation is known, the small steps in clearly bounded systems can be nicely predicted. However, the danger is that the effect of the EHS may degenerate into a succession of such Pavlovian reactions that we elicit from nature. What is most in danger from this is the chance of self-ordering in the large continuous areas where we may be amazed by an unpredicted course of development. Debate at the programme level consequently has a cultural component too and lends itself to interdisciplinary discussion. In the Netherlands arguing for adventurousness (and mystery) is more or less absurd. Nevertheless, it would be a pity if we did not succeed in rising above the highly technocratic debate on natural target-types. The prospect of the complete overlay of the EHS with natural target-types deprives this honest but not childish project of a large part of its soul even before it starts. The contrast between determinists and people who do want adventure runs right across the disciplines and seems to me to be more essential than magnifying the supposed contrasts between landscape architects and landscape ecologists. But perhaps this sort of patchwork of safe compromises and collections of species-oriented hobbies is precisely the nature this country deserves. The great mystery of the Dutch landscape is after all the lack of mystery.

Dirk Sijmons
An adaptation of the introduction to the opening of the exhibition at the fourth Locus seminar on designing natural development on 23rd April 1993. This talk is included in the exhibition catalogue (published by the Stichting LOCUS) and thereafter appeared in 'Landschap' magazine published by the Werkgemeenschap Landschapsecologisch Onderzoek, (10), 2, 1993.

1. Sijtsma, F.J., et al., Effectanalyse Ecologische Hoofdstructuur, Stichting Ruimtelijk Economie, Groningen, 1995.

2. RMNO, Vijf visies op natuurbehoud en natuurontwikkeling, Raad voor het Milieu- en Natuuronderzoek, The Hague, 1988.

3. See also 'Vliegtuigstrepen in een wolkenlucht' in: Feddes, F.J. (ed.), Oorden van Onthouding: Over natuurontwikkeling in een verstedelijkt Nederland, Nai uitgevers, Rotterdam, 1998.

GREEN HEART?
GREEN METROPOLIS!

In 1908 the Algemeene Nederlandsche Wielrijdersbond [Dutch Cycling Association] celebrated its 25th anniversary. To mark the occasion it published four books on the beauty of our country. The authors went out by car, bicycle, skates and boat to sing the praises of the Dutch landscape. Birdsong in the silent polder! The wealth of flowers in the spring meadows! The twisting rustic lanes with windmills, old farms, bridges, ditches and grazing cows. A cycle ride through the farmland and a picnic at the waterside. It could not be more Dutch than that. The books draw a picture of what was to grow into an almost indestructible ideal in the following decades; the ideal of the modern urbanite who in his spare time goes out to enjoy nature and the charming landscape.

A twin phenomenon
The Green Heart, as the area enclosed by the West Holland conurbation is called, is the policy-makers' expression of this ideal. The Dutch cities of the west have grown up in the form of a ring, largely due to the exceptional hydraulic and soil characteristics of the land, and this encloses a large inner area. These twin phenomena have since the fifties been known as the 'Randstad' [Cities round the edge] and the 'Groene Hart' [Green Heart].

The Dutch landscape does not derive its characteristic features from savage and unspoilt nature. Outside the city the landscape is primarily determined by the form of agricultural use. And with the farmer as the manager of its landscape, the Netherlands was always a richly blessed country. We only troubled ourselves about the fine landscapes that were sacrificed to city or industry and about pollution. In spite of this the conviction remained that agriculture could manage the largest part of our countryside in such a way that a situation was maintained that was attractive for recreation or, seen most optimistically, would arise as a 'by-product' of agrarian activities. This was of course a very practical idea and everyone who sits fishing in a polder ditch on a quiet spring morning or skates from Schoonhoven to Oudewater on a fine winter's day will be grateful for it.

And yet things are not right in the Green Heart. There are certainly still silent beautiful places, but their number is decreasing at an alarming speed. Nowhere in the Netherlands have the small towns and village centres grown as fast as here. Apart from housing, it is also new infrastructure, industry, new forms of agriculture and other accessories to modern life - rubbish dumps for example - that are also threatening the Green Heart from within and without. The heart is shrinking and the green is rapidly turning yellow.

The dwindling of the Green Heart is a consequence of miscellaneous claims by society on space. The expression 'the heart gets smaller' immediately exposes the weakness of the concept: the Green Heart lacks geographical boundaries anchored in the landscape. It has a heart of paper. It figures chiefly in policy documents. And however forceful the statements used in these documents may be, verbal protection is not sufficient. Agriculture plays a key role in the insidious process of the Green Heart's shrinkage. The counter-pressure agriculture is able to put up against urbanisation is declining in strength. Since the fifties agriculture has in social terms lost a great deal of importance. A more serious matter is the fact that the economic resilience of traditional agriculture is increasingly being put to the test. Production that is bound to the land (stock and arable farming) is doing poor to middling. Future prospects, in the light of increasingly market-oriented management and decreasing European protection and regulation, are especially sombre for arable farming. The government measures needed to save the environment do not make it any easier for the farmer either. It is therefore not surprising that the enthusiasm for farming among the present younger generation has dramatically decreased. It is partly as a result of this that many hectares of farming land have fallen prey to other uses, not only in the sphere of influence of the larger cities, but just as much in the surroundings of such provincial towns as Gouda, Alphen and Woerden.

Death by Gladioli

What is the state of the green 'content' of the Green Heart? Insofar as the beating of the green heart is sustained by the agrarian cultivated landscape it is not a very cheerful story. The first problem is that of accessibility. A tough and stubborn problem. The preamble to the 1931 Amsterdam 'Boschplan' was already condemning it:

'The polder land round Amsterdam, as beautiful as it is with its broad and peaceful waters, its intimacy and its hazy distances, and however much one can enjoy its beauty, withholds from its admirer important and essential elements which elsewhere make time spent in natural surroundings so salutary. The recreation (or re-creation) experienced by the city-dweller, who is so tightly restricted on every side, lies not only in the enjoyment its beauty offers the eye and the healthy exercise in fresh air, but also in the freedom to go where one wants, in contact with the plants, animals and soil. In the beneficence of silence and in the purity of life one feels around one, and lastly in the contrast between the free grouping of objects in nature and the strictly ordered life of the city.

The polder land cannot at the moment be entered except by road, with every square metre used for production, and the ditches hold the walker within narrow confines. The only places in the middle of the countryside where one can relax is on the broad shoulders of the dykes and certain roads.'

There has not been much improvement since then. A lot of new recreation areas have of course been laid out, but accessibility to the agrarian countryside has only declined. It was only by means of major administrative efforts that it was possible to establish a few cycle routes along private roads on agricultural land. At the present moment no less than 4.5 million city-dwellers live around the inaccessible property of about three thousand agrarian landowners.

In the course of the seventies it appeared that we could not expect economically profitable agriculture also to serve the interests of good nature conservation and maintain a richly filled landscape. The demands the government can make in this respect would soon undermine the viability of the agricultural sector. The fact that after almost thirty years, subsidy schemes to encourage private nature conservancy have finally caught on among farmers is

On the back of mum's bike from one cheesemaking farmer to the next, a landscape to which developments in agriculture will gradually force us to say goodbye.

a sign of how great the need has become rather than a sign of the wholehearted embrace of nature conservancy. Furthermore, in the light of the problems in the Randstad it is too little, too late.

The landscape value of the Green Heart hangs more than ever in the balance. An outing in the area no longer provides the pleasant relaxation that was so natural at the time of the Boschplan. A picnic where the muck-spreader has just passed is no fun at all. Few find the view of silos and groups of corrugated iron buildings attractive. Even night-time darkness has become a rare commodity, and that here in the country! The degradation of the landscape in the Green Heart is partly the consequence of the intensification of arable and cattle farming. But the greatest changes have been brought about by those branches of agriculture that are doing well economically: knowledge and capital-intensive production. Bulb cultivation, greenhouses, tree nurseries and intensive cattle breeding are the strong growth areas in agriculture. And it is precisely these businesses, linked as they are to the city and urban infrastructure, that put up resistance to advancing housing construction and industrial sites. The space occupied by this sector in the Green Heart has increased substantially. We have to see this knowledge and capital-intensive production with its industrial features as a part of the urban fabric. The radical transformation of agriculture at once turns the notion of the farmer as a conserver of nature into a fantasy.

From VINEX to ZESNO

Should we mourn the possible loss of the Green Heart? No, say the cynics. Why hold onto the idea of a well-spent free Sunday in an area that consists of an inaccessible, polluted, monotonous succession of acid-green pasture sown exclusively with tetraploid English rye-grass and where peace and quiet are nowhere to be found? Why should this take the place of a much less abstract and generally shared desire for a house with a garden in the proximity of a town? It is not without reason that the image of the endless sea of houses in Los Angeles has recently cropped up more regularly in professional journals.

However, the cynical view of the decline of the Green Heart, which has been encouraged by a government seemingly incapable of turning the tide, disregards the unique opportunity to reshape the Green Heart into an area of superb outdoor areas and allure. Just as Amsterdam got its Vondelpark in the 19th century and the Boschplan in the 1930s, the Randstad with its huge concentration of population also needs sizeable green counterbalances in its immediate surroundings. Because, although the classic Sunday cycle ride is no longer the model for the modern city-dweller's varied leisure activities, the need for space, freedom and peace is still equally pressing.

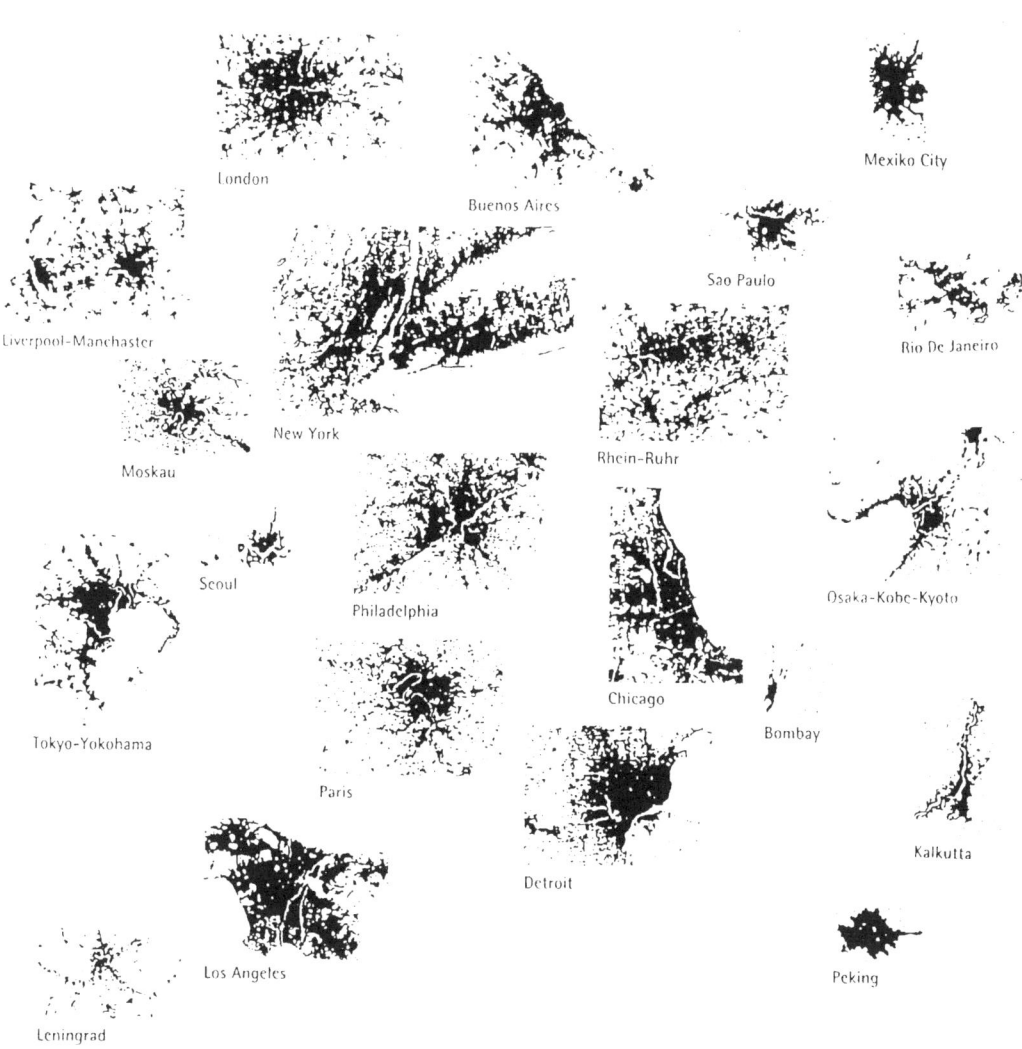

A comparison of patterns in major metropolitan systems shows up a number of similarities: for example, the maximum distance the city-dwellers in a random urban system have to travel to find the first unbuilt area is about 5.5 kilometres. There are considerable differences in the size and standard of design of these 'chlorophyll grains'.

Even more so because almost all the locations in the enormous VINEX[1] housing programme (and the succeeding VIJFNEX and ZESNO) have a common Achilles heel: they are all in the 'second and third choice' categories. The fine locations, where it is not hard to build attractively in an appealing setting, are almost all used up: hardly any more can be found. If city-dwellers still want to be able to find the space that fits their leisure activities, and preferably in walking or cycling distance, such places will have to be created or protected before they vanish.

Creating and protecting are two essential concepts for the future of the Green Heart. Parts of the area are more than worth protection, in most cases for cultural historical reasons and sometimes for their actual or potential natural value. Effective protection needs local sharpening of the present restrictive policy. Where this quality is lacking, goal-oriented investment should make up for it. The investments can be realised by incorporating them into the planned development of the adjoining urban extensions. If the Randstad metropolis wishes to be assured of a rich, varied and usable countryside this century, action must be taken now. The Green Heart as an administrative concept is the only means available to halt the sell-off of what remains of the countryside in Holland. The present concept has spent its force. It is ideologically outdated and the programme no longer suffices. There are two possible ways of charging up the concept with new meaning and energy.

A new grounding

First of all the Green Heart deserves better geographical and programmatic grounding. At the moment it is fragmented into a number of peat meadow areas, pond areas, drained land and ribbon development along old peat rivers. Some of these elements have a landscape or ecology value. Others, meaning the drained land, are of much less value, but are extremely well suited to a number of other purposes of which the Randstad has an urgent need, such as locations for suburban housing. The beautification of the Green Heart as a whole must be replaced by a more selective strategy whereby the parts that deserve it are protected and enriched and others are surrendered to the development of precisely defined programmes. This strategy should lead to recognisable units and a countryside with clear boundaries which can also actually be maintained.

Secondly, those parts of the Green Heart that are valuable as landscape are crying out for an active investment policy of a higher order than currently provided for. These investments should prevent the preservation of the Green Heart being dependent on agriculture alone. The elements that appear most suitable for the development of a green infrastructure that can withstand the ravages of time and for the absorption of the ever-changing urban programme would in the main seem to be large natural areas, accessible to city-dwellers and combined with utilities such as drinking water extraction and the generation of energy.

One of the most important qualities we shall have to aim for is that of the large format. This is the indispensable condition for the provision of peace and a feeling of freedom and adventure. The only way to enable natural values to coexist peacefully with the city-dweller's recreation is to create large areas. The time has come to safeguard the last remaining large continuous areas. This means areas of the size of the Vechtplassen, the Biesbosch and the Kagerplassen. In this chain only the Biesbosch has adequate planning protection. The other areas are exposed to imminent fragmentation. They can be compared to 'green thousand-guilder notes' which, if we wait ten years, will be exchanged for nine notes of a hundred guilders (if agriculture has not yet chased away all the meadow birds by then) and a little loose change. The ANWB [Dutch equivalent of AA or RAC] and the World Wildlife Fund are thus not allowing themselves to be drawn into the narrowed question whether one is for or against the Green Heart, but argue for goal-oriented investment one level lower down. It is preferable to make the effort at this level than to enter into a strategy of defeat in far too large a 'Green Heart' by way of a homeopathic dilution of policy.

When do we switch to plan B?

There remains the question of the financial and administrative guarantees for the implementation of this sort of strategy. Because if we no longer see agriculture as the natural creator of our landscape, we relinquish the possibility of getting a cheap ride from an economically healthy power. The unique cohesion between recreation, nature and urbanisation policies found in the Netherlands in the thirties gradually fell apart after the war. Now that large numbers of homes are being built as part of the VINEX operation, it is extremely important to pursue integration once more. To this end the policy and the finances must be astutely linked to investments in vegetation and landscape. The chances of success increase when, as a result of the better geographical anchoring of the Green Heart, the valuable landscapes are coupled to the surrounding major cities. These cities actually differ from each other far more than the uniform concept of the 'Randstad' would lead one to suspect. The major cities and urban complexes would have to adopt an identifiable area in their immediate surroundings.

The policy concept for the Green Heart should evolve from an agricultural area which for a long time has no longer been able as a matter of course to offer natural values and a beautiful landscape, into the consideration of a Green

Big is Beautiful (1): The relationship between animal populations and the size of marsh systems.

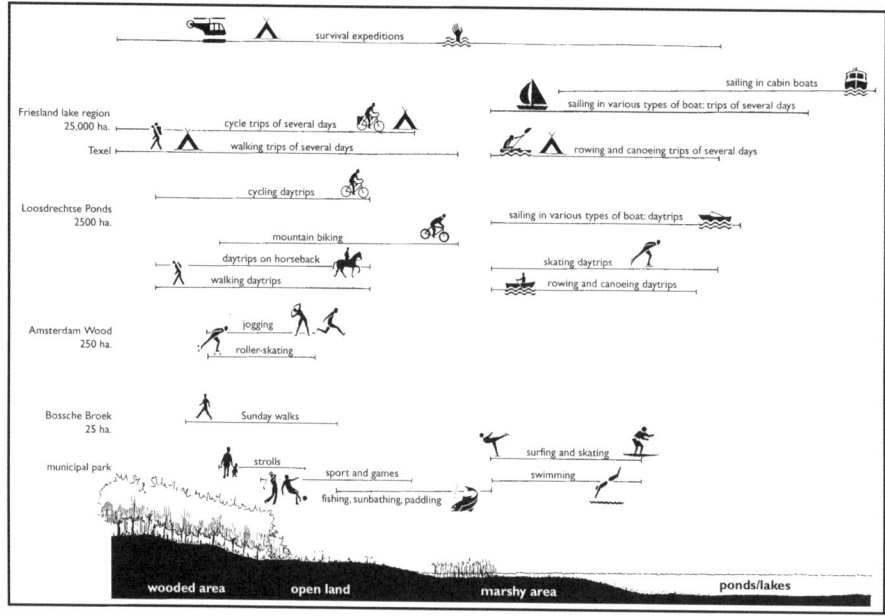

Big is Beautiful (2): The relationship between surface area (or network length) and recreational possibilities set out in a diagrammatic cross-section through the West Netherlands.

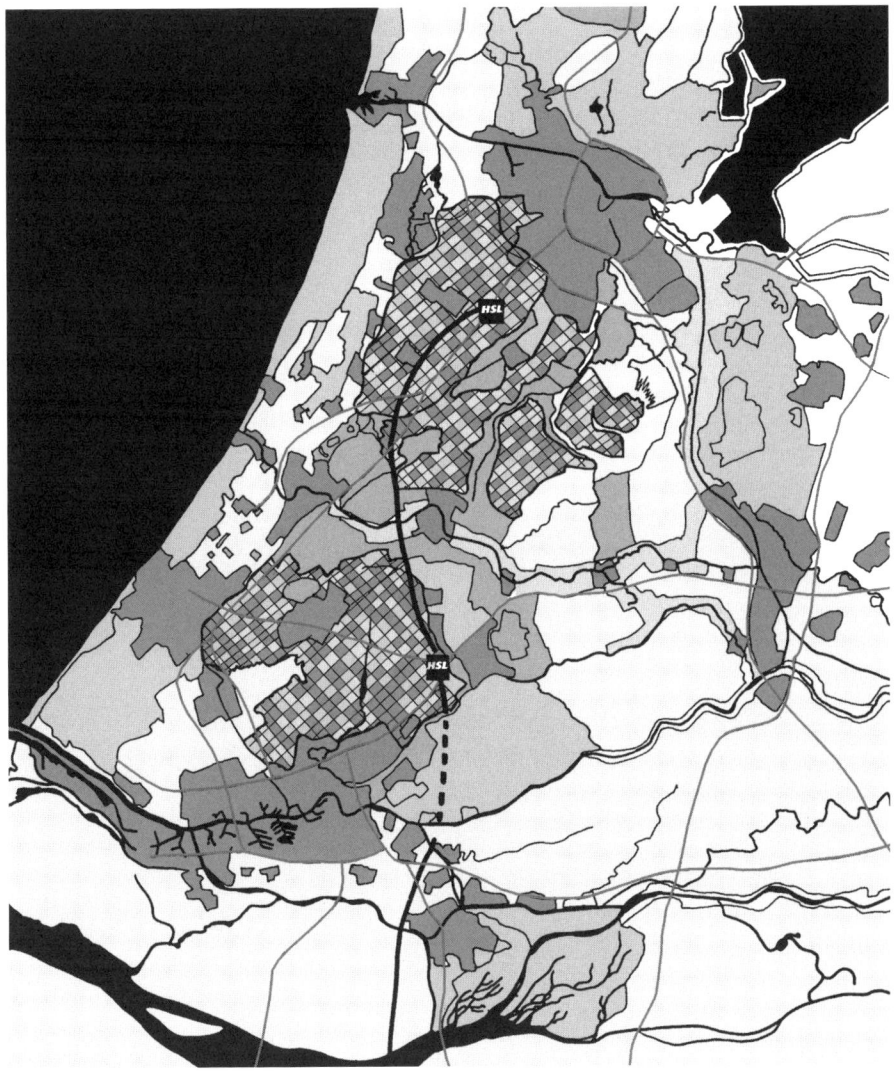

'Overholland!' presents an alternative strategy for the Randstad and the Green Heart. The 'green thousand-guilder notes' are all safeguarded and designed so that recreational possibilities of unprecedented allure remain available in this nascent metropolis. New natural environments arise out of the adaptation of the Randstad water system, which dates from the sixteenth century and in terms of urbanisation cannot carry any more load. In peaty areas the water level is raised in order to set peat growing locally again, mainly to increase the storage capacity of the Randstad by means of the absorption effect, and thereby to provide perfect water for horticulture. In the zone on the banks of the Vecht and the Old Rhine drinking water is extracted. The drained areas of land are undergoing a transformation for the fourth time: the digging of living peat gives rise to ponds which are then drained again and in this plan are changed into urban land. They provide space for a relaxed form of urbanisation in a mixture of activity and agrarian knowledge- and capital-intensive production. The key is completed by monofunctional agro-business complexes and landscape monuments. (See pages 144-145).

Metropolis in the West Netherlands. This is not therefore an end-of-year planning party with the aim of cheerfully selling off the Green Heart to be the first to urbanise the most beautiful Arcadias. No, on the contrary, great effort has to be put into a regional design for the Randstad as a whole in order to give the now rapidly weakening green heartbeat a new impulse. Estimating the force of the actual environmental changes, we have in political and professional terms about five years to think up 'plan B' and set it in motion. The position of the Minister of Housing, Regional Development and the Environment is reminiscent of that of the Minister of Foreign Affairs after the Wall came down. A radically changed context requires a response in policy terms, but at the same time the continuity of policy requires caution. This minister does not seem to have found the answer. She opened the debate on the Green Heart only to declare it closed as soon as she could. The decision to dig tunnels for the high-speed train under part of the Green Heart shows how much the policy-makers have lost their way, blinded by their own metaphors regarding the 'valuable natural area, the Green Heart'. This 900 million guilders, which will probably escalate to about 2 billion (?) could have been spent infinitely better on concrete projects in the landscape. A link has to be made between making our cities denser and more attractive and opening up our countryside. If we neglect this, the result for the inhabitants of our compact cities will be a lose-lose situation at a time when everyone is talking about win-win.

Noel van Dooren and Dirk Sijmons
This text is adapted from an article in a special Randstad issue of the Stedebouw en Volkshuisvesting magazine (1995 - 9/10). It is based on the report of the same title on the possibilities for recreation and nature in the Randstad which the ANWB and the WWF commissioned in 1995.

1. Fourth Memorandum on Physical Planning Extra, (Nickname: VINEX) Ministry of VROM, The Hague (1994)

BLUE SURPRISE

METEOROLOGY IN THE RIJNMOND-SCHELDEMOND AREA

Explorers of urban culture without a programme. Pushed forward by and operating under cover of the cultural institutions of the city. And the population of Hoeksche Waard are in great fear. Is this the starting signal of the inevitably increasing influence of city and port? And what will be the impact of this on the social and spatial identity of the region? Hoeksche Waard lost its insularity in the slipstream of the execution of the Delta Works. The region was able to retain its own character because it always appeared to have 9been skipped in the hurry of reaching the blue heart of the Delta or getting back to Rotterdam as soon as possible. Gradually, however, a cumulus cloud of – mainly urban – items of the programme are starting to build up over Hoeksche Waard. Possibilities of accommodating glasshouses and extensive areas for harbour-related activity are being explored. Besides, Hoeksche Waard seems to have been discovered for suburban living at twenty minutes' distance from Zuidplein in Rotterdam, as is evident from the rising prices of real estate. At the same time the present economic bearer of the region, arable farming, is faced with a difficult period. In the EU the conversion is being made from a product-oriented subsidy system to a system more directed at the world market with limited income support at most. Even now it is starting to dawn on the Dutch centres of arable farming how weak the competitive position is in view of the scale of the Dutch farms, the relatively high land prices, and in the light of expanding environmental legislation. In addition, there is the expected post-2003 expansion of the EU with inexpensively producing agricultural countries such as Hungary and Poland. In the Netherlands the perspective for products and crops which are dependent on price competition will soon deteriorate.

The essence of the problem is to be deduced from this: urban high-pressure regions situated at a short distance from each other (Rijnmond and Scheldemond areas) and an agrarian low-pressure region (the sea-clay regions of the Zeeland and Zuid-Holland islands and West Brabant).

Ambition

Drastic spatial and social processes of change will result from this field of tension. Our ambition in positive terms: guiding these processes in such a way that an attractive (urban) landscape arises for the people living and working there as well as a landscape whose spatial and social identity and possibilities of use are so evident that Hoeksche Waard will be etched on to the mental map of the city-dwellers. This psychological link is the only chance of there being an enduring and positive development. In order to achieve this it will be necessary to make the course of agricultural development the central theme of the design. If this is omitted, the result will almost certainly be a postmodern palette of farming styles and cluttered urbanization.

Formulated in negative terms the ambition is 'never again to permit another IJsselmonde', where with the best intentions of all the sectors an impotent and fragmented non-landscape has arisen these past thirty years.

Territorial choice

On the scale of the 'Euregion' of Rijn-Scheldemond, there are a number of do's and don'ts involved in giving shape to such an ambition. In the first place it is important to bring up the construction of the A4 for discussion. Construction of this road does not only score badly from the point of view of capacity, the indirect spatial effects resulting from it will also largely obstruct the view of an attractive perspective for the future. A diagonal area the size of Rotterdam South will arise, attracting the sort of nondescript mixed industrial site that makes little use of the specific qualities of the region. Even more important is the cause and effect chain started by such a link with the A4 corridor. It is the extension of a ladder structure between Rotterdam and Antwerp, some kind of double 'cable chute' which will result in a sort of homeopathic dilution of the programme. This in its turn causes each municipality to launch its own little industrial site with the result that nothing will be quite successful anywhere, which implies the continuation of a wasteful use of space. Fragmentation and disintegration will advance on a broad front so that, all in all, the enormous opportunities available to make a clear territorial choice will be killed in the 'polder model' of consensus. We propose utilizing the combination A16 and HSL (High Speed Line) as the exclusive economic zone between Rotterdam and Antwerp. The 'twist' in it and the 15 minutes' loss of driving time this yields are our daily peace offering to diminishing the rush in the relieved blue heart of the Rhine-Scheldt Delta. The A29 is to be geared to, and where necessary profiled for, utilization of its original quality: the most beautiful parkway of the Netherlands. Starting in the heart of Rotterdam it opens up all the great phenomena of the Delta landscape. Industrial sites are kept at a dignified distance, the landscape itself is the high visibility location. Apart from being a halting place for ongoing motorists the so-called 'Aires' are direct links between the highway system and the finely-woven recreational networks for walking, cycling and sailing.

WATER MANAGEMENT

Water management forms the basic layer of spatial planning. Gradually different views are emerging on dealing with the hereditary enemy. An enduring strategy for coping with the consequences of the rising sea level consists of at least two parts: a vision on the development of the morphology of the coast, and on the way we drain off our river water. Both accounts have one common denominator: the insight that we should once again make natural processes, such as erosion and sedimentation, our allies. Under penalty of a struggle lost beforehand against harsh, inelegant civil-engineering methods. Natural engineering proves to be civil engineering for the advanced. The strategy of the past century - keeping the coastline taut and as short as possible - is supplemented with a revaluation of the significance of the permanent drainage of sediment by the rivers through the formation of a protective front delta. The great challenge is to restart a large-scale sediment transport. The designation of overflow areas and overflow polders throughout the entire Rhine branch from Switzerland up to the estuary plays a threefold role in this respect. Because of the retention capacity it will then be possible to drain off extremely high river water more gradually; more sediment will be carried along by the river in its flooding and this will yield an attractive river-related landscape. In the south-west of Hoeksche Waard a number of polders are acquired as overflow areas.

Salt-fresh gradient

In our planning area the Haringvliet sluices must be reopened - while retaining a flood barrier, of course. If it becomes a tidal region again, the sediment will also be removed. This is highly necessary, since the locked Haringvliet has literally become the sediment drain of half of Europe. An open connection between the Brielsche Maas and the sea will also be provided. The Spui will become a tidal region again. In the upper part of Hoeksche Waard some regions are 'de-poldered' so as to increase the basin-storage capacity of the system.

This restoration of the salt-fresh gradient, also due to the strongly improved quality of the water, may have quite a few surprises in store in the coming decades. Will the sturgeon, of which the last specimen was caught in 1955 in the Nieuwe Merwede, return to these waters?

Water for agriculture

There are problems, too. Since Hoeksche Waard will be surrounded by brackish water again, the supply of sufficient and high-quality fresh water for agriculture will have to be safeguarded. We propose leading the water surplus in Alblasserwaard by means of fresh-water pipes through Hoeksche Waard and Voorne-Putten to the users in the Westland. In a departure from the provincial plans, which provide central ongoing water pipes, we suggest having Hoeksche Waard, after the inlet at Puttershoek and the distribution point at Strijen, fan out into six imposed waterways which can then form the basis of a new agricultural high-water system. In east-west direction the Waard will be marked by wide and visible water. At present this is only the case at the Binnendijkse Maas. Furthermore, the retention of good, fresh rainwater in the region will be made possible by storing water in the peaty profile of Oude Land van Strijen. This sub-region operates as a water battery connected to a newly constructed high-water system. The greater part of the farms in the region will therefore get the possibility of hydrological precision control at farm level and hence a wider choice of crops. This flexibility is of vital importance since there is no definite answer to the present agricultural problems. A wide range of various farming styles should be made possible in the region: from farmers who see a future in an internationalizing market strategy to farms which are more aimed at a regionalizing strategy. All the intermediate forms of farming will also occur in the region. The new water system will enable farms to deal with these uncertainties.

New margins

The interventions in the water system not only create new conditions for use. Locally they will also provide new margins, such as the zones between the high-water canals and the dikes. This will also benefit the public character of the landscape, and the imposed high-water canals and the accompanying viewing paths will provide a recreational route covering a considerable distance. Apart from their opening function, the water interventions will also create new isolated places, such as the Ambachtsheerlijkheden island in the Haringvliet. Besides, new contrasts will arise: the polder of Goudswaard surrounded by osier-beds is a good example. The plan has seized upon these new regional characteristics with both hands so as to create the differentiation the region sorely needs.

Transport

Water also has an important transport function. From the Maas plain to the Drecht towns the river branches constitute the backbone of an ever finer-

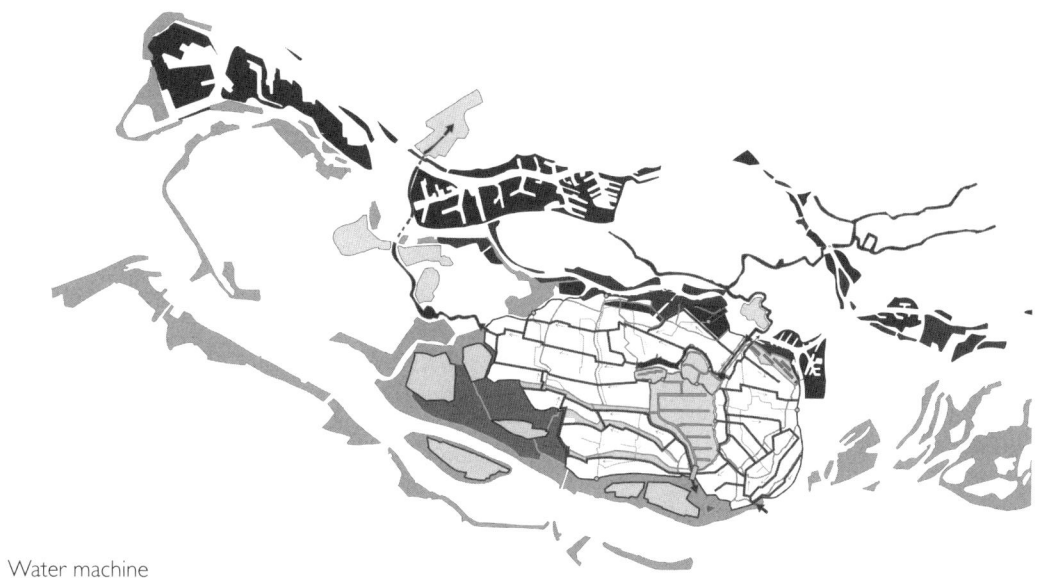

Water machine

grained series of harbour and industrial sites. If it is up to us, the new industrial sites in Hoeksche Waard should also be more oriented towards opened up waterways than just towards the road network.

AGRARIAN AND AGROCHEMICAL LEGEND

We see three opportunities for agriculture in Hoeksche Waard. However odd this may seem, the first has to do with the proximity of the petrochemical complex and the port. The answer to the environmental problem should not only be formulated by agriculture. The petrochemical industry must also take a different course. It is expected that the environmental levies will see to it that fossil oil is only used for very high-grade applications. Biomass will increasingly be considered raw material for the processing industry, but not by converting an enormous bulk production of biomass into a raw material similar to oil. It can be done more cleverly and in a manner offering opportunities for the specific situation of the Netherlands. The new perspective more elegantly utilizes the organic structure already created by nature in the plants. All the parts of the plant can be used as raw material, residues can be converted into bio diesel or naphtha and the remaining parts converted into energy in the bio oil burner. This approach is called 'integrated plant conversion'. Research in Wageningen shows that hemp and flax offer opportunities in the Dutch situation. Everything is used, from the ethereal oil to the fibres which have likely applications as reinforcement material in synthetic products (e.g. for the car industry or as absorption medium in diapers). Numerous semi-manufactures and auxiliary materials for petrochemistry can also be produced in this veritable cascade.

Agrochemistry: closing cycles at a regional level

It is proposed that farmers should be included who are interested in an agrarian experimental garden for these kinds of crops, an agrolab where a Rotterdam agro/petrochemical complex can experiment with the new raw materials at a practical level. The double water system has the flexibility to respond to new demands because of the wider choice of crops. At present it is flax and hemp, in twenty years it may be other crops whose possibilities may have to be investigated.

So far a commercial breakthrough has failed to occur. Advanced non-food applications on an industrial scale require an absolute certainty of supply. Consequently, the supply of raw materials should not solely depend on Dutch production, but will also have to be purchased elsewhere. The port plays an indispensable part in this. Nor should other semimanufactures depend on one single resource. The risks have to be spread over various crops, various resources (also organic waste from the city for bioconversion) and production areas. This is called the Multi Biomass Plant (MBP) concept.

What is new is that for integrated plant conversion the whole plant must be harvested. The transport costs may easily rise in the case of such bulk. In the region itself the primary processing has to be realized in an agrorefinery. Transport up to 50 km appears to be feasible from an economic point of view. In this refinery the plants (hemp, flax, coleseed, grain, willows) are divided into easily manageable (and transportable!) chunks for further processing in the processing industry. The residues are converted into energy, residual heat and CO_2 in the oil burner of the agrorefinery.

Hoeksche Waard offers opportunities for this development, when synergism is developed from the unique combination of the petrochemical complex, the advanced food industry, a large port offering life security as well as scientific know-how in land development and genetic engineering, and last but not least the practical know-how of the farmers who were still growing flax until 25 years ago. An agrochemical complex in the making.

Mixed farming: closing cycles At farm level

The second course is the course of new-style mixed farming. Here, too, the cycles of energy and matter are cleverly closed. Not, as above, on an industrial

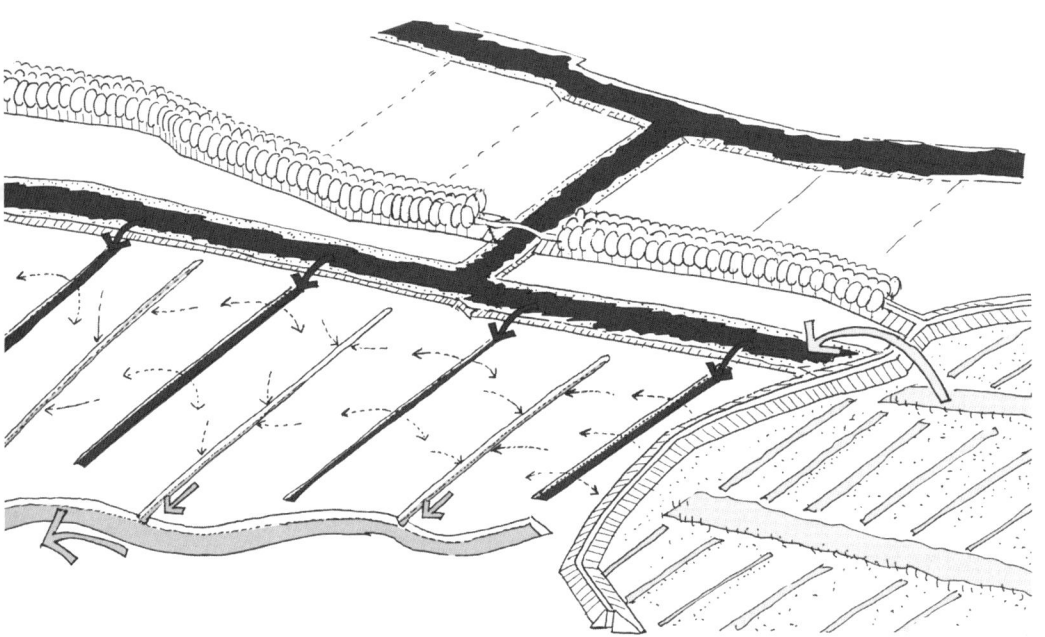

Detail of the water machine showing the forkation of the high- and low-watertable network.

scale, but within the farm. The renaissance of mixed farming is a reaction to the conclusion that the current specialized agricultural production systems are not enduring. They are characterized by narrow and one-sided cultivation plans, nutrient surpluses, a high input of fertilizers, crop-protection materials and fodder, and have to cope with (latent) unemployment due to the small scale of the farms. The mixed-farming system reduces the use of external input and produces more efficiently by the use of home-grown low-nitrogen and high-energy fodder, by using residues, by a more efficient use of the nutrients in manure, by including grass parcels in the rotation, by widening crop rotation in the cultivation plan and finally by an optimum input of papilionaceous flowers which bind nitrogen from the air and therefore operate as green fertilizers. This will also result in a better employment situation and more effective spread of the income risks.

Broadening the countryside economy

For a farm innovation is also possible by orientating more towards the regional market. The proximity of the city is an advantage. There are opportunities for milk products, biodynamic or eco vegetables, fruit and fruit products, special applications of grain (Hoeksche Waard beer!) etc. These market segments are growing steadily and are expected to serve between 10-20 percent of the consumers, whether or not through direct market sale or subscriptions. Besides, we also propose having farmers profit from the rise in the value of land for residential purposes. The traditional 'camping at the farm' can be locally extended to 'building at the farm'.

Agriculture act

Taking advantage of these three opportunities requires cooperation. Cooperation among fellow farmers and the development of a vision at the scale of Hoeksche Waard. It requires the forming of new alliances, creating new business and functional relations. The result: an 'agriculture act' which will be difficult for the competition to follow.

THE JUMP SOUTHWARD

'Just building-on' in Hoeksche Waard is probably the gloomiest perspective conceivable. 'Another IJsselmonde' will almost certainly be the consequence. What we want to aim at is making an urban Bob Beamon-jump from Rotterdam to Haringvliet. A jump southward. The south coast of Hoeksche Waard where an introverted new urban residential environment contrasts with the restored vastness of the tidal region: the cleared island of Ambachtsheerlijkeid (1) *(the numbers refer to the plate of Blue Surprise in the colour section of the book)*, equally interesting for the Zuid-Holland and West-Brabant housing markets. The south, where in the margin between the taut framework of the dikes and the new high-water system a new informal occupation produces a double ribbon (2). The southern overflow polders, where like a kind of 'Rotterdam holiday land' simple but high-water-free cottages are concealed among the osier-beds along the opened-up edges (3). The urban programme makes the jump southward and elegantly lands in the glue joints created by the transformations in hydrology and agriculture. The latter will profit financially from 'building at the farm' and will thus increase the possibilities for housing as well as recreation.

Dirk Sijmons, Yttje Feddes, Lodewijk van Nieuwenhuijze & Ruut van Paridon, Blue surprise is the H+N+S contribution to the manifestation AIR Southbound, 1998 and was first published in: Anne-Mie Devolder (ed): De Hoeksche Waard. New Landscape Frontiers. Thoth Publishers, 2000.

SUBURBIA

Never before in history was nature overrun on such a scale and at such a speed as in America during its cultivation at the end of the eighteenth and first half of the nineteenth centuries. In the wake of the frontier pioneers and their great trek, the mania for cultivation among the first colonists raged over the land like a storm, a devastation that left behind it uprooted forests, prairies razed to the ground and drained peat marshes. The new cultivated land presented the cheerless appearance of improvised constructions in the midst of bare, still

The 'Catalogue House' as an instrument in the nineteenth-century American civilisation offensive.

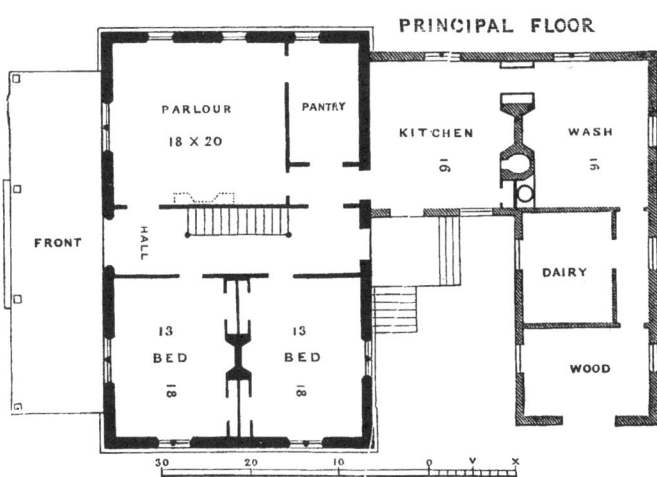

unaccustomed fields and pasture. Then a gradual process of adaptation to the new circumstances started. The land was arranged more on the basis of plans in order to combat erosion by wind and water, and the farmstead was supplemented by vegetable gardens and orchards. Attention was also paid to the embellishment of the farm and the country houses of the merchants and manufacturers who settled with the first wave of cultivation. Freed from their ties to the old continent, the pioneers sought a truly American style of building. Under the leadership of the influential landscape designer Andrew Jackson Downing, two authoritative periodicals, the American Agriculturist and Horticulturist America presented this quest as an essential step towards a new civilisation in the new America. It led to the introduction of new prototypes for the house, the farm and the farmyard. The examples in the magazines were copied all over America with countless variations in taste and material. The catalogue house was born and so surprisingly enough began its stormy career as the figurehead of a burgeoning American architecture. The campaign for the expansion of these architectural prototypes not only had an aesthetic background, but also had to be understood as an instrument in the development of a national consciousness of the confederate state.

The rise of the catalogue house

After a delay of about two hundred years, the ready-made house suddenly landed in the Netherlands, encouraged by the favourable wind of a liberalised housing market. In the countryside, where from time immemorial the built area expanded plot by plot, the catalogue homes offered by building companies enjoyed striking popularity. Architects have always turned their noses up at this off-the-peg market. In so doing they refer to the sanctity of the personal relationship with the client, which is as it were sealed with a unique home. Now they have to watch with envy as the instant house captures the housing market. The architect has sidelined himself. The architects can now only assert themselves in complaining rearguard actions about Gamma [a do-it-yourself supermarket] fencing. Leafing through a volume of the least-read but most influential architectural magazine in the North Netherlands, 'Kavel en Huis', it soon becomes clear why the catalogue home is gaining such popularity. People who cannot face explaining their motives to an architect, or the nerve-racking coordination of the building, or the oceans of time spent on things they do not actually understand, and are also aware of everything that can go wrong, nowadays buy a house the same way they buy everything: go shopping and choose from a range of tried and tested articles. Not a huge assortment, but compared to the homogenised car market the house market offers considerable

Some of the country estates were preserved. There is hardly a single seventeenth-century country house left. Note the Gamma fence. Is this a catalogue house?

Suburbia

The catalogue house, architectural enemy no. 1?

choice, right down to the colour of marble in the kitchen. In addition, a lot of companies guarantee high-speed completion of the house within four or even three months. It is no wonder that more and more people are buying a house as if it were a caravan or a sofa. In short, if you think of the catalogue home as a problem, you have to realise what a formidable opponent it is.

'White Mould', its spread and control

The North-East Netherlands includes some marvellous man-made landscapes. In addition, the night sky there is black and silence still prevails. Add to this the relatively low land prices as a consequence of collapsing agriculture and the popularity of this area among well-off older people and people in search of a second home (especially the target-groups for the catalogue home) is easily explained. The result is that the most beautifully located villages are very rapidly developing incrustations of mostly immaculate white-rendered detached houses. This phenomenon is called the 'white mould' for the suffocating consequences it has on the old village and its community. Local councils often approach this development somewhat equivocally. It is readily admitted that the new buildings do not deserve any prizes for beauty, but there are advantages too. The building work and the arrival of new consumers are a welcome stimulus in this area of low economic activity. The idea seems to be that with a well-considered zoning plan and keen planning inspection, unwanted growth can be kept down and the rough edges smoothed off.

Counter to this hospitality (not untainted by opportunism), critics say that one should not make oneself so dependent on an influx from outside, especially from the Randstad. They consider it to be a dangerous illusion that by offering a surfeit of well-accessed building sites (attractive housing plots and also industrial sites) the economic motor will pick up once again. It will irrevocably lead to a sell-out of their own qualities while the area itself will barely profit from it. The critics prefer a scenario in which the North adopts a self-assured attitude and works on the development of its own qualities.

National policy and the unintended consequences

The policy of the 'compact city' contributes unwittingly to the rapid growth of suburbanisation in the northern provinces. We are driving away too many city-dwellers by means of well-intended environmental measures which have not however been tested for their consequences on a larger scale. And that is annoying for the environment, because recent research has shown that the city and its inhabitants score better on almost all environmental parameters than the inhabitants of smaller towns and the countryside. Every city-dweller also receives higher marks for his environmental efforts even without additional measures. The measures taken to discourage the use and ownership of cars so distorts the balance between the city and its surroundings that unnecessary push factors are added to the strong pulling forces of suburbanisation. The transformation of the city into a sort of "environmentalists' model community" may in the long term have unforeseen and much more negative effects on the environment than a more relaxed view of city and urban life. The point of the state's policy should be to improve the city's competitive position in order to counteract the enticements of suburban living. The city has to be made more attractive and complete in order to continue to hold onto potential deserters (both inhabitants and businesses). The measures may range from the involvement of companies in the distribution of housing in order to accommodate employees who wish to live closer to their work, to the development of suburban habitats and 'sun-belts' on the margins of the regional public transport system.

In addition to this there is a less obvious factor at play. The combined effect of our Environmental Planning, the Building Act and regulations on building appearance have the additional consequence that 'rear sides' are systematically regulated away and smoothed out. Stately formal facades facing the public road and informally unregulated 'rear sides' away from the street, as were built up to the beginning of the last century, offer unprecedented flexibility at the house, block and city levels. The present monstrous alliance between the mania for organisation, hygienism and architectural perfectionism more or less excludes any form of adaptation of houses and blocks to personal wishes. The influence of this restrictive policy on the rapid spread of the 'white mould' is indirect but powerful. When it comes down to meeting individual desires, the new housing estate, with at the most a well-designed garden shed, is not on the side of even the simplest of detached houses. It is therefore no surprise that suburbia wins out splendidly over the city.

The time is gradually approaching when fundamental reflection is needed at a national level about what we want to regulate and what not (see also: 'The Netherlands, kunstwerk again'). There is an administrative component involved, but also a planning one: what do we want to establish formally and what do we leave free? It would be a good thing to reintroduce 'rear sides' into our plans for new buildings in urban areas.

Landscape differences and new housing environments

Adjustment of national policy may curb the 'great trek' to the north and other parts of the country but it cannot stop it. A purely defensive approach to this wave of migration, with both feet on the brake, is bound to end in failure. But this approach also misses opportunities to turn the arrival of the immigrants to the advantage of the area. Possibilities must be sought to guide these developments in such a way that they can end up in a meaningful way in the topography of the landscape of Friesland, Groningen and Drente. The existing distinction between landscapes can be used fruitfully in the implantation of differing housing environments. This sort of approach offers the prospect of the location of housing in rural areas that is unlike the stereotype image of villages expanding in identical ways with nondescript catalogue houses.

An example: the Lage Midden in Groningen

The province of Groningen is also faced with a rising flow of 'immigrants' looking for a rustic abode. One might say it was the overflow from the intensive building on the sandy ground of the Hondsrug. Infection by the white mould is a real danger, more so because the problems in agriculture create favourable conditions for it. The imminent shrinkage of the agricultural

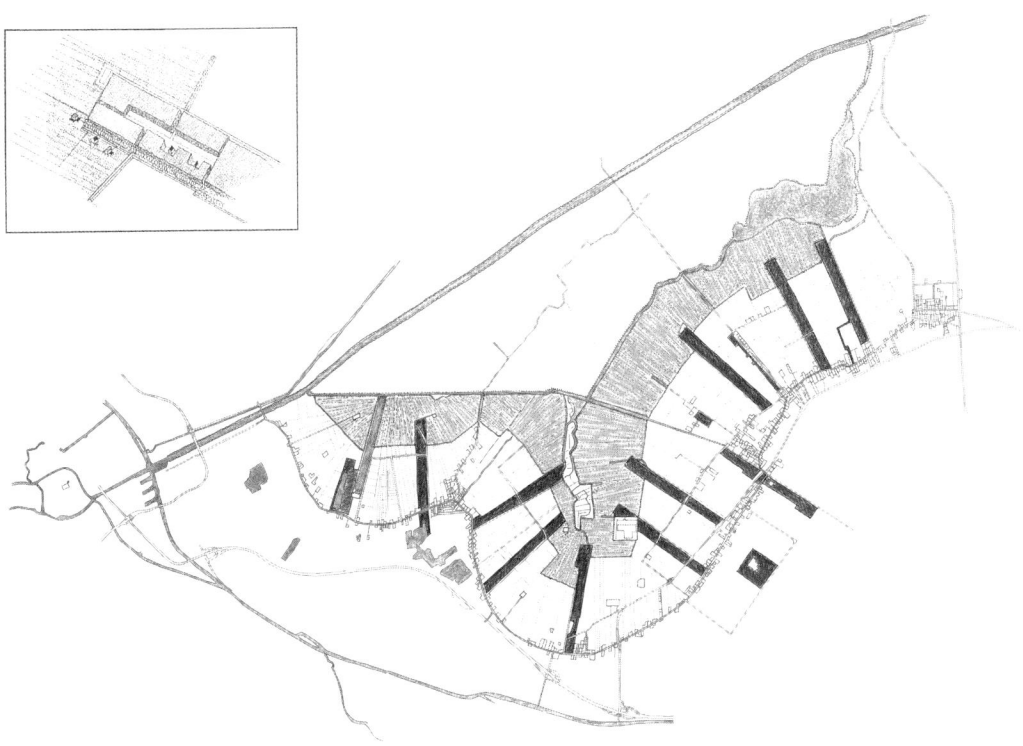

The linkage of two newcomers alien to the area, natural development and suburbia, presents a surprising prospect. The natural development plan has been worked out as an alternative to the present ecocratic plan that turns its back on the landscape (see illustration on page 91). The alternative plan works with the same programme but looks for a connection to the landscape and culture in a different way. The soil to be removed is raised into long cunettes on which woods are planted. The natural wood component is located where the woods adjoin the marshy wilderness. This links up with the tradition that in the landscape of Groningen trees are a sign of human presence. In the new wooded space is offered for detached houses at various price levels. This also provides an architecture-proof solution to the white mould. Natural development is literally connected to the city where the supporters of nature conservancy are to be found.

area might well affect Groningen disproportionately, considering its extensive arable acreage. The release of agricultural land encourages a decrease in land prices and opens the door to other functions and new land users.

At the same time, in Groningen as everywhere else, plans for natural development have been made. What the plans have in common is that they are often rather introverted and turn their backs on the existing landscape. A good example of this are the plans for natural development in the landscape of the Groningen 'Wolden' in the Lage Midden area, since time immemorial a transitional zone, a peaty intermediate area between the sand of the Hondsrug in Drente and the marine clay of North Groningen. The plan displays a dull exercise in filling in with various types of natural objective. The motif of the plan seems to have been informed mainly by the wish to link together existing property round the Schildmeer, along the Duurswold drainage canal near Woudbloem, and further on towards Hunzedal. Altogether this amounts to a respectable portion of the province of Groningen (about 1500 hectares). In a country where you need planning permission and an architect's plan for a skylight, you can immediately carry out a project of this sort of size, with massive consequences for the character of the landscape, without a designer being involved at all.

The 'lichenisation' of the white mould

The Natural Development Plan offers the perfect chance to interweave suburbanisation with the existing man-made landscape in a meaningful way. It provides an opportunity to allow this new programme to find its place in a natural way in the topography of this marvellous area.

The combination of influences from outside the area, suburban village extensions and natural development may yield a symbiosis that very closely resembles the fusion of moulds and algae into lichens. In fact we use the term 'lichenisation' of housing. In our thematic elaboration, which is explained further in the 'plans' section, we show that this can be given a form that produces elements that fit the charm of the landscape. In this proposal the occupation strategy is oriented towards the accommodation of habitation in new strongholds and rubs up against the natural development zone towards the Schildmeer.

In this way the Groningen landscape undergoes the transformation in full awareness. In this way the two exogenous factors, new natural areas and suburbanisation, can become interwoven with each other in a meaningful relationship with the continuing agrarian function. Estimates are that this method will quite simply provide the capacity to cover all the demands of suburbia for the next fifty years.

This example shows that the administrative level that connects local authorities provides for new opportunities. Genuine solutions can be formulated on a landscape-wide scale. We should not conceal the fact that it is also the most difficult. For a plan like that at Slochteren, not only is collaboration between local authorities essential, but the planning bodies of the rural area and Environmental Planning and the Housing Act also have to be well geared to each other.

The provincial and the cooperating local authorities have an important part to play in implementing these plans. Not only as coordinators but also as developers, together with landowners and market forces. Projects like this are interesting investments for the various ecological funds run by banks. There is a smart route to implementation that starts with changing the block used for organising land, the purchase of land with an aggregate value clause and the creation of a land-use plan implying authority to introduce changes. This is followed by afforestation, taking advantage of various EC subsidies, and locating, thinning and cultivating it in such a way that the new zones or parts of them can be classified as country estates under the new natural beauty act. And lastly, what about the original owners? The farmers who put in their land share in its increase in value by means of the aggregate value clause. The combination of natural development and habitation is unrolled eastwards from the city. If the conservation plan has to be introduced more rapidly the land needed for the zones can be acquired in the framework of the land use plan in order to raise the cunettes and thereby give the wood a head start. All this has created a housing land capacity that will last Groningen for 25 years.

If we cast our eye over all this, the main problem is not so much that a lot will change, but rather that the first signs (the plans and projects) indicate that much of it will be completed carelessly or, which is worse, lovelessly. It seems that the provincial authorities have no ambition to handle these changes in a purposeful way either. It is to be hoped that the interest in architecture that has taken hold of the city of Groningen will soon catch on in its surroundings. It is high time a vigorous landscape policy was developed. It will then no longer be enough to mark the various types of landscape on a map and formulate a handful of regulations. It comes down to effectively deploying the landscape-forming processes currently in action under our very nose in order to create a new, living man-made landscape. Dialogue with the area and the use of landscape designers can then provide for a meaningful spatial expression of this programme and for a close relationship with the existing landscape. The motto is: development in a way that retains the pride of the land.

The local authorities' answer to suburbanisation

The question is how to guide suburbanisation without such a fine opportunity for natural development plans presents itself. What can a councillor in a small rural district, with little official support and no experience in commissioning work, do with the average land division plan for six or seven houses? The answer is: a surprising amount! The first recommendation is not to rely on the Building Inspectorate alone. The Building Inspection Committee can never make a good plan out of a bad one and can at best raise a mediocre one to minus six. If everything depends on their recommendation it is already too late. It is preferable to work on a project basis and make the intentions obvious in an urban development plan, even if only basic, but in most cases this will not be in order or can no longer be put in position 'in time'. In such cases all manner of things can be done in the sphere of indirect regulation. Simple rules such as building lines, imposing requirements on things that are not normally subject to building inspection, such as the design of plot boundaries, or the proffering of a particular assortment of trees. If one is intent on keeping catalogue houses out of the borough, effective means include regulations on the materials used, possibly combined with a single 'unusual' requirement (e.g. every house has to have a verandah). Local building orders can also be employed within certain preconditions. There are in other words more than enough ways of tinkering with the environmental quality of this sort of small assignment using gentle and indirect regulation without lapsing into cavilling.

Dreamteams

Bouwbedrijf Hiemstra - Erna van Sambeek

Stegewerns BV - Giorgio Grassi

A. de Bok & Zn - Wim Quist

Wed. Joustra - Kas Oosterhuis

Van Eesterveen Bouw - Gunnar Daan

Koop Tjuchem B.V. - Coop Himmelbau

And what about the catalogue house?

If, in spite of everything, we insist that the catalogue house is contrary to good taste, one last resource remains: improve the quality of the content of the catalogue. Why should we not provide an attractive ready-made range?

Why not take up the challenge and link the northern building companies with one or more architects and give these duos the task of designing a good serial product? The competition between good and bad taste can then really get going. I am afraid that the result would disappoint a great many architecture-lovers. Personally, I prefer to put my money on an 'architecture-proof' landscape solution.

Dirk Sijmons
This is a compilation from two talks at the two 'Keuning congresses' in 1996. The topic of the September congress was 'the Lage Midden in Groningen, the Wolden', and was reported on in Noorderbreedte 6a, 1996. The talk is there summarised under the title 'Wonen in de natuur' [Living amidst nature]. The second congress was devoted to the area between Assen and Groningen, the 'Koningsas'. An extensive report is to be found in the publication 'Stadslandschap in ontwerp; visies op Assen in a nieuw stadsgewest', which Hans Elerie edited for Regio-PRoject in 1997. The text of the talk given there is printed under the title 'Wat te doen' [What to do].

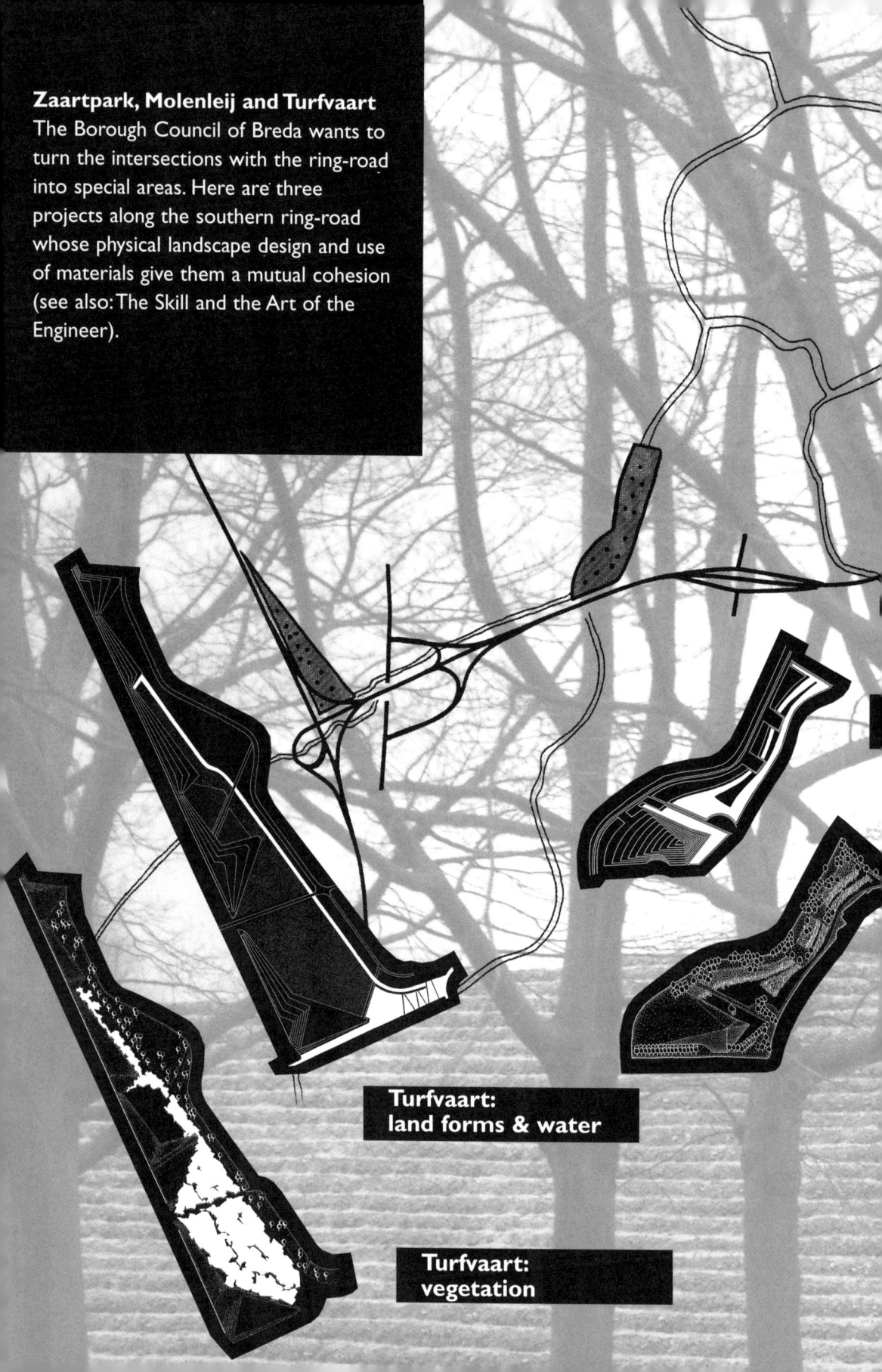

Zaartpark, Molenleij and Turfvaart
The Borough Council of Breda wants to turn the intersections with the ring-road into special areas. Here are three projects along the southern ring-road whose physical landscape design and use of materials give them a mutual cohesion (see also: The Skill and the Art of the Engineer).

Turfvaart: land forms & water

Turfvaart: vegetation

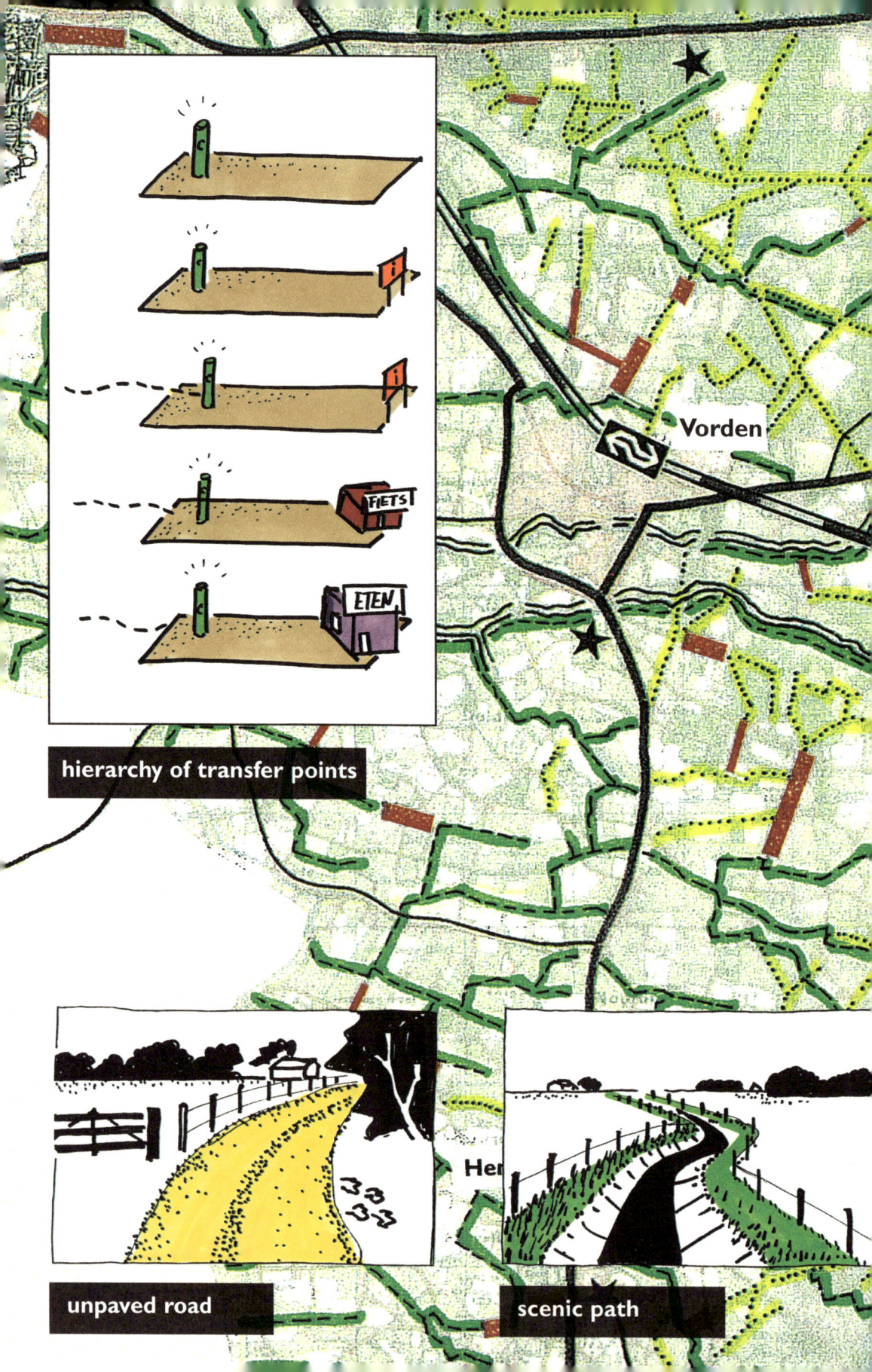

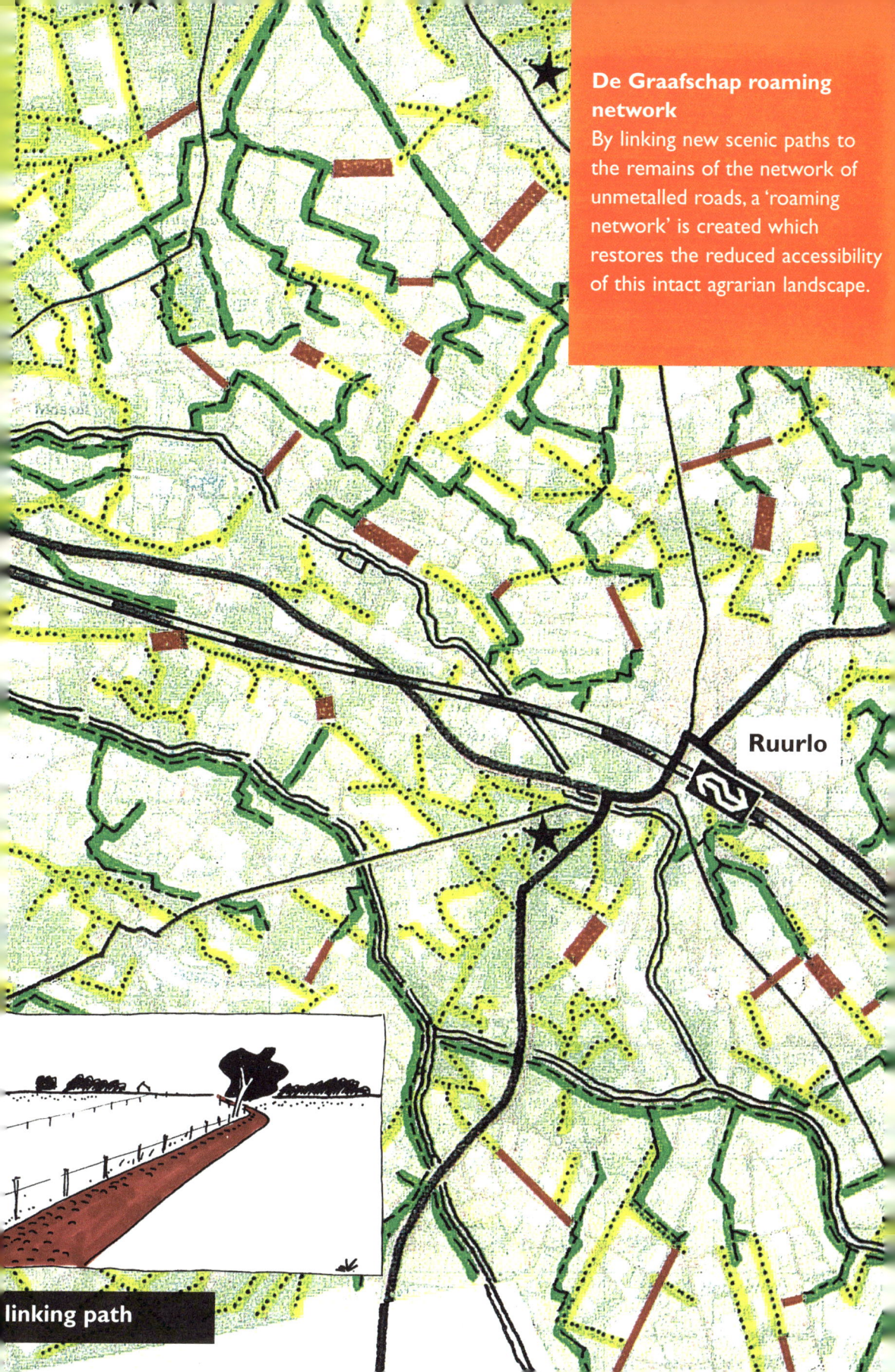

De Graafschap roaming network
By linking new scenic paths to the remains of the network of unmetalled roads, a 'roaming network' is created which restores the reduced accessibility of this intact agrarian landscape.

Ruurlo

linking path

NOW

BANKING OF NATURAL SITE

REMOVAL OF SOIL: DREDGINGS > RAISING OF BUILDING LAND

MAKING WASHBOARD

SETTING WATER LEVEL & PLANTING BUILDING LAND

NATURAL DEVELOPMENT & LICHENISATION OF BUILDING AREA

Housing & De Wolden

Groningen is also in danger of becoming infected by the 'white mould' of nondescript catalogue homes. In response to this, an architecture-proof landscape has been developed in which new residential and natural development areas are generated 'in conjunction' in new settlements. Small woods that make reference to the Groningen 'borgen' provide space for the future housing zones (see also: Suburbia).

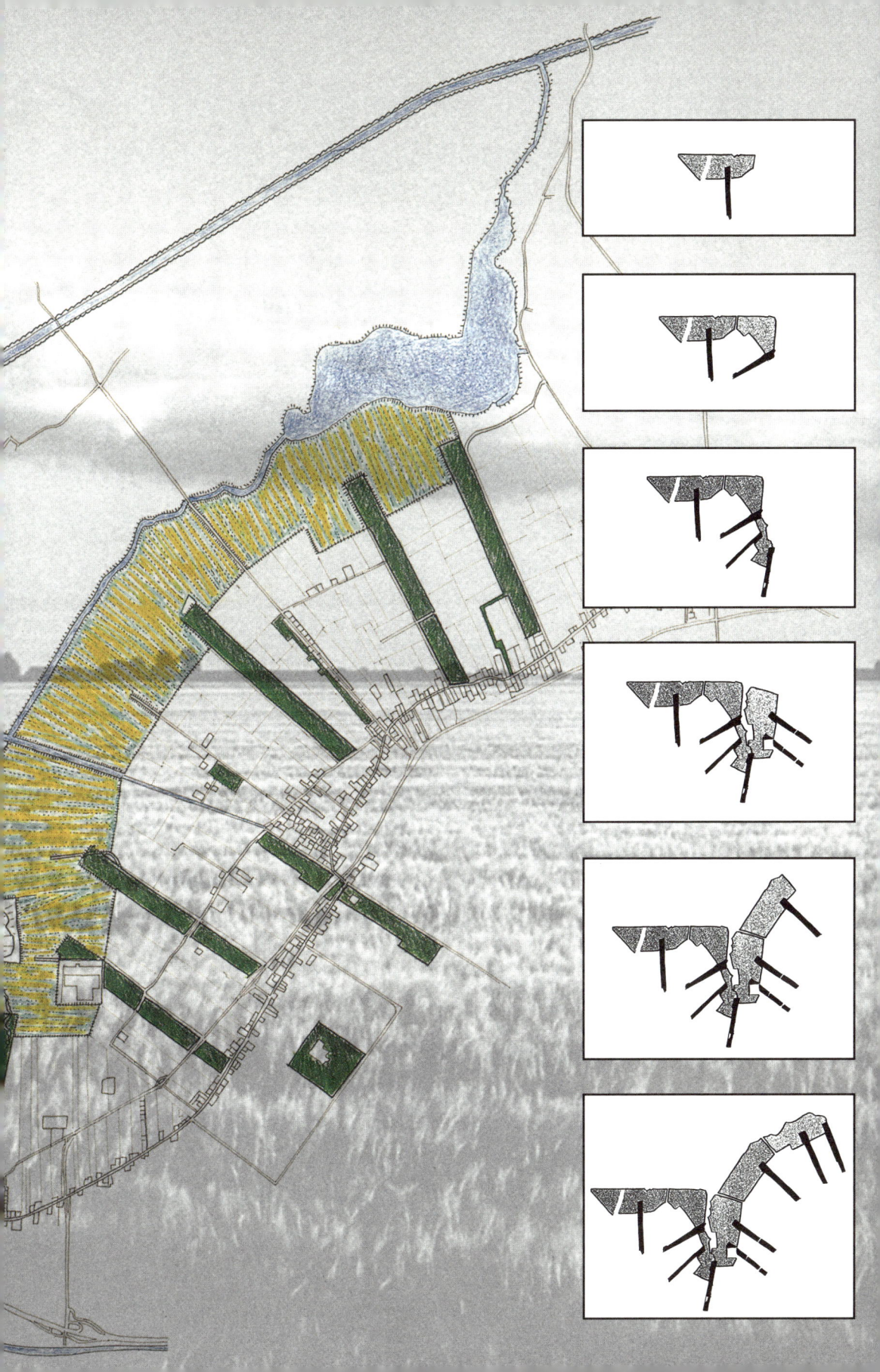

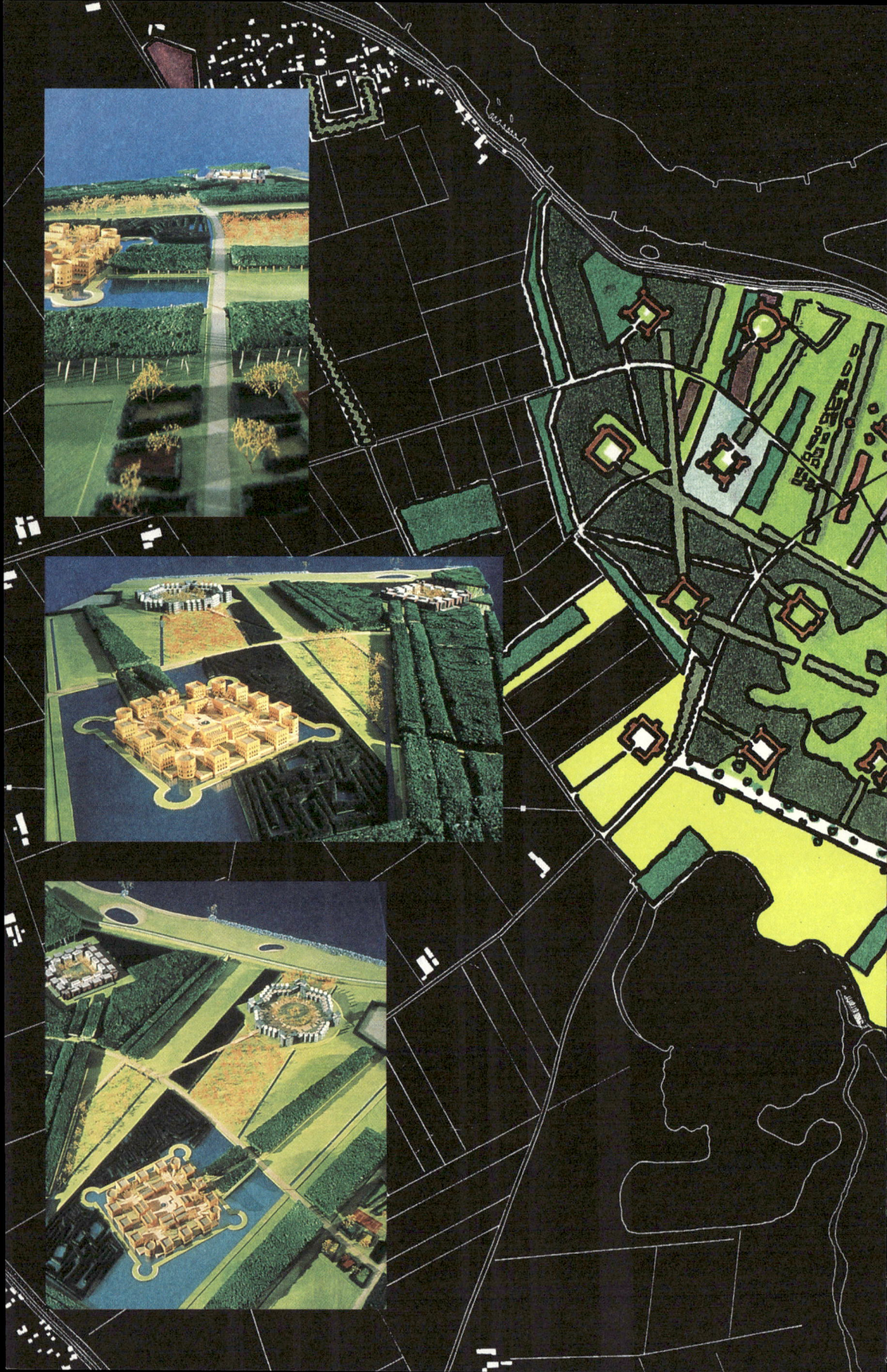

Haverleij
An alternative to the dreary repetition of semi-detached houses. In Haverleij the houses are clustered and the surrender of a part of the private garden is compensated by turning the land so saved into a 'country estate'. (see also Brabant: a possible continuation).

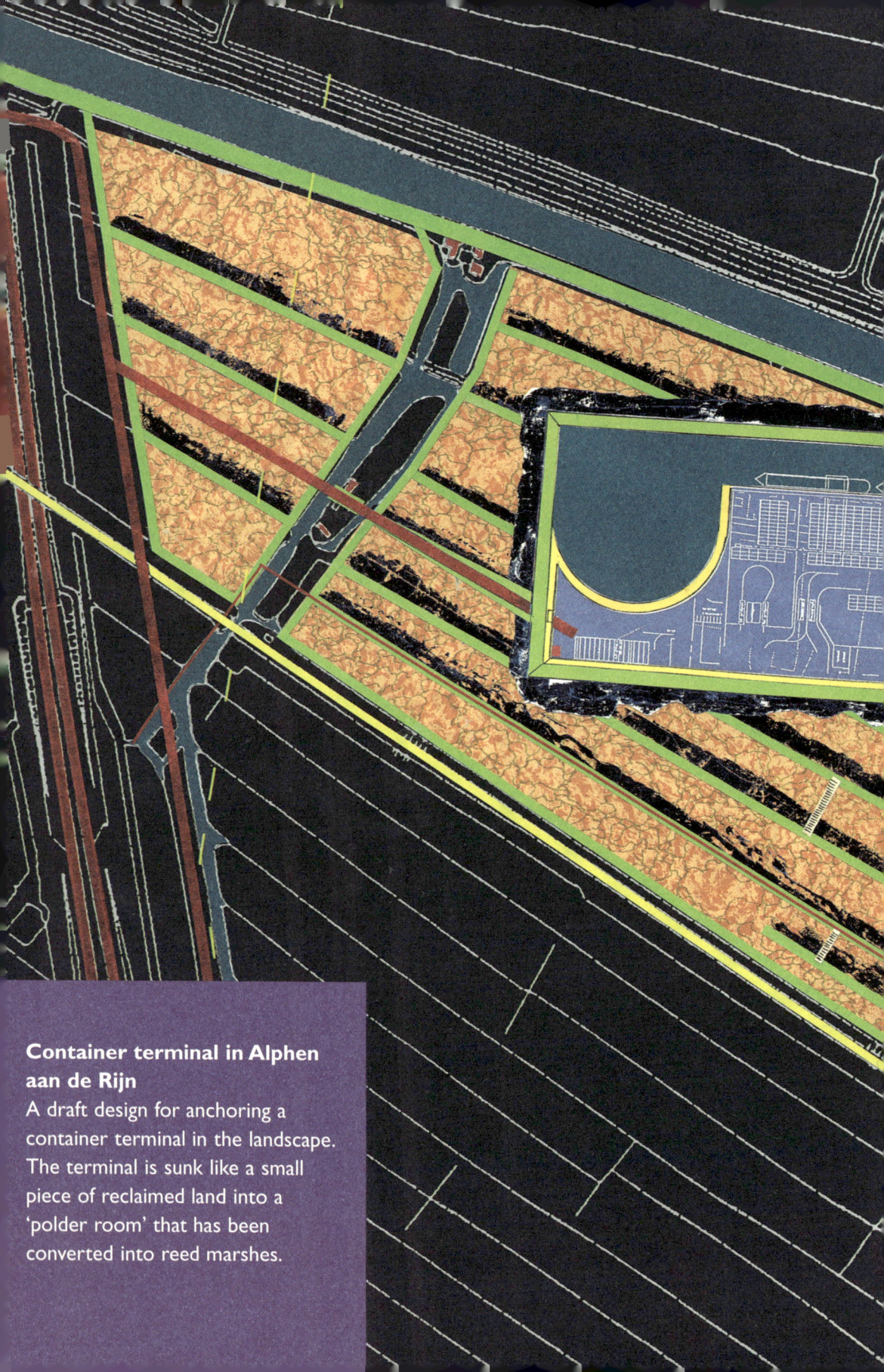

Container terminal in Alphen aan de Rijn
A draft design for anchoring a container terminal in the landscape. The terminal is sunk like a small piece of reclaimed land into a 'polder room' that has been converted into reed marshes.

Dreumel

Druten

Dyke improvement in Afferden-Dreumel

A design for a twenty-kilometre long river dyke along the Waal, for which an asymmetrical and concave cross-section was devised. Its asymmetry is brought to life by means of a 'wet' marshy base at the foot of the outer slope as a transitional zone before the natural areas in the foreland. A raised mowing path marks the boundary between the inner slope and the cultivated land (see also: The Skill and the Art of the Engineer).

Waterland Neeltje Jans
A dune carpet, a car park and a starfish promenade transform the former construction island Neeltje Jans into an attraction park.

Blue surprise Hoeksche Waard
Reorganisation of agriculture by means of a new water system, as the only worthwhile basis for an urban landscape with new meaning.

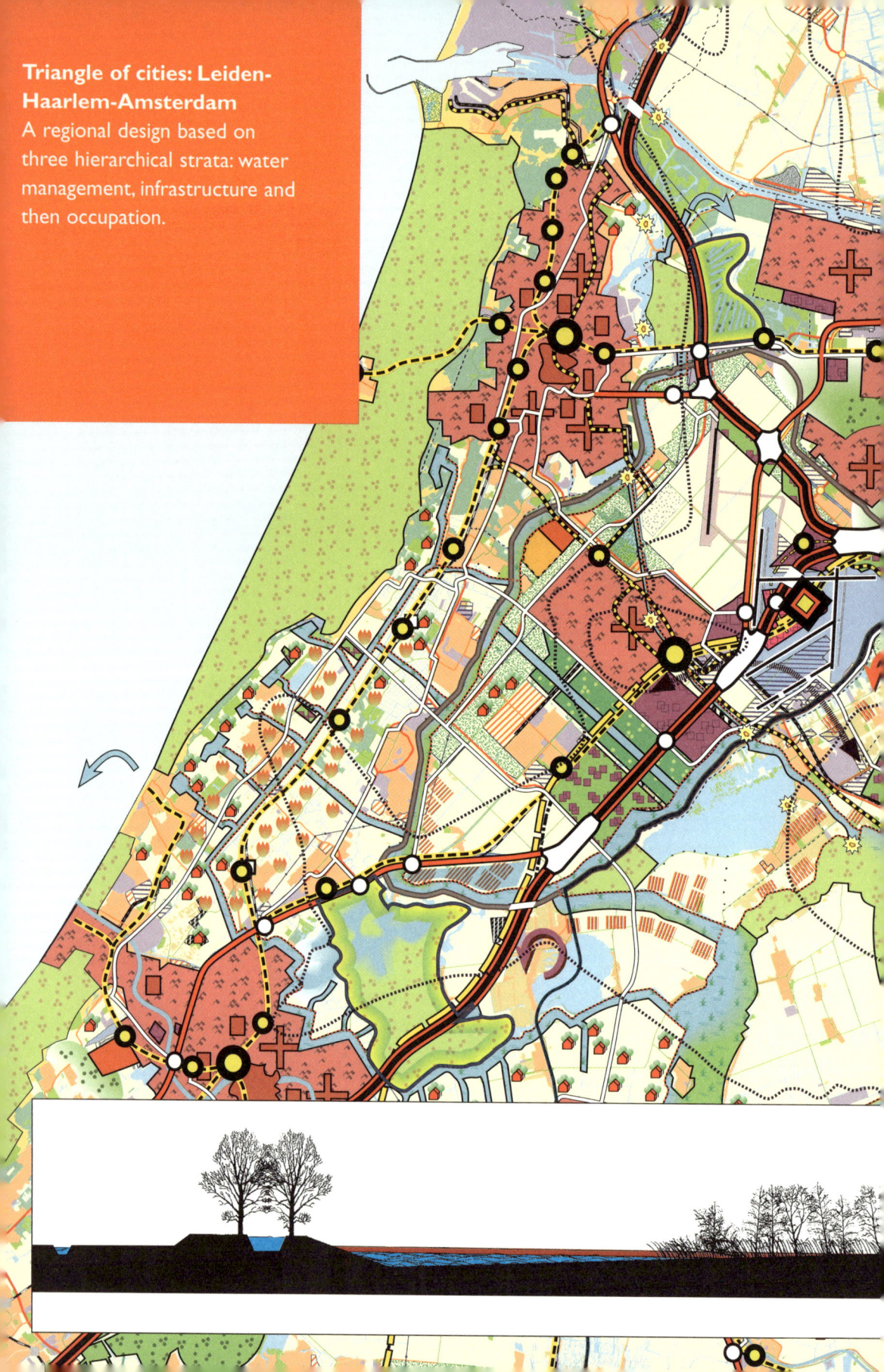

Triangle of cities: Leiden-Haarlem-Amsterdam
A regional design based on three hierarchical strata: water management, infrastructure and then occupation.

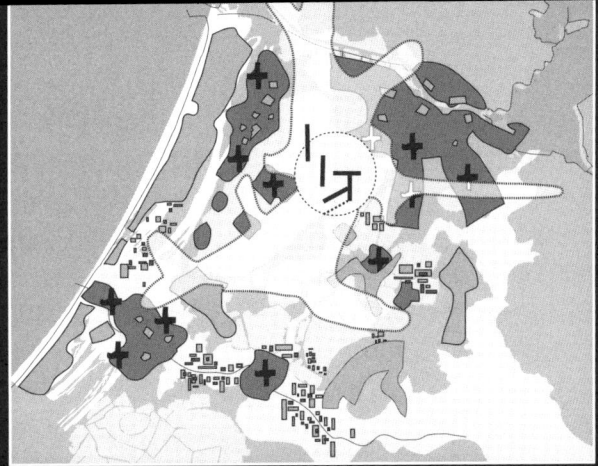

New conditions resulting from infrastructural planning: intersections in public transport network and industrial areas

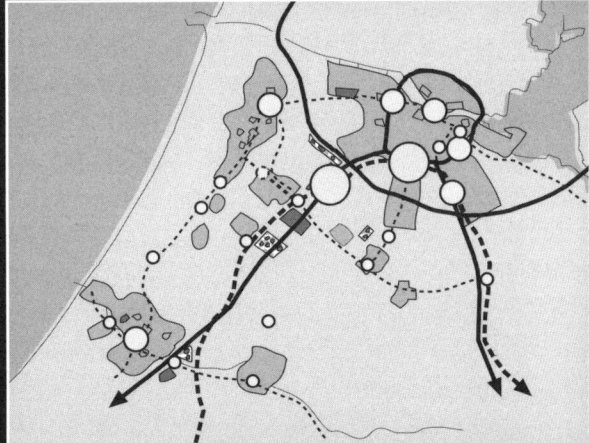

Interactions between red and green: a major task for urban projects in combination with a new stimulus for the Green Heart. The local ecology and the airport's sound contour serve as guidelines for the location of new, scattered housing and industrial sites.

New conditions as a result of water planning: introduction of the intermediate drainage pools.

Outdoor recreation.

ROTTERDAM, HOLIDAY ZONE

The time when the government made accurate estimates of city-dwellers' need for open-air recreation is definitely behind us. This counter is closed. The square metres of all types of green amenity to which everyone had a right have been translated into a recreation programme for open spaces, crystal clear and scientifically based. With mild nostalgia we bad farewell to these estimates of needs that exposed the great lack of fishing water in the Veluwe ['upland' area] and the flagrant lack of woods in the Waddenzee [off the NW coast]. The government policy which juggled with such terms as 'daytrip recreation locations', 'route-linked terrestrial recreation forms', 'recreational co-use' and 'amphibious leisure activities', has recently, entirely in keeping with the spirit of the age, been swapped for the market, which from now on has the task of providing amenities.

The disappearance of this scientific basis makes it risky but not impossible to say anything about future recreational behaviour in the Rotterdam region. As a tribute to this former area of government meddling I shall speak in the terms used in estimates of needs when I identify target groups and chart developments in what is on offer. Who is still prepared to show themselves in the open air? Who is in search of recreation ('the recreation of the whole being' or in more Rotterdam-like terms, 'the reproduction of the capacity for work') and, lastly, what subset can be constructed between these two groups that leads to open-air recreation?

The elimination of government policy appears to coincide with a substantial part of the traditional target-group, the average metropolitan family, saying farewell to open-air recreation. Leisure time is increasingly spent indoors. In addition to events attended in large numbers, which are increasing in number and cost, the home plays a key part in leisure activities, not least as a result of the time spent on 'home design' itself. Dutch people 'home design' their heads off in bigger and bigger houses. Home design is many Dutch people's favourite leisure activity. In this group, full contact with the open air takes place mainly when they are working on their gardens. The annual turnover of garden centres, garden furniture and nurseries is more than 2 billion guilders. In addition to the eternal hobby dens and handyman's sheds, telecommunication, audiovisual media and computer entertainment also occupy a massive amount of free time. Cubic metres, a reasonable amount of freedom to convert the house (additions and decoration) and sound electric connections (!) are the most important environmental ingredients for these forms of leisure activity.

The benefits of the amenities created in recent years have not gone unnoticed by the hard core of the heterogeneous group which for convenience' sake we designate as the traditional target-group for open-air recreation policy. Among this group the 'shadow city' will become even more important than it is today. This is the parallel universe where mutual solidarity and helpfulness exist, where you know your neighbours and where conviviality reigns supreme: the camping site. This spatial emancipation of the neighbourhood feeling will indeed only assume other forms and probably also appear on the market (and on the map!) in more luxurious variants. The time one spends on a camping site or holiday home parks will continue to increase: preferably from Thursday evening instead of Friday evening, until Monday morning and including all holidays.

It is to be expected that other groups will also follow this example and will set up similarly homogeneous leisure ghettos. In America this process is even taking place on the ordinary housing market. The urge to spend one's time exclusively in an environment of like-minded people can be taken to absurd extremes (the most extreme example I know is a guarded housing enclave in Los Angeles for middle-class homosexual Spanish-speaking men who like sport). In the Netherlands this tendency is mitigated by resistance to segregation in environmental policy. But in the leisure zone we shall call 'Rotterdam, holiday zone', these forces of social self-organisation will certainly leave their traces. The shadow city is more segregated than its more politically correct nephew: the official city.

This brings me to the New Dutch. Most well-off people will be making their wishes known to the accommodational recreation market between now and about twenty years' time. For now, it is mainly of interest that the sites for one-day recreation at cycling distance from Rotterdam, such as Bernisse and the Rotte Meren (constructed some time ago to allow the pale inhabitants of the city a day in the open-air with their family) have now been discovered by several groups of new Dutch people ranging from the softball teams from Japanese companies to the Turkish and Moroccan families that picnic there almost every summer weekend. The new forms of collectivity have given these sites an unforeseen second wind.

At the other end of the spectrum there is a group that is interesting in this respect, whom I would like to characterise as the 'Horizon Broadeners'. It is a group which, in its annual activities, is mainly linked to the active adventurous holiday. People who book an action trip every year. This year walking in the

Indoor recreation

Andes, next year wild-water canoeing on the Colorado river or, closer to home, walking a grand randonné in France or wandering the tangle of public footpaths in England and Ireland. For more people every year the focus for trekkers is the 'Op Stap' travel fair. These people do not necessarily come from higher income brackets in everyday life. Horizon-broadeners with minimum incomes will also find something to suit them in the range of holidays offered. However, people in this group have often followed higher education. The pattern governing all articles on the market will also apply to the boom in active and adventurous holidays. The trendsetters come home with something new and after a while others want the new product too. In their weekly lives these recreation pioneers will want to experience these activities on a smaller scale. This offers the opportunity to build a bridge between this social trend and the creation of new natural settings and wilderness: the 'uncharted reserves'. Places where you can escape from our overregulated society and where for once you cannot tell from the yellow tops of the posts that you are an hour and a half away from the car. In these places the recreator does not have the steward breathing down his neck, but is in fact invited to partake of adventure off the beaten track. This is a new freedom for the city-dweller but also the natural setting, which can here go its own way without the nature conservers and unimpeded by natural target-types. This is still possible, even in our open space, raked over as it is, as long as some rather larger continuous areas are created in a few strategic locations and as long as the network is long enough. This sort of place provides the perfect setting for a daytrip on foot or by canoe, or trying out one's equipment for the annual trip, which seems to be getting more expensive and extensive by the day.

In-house recreation

Amongst the youngsters, pensioners and long-term unemployed, a varied group of people with lots of free time, we find the group without an agenda. The spatial expression of this group's behaviour in the open air may add interesting new items to the key on the map of Rotterdam, holiday zone. Special forms of active participation in the landscape and market gardening will arise and other forms will make a comeback as has the allotment. This is an opportunity for environmental policy in Rotterdam. If the authorities still see something in laying 'green arteries' throughout this region it should, with an eye to the future, act quickly. It should be seen as a warning that land prices have risen so much that green projects only seem to have a chance of succeeding when they are developed as 'working landscapes' in combination with the construction of industrial sites. The purchase of land should have absolute priority. At the moment, all the money can best be spent on acquiring land in the region on a large scale and by private means in order to safeguard public accessibility. Spending money on design and management can wait for later. In the meantime a lot can be left to spontaneous natural and recreational processes and can also be saved from the cost of management by handing over parts of these sites (for the price of the interest or free) to particular population groups. There are enough enthusiasts who would like to manage a small natural area in their own way, as a sort of twenty-first century allotment. Those without an agenda appear to be perfect for the task of bringing this 'people's nature' into being.

In-skull recreation

One can descry a special subset in the group that goes through life without an agenda: the Sages of Rotterdam. This growing group will, by conviction, lack of money or a combination of the two, increasingly turn away from the 'senseless dragging of people and things around the planet'. On the basis of the insight that tourism adds nothing to human existence, these sages will increasingly seek the possibility of going on holiday on a single square metre. Partly by getting away in a virtual sense (indoors or even 'in-skull'), and partly by taking advantage of new modest amenities in the countryside. This group uses the 'uncharted reserves' for taking the haste out of existence. This also gives the government an initial instrument for the pursuance of temporal as well as spatial (environmental) policy and at the same time devoting the right attention to the programme with the lowest social dynamic. The amenities that will be introduced here are the foci of a new spirituality. It is conceivable that inside these new grains of chlorophyll in the Rotterdam region the new act on the disposal of the dead might lead to the growth of all manner of unusual funeral and mourning rituals.

Cutting across all these groups in Rotterdam, holiday zone, there will be a great need for small plots for modest second homes. In this situation the government might well waive the building inspection regulations (an experiment that would certainly be supported by the chairman of the BNA [Dutch Architects' Association]). In order to prevent people from occupying them all year round they could be limited to water and drainage connections, without energy supply. One would have to provide that oneself. The exterior of

| | RECREATION WITH ACCOMMODATION | | | | | |
| | *recreational city* | | | *shadow city* | | |
	indoor	event	recreation ground	camping site	datsja	allotment
Traditional	✓	✓		✓		✓
No agenda (old)	✓	✓		✓		✓
The Sages of Rotterdam	✓				✓	
No agenda (young)	✓	✓			✓	
New Rotterdammers		✓	✓			
Horizon-broadeners DALO	✓		✓			
WELO		✓				
JALO						

= LANDSCAPE

these dachas built for and by Rotterdammers will turn out much more paradisaical than the expensive and sterile imitation architecture of the 'Goesse Sas' or 'Port Zeelandia' sort further from the city.

Can all these developments still be fitted into this urban region, woven as it is with streets full of underground piping, petrochemicals and architectural organisations? Yes it can, as long as an effective environmental policy is pursued that reacts alertly to existing initiatives and developments that have been set in motion. The future peat heart of the Krimpenerwaard is, as well as a natural development zone, also a perfect candidate for the regional 'uncharted reserve', followed closely by the Biesbosch, the future national park and the other attractive areas that come into being along the Haringvliet when contact with the tides is reestablished there. The Hoeksewaard in particular is a decisive factor in the development of Rotterdam, holiday zone. By safeguarding for the future the agrarian function in the strongest parts of the area and by making planned use of the released sites in the weaker areas (in the Land van Strijten) for the development of a mosaic of professional agriculture, urban nature conservancy, urban agriculture and the dacha sites, this waard [holm] will be able to grow into Rotterdam's pleasure ground. The Hoeksewaard and the Dordrecht island on the southern flank of Rotterdam are perfect locations for the construction of sun-belts with the more exclusive housing this urban district so much needs. So even the happy few will be favoured with a place in the sun in Rotterdam, holiday zone.

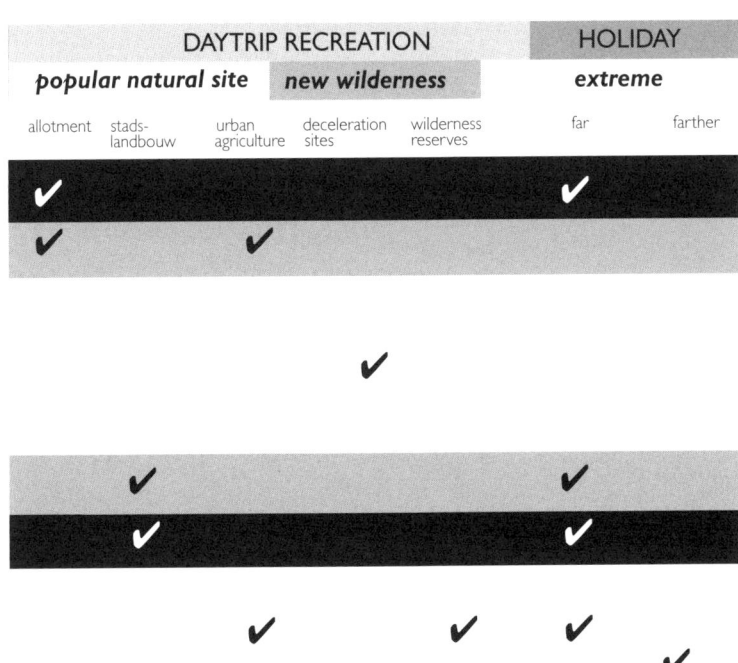

Rotterdam, holiday zone

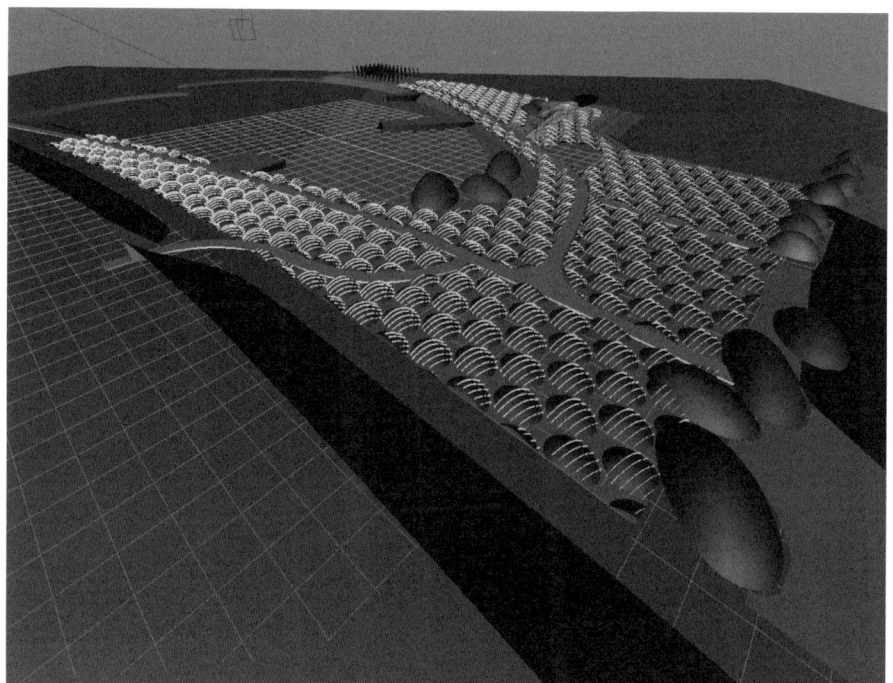

Amusement parks and events are gradually drawing more people than ordinary recreation sites. This is a design for a theme park on the former site-island Neeltje Jans in the Oosterschelde estuary. 'Waterland' is intended to present the subject of water to a broad audience in spectacular demonstrations and experiences. H+N+S drew up the site plan (see pages 140 & 141).

On balance, there looms the image of a more relaxed and primarily less centralised development of the city and urbanisation. In this vision, the southern flank of the Randstad manifests itself as an arrangement of linked areas where high and low dynamics and red and green can exist alongside each other. To this end, the counter which the government closed just now will have to be opened a little again. We should not deceive ourselves that cocooning has replaced open-air recreation forever. Even the oft-heard cry that it all comes down to offering people a detached house with a bit of land and plenty of storage space under a blue suburban sky, and then just rolling out the carpet and making no further investment in the countryside, is very short-sighted. The government and private individuals can change the urban landscape in the southern flank into Rotterdam, holiday zone. The opportunities are waiting to be taken.

Dirk Sijmons
A contribution to the collection of articles entitled 'Leefstijlen in de 21ste eeuw' (ed. Arnold Reijndorp. et al.) published by Nai uitgevers in 1997.

DESIGNING WITH LANDSCAPE ANTECEDENTS

The future does not exist. There is only a past that grows. (Karra Elejalda, 1997)

It is true. We have all become more cautious than our ancestors. After a hundred years industriously developing the driest and wettest of Dutch land, after the standardisation and canalisation of streams and rivers, after urban expansion and land consolidation and after the construction of numerous new roads and railways, the last three to four decades of the last millennium will go down in history as the time when the apparently endless changeability of the landscape was first systematically and successfully brought up for discussion. Systematically, because, in addition to archaeology, the landscape as an artefact became the object of cultural historical research. And successfully, because it turned out that the results of this research could be applied to environmental policy almost without financial resources and contribute to the extremely rapid institutionalisation of the phenomenon of landscape conservancy.

This increasing interest in our country's topography and the gathering of knowledge in universities and state institutions is backed up by a feeling (not to say sentiment) broadly held in society that the unbridled development and intensification of the countryside and the postwar reconstruction have done the landscape more harm than good. The reaction to this is expressed in ministerial documents regarding nature and landscape conservancy in the seventies. 'The realisation of the significance of the cultural historical heritage in the environment in which we live, work and spend our free time should be reinforced. Many know that man is reliant on nature for his physical survival; but the significance of the surroundings in which our past history can be identified has probably not been sufficiently realised.' The rapid growth of the policy area means that the question can be asked whether historical-geographical understanding can possibly mean more than just bringing up arguments for the curbing, blocking or – as in the government decision regarding the route of the high-speed train through the Green Heart – putting a stop to investments in the rural areas. Research into the history of the landscape is seldom used for any other purpose than active landscape conservancy. And up to now the reverse has also been true: the research is only made legitimate by the desire to conserve the landscape.

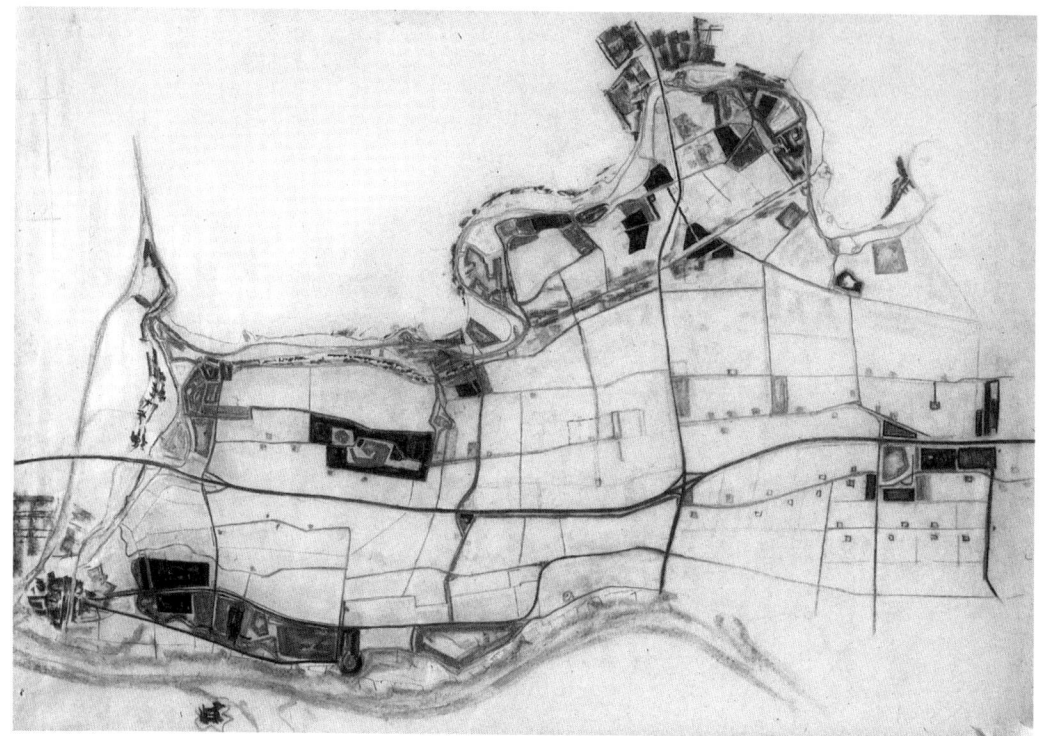

The embankment sand needed for the construction of the Rijksweg 15 arterial road between Nijmegen and Rotterdam was taken from deep sand pits at regular intervals along the route. The lakes that were so formed have all been laid out for daytrip recreation. The design for the Lingebos, which was drawn up in the sixties by the landscape designers of the Forestry Department, offers an attractive exception to other, generally formless recreation areas. The design brings the history of the landscape back to life, and does so on two levels. The meander-shaped lake shows that the arm of a river was located here in the age of the natural river system in the Mid-Netherlands. In addition, in this particular layout the combination of water and woods refers to the phenomenon of the duck decoys which for centuries marked the inaccessible marshy backlands between the major rivers.

The basis for the museum-like approach to landscape history is for that matter also to be found in the abovementioned documents. In 1977 the Minister of Welfare, Health and Cultural Affairs wrote: 'In the framework of landscape conservation it is abundantly obvious that it is interwoven with the cultural objectives of welfare policy, in the form they take in museum policy and the preservation of monuments.' And there's the rub. The methods and techniques of historical research in art, architecture and garden design are, mutatis mutandis, applicable to landscapes, but the range of instruments available to the Department of Monuments for the preservation of interesting relics is simply unsuited. Whereas old architecture can be restored and used for a new purpose without changing its form or appeal, the cherished landscape slips through one's fingers like sand. In architectural terms, the landscape is simultaneously interior and exterior: its formal qualities cannot be isolated from the functional and constructional dimensions. It is extremely hard to judge landscape in an artistic sense, since after all it never results from one single wilful or brilliant creator but is always a support for collective meanings. Nor can it be moved, exhibited or purchased, or at least only partly and then usually in fragments. And on top of this, it is never finished.

This last point is probably one of the most important reasons why environmental designers such as landscape designers, who generally move into action when something in the environment has to be changed, cannot often make use of the results of cultural historical research. As Taverne, the architectural historian from Groningen once tellingly wrote, to environmental designers the conception of a landscape or urban transformation or addition is roughly equivalent to a mechanic tinkering with a running engine. Landscape designers analyse their field of work in dynamic terms and see the landscape as the result of systems and processes. Historical geographers tend to see patterns and objects with differing degrees of intactness, age and rarity. As long as this sort of knowledge does not work towards increasing the quality of the adaptations and additions to the landscape – which will after all be constantly occurring – but only lead to prohibitions, historical geographers and landscape designers will continue to operate on separate lines.

But of course there is more going on here. Landscape designers have not yet responded adequately to society's call to act in dialogue with the history of the landscape. They have in their turn not yet turned out to be sufficiently capable of incorporating cultural historical awareness into their plans. Or, in other words, of speaking a spatial language in form and material that satisfies the need for a balance between the familiar semi-natural environment and the renewal it is occasionally subject to. In this area there is a great discrepancy between the undisputed motivation – expressed in a variety of ways – in landscape design plans, to look for a link with the genius loci (or the genius regionis as Johan Meeus called it in the 1992 essay collection 'Artivisual Landscapes': the character of a place) and the actual design skills needed. Since landscape design will be called upon for this skill more emphatically than in the past, it is best to study the relationship between landscape history and landscape design in greater depth than has been the case up to now.

Up to now the landscape design plans that attempt to be consistent with the history of an area's occupation have followed the patterns of the past far too closely. The design of the new landscape is often seen as an endeavour to make a faithful copy of the former pattern of the landscape. In plans like this the relics of the old situation are visible in the form of land division patterns and lines of vegetation. They form the starting point for the restoration. But because, for the reasons mentioned above, complete restoration of a landscape is hardly ever possible, efforts at restoration result in historical stylisation. They are seldom satisfactory because they are neither one thing nor the other: neither genuine facsimile of the topography nor a contemporary landscape. A landscape's understanding of history and the transformation of this knowledge into contemporary design inspiration demands something other than just respect for what there was.

A look at architectural theory may clear things up. A few years ago a debate arose among the architecture critics Tzonis, Lefaivre, Jencks, Frampton, Taverne and others about a specific approach to architectural design that had made itself apparent several times in the course of history (including recent history). In the end the critics agreed on the name for a working method that differs from other historical architectural movements in that it is not based on classical architectural formulae, ideal architectonic types or universalist schemes, but on concrete, region-specific models, structures and patterns. Since then, in imitation of Alexander Tzonis, this approach has been called 'critical regionalism'. The author repeatedly pointed out that regionalist architecture, much more than other architectural styles and movements, aims for the restoration of the social relevance of building by looking for explicit links with movements for political emancipation. Critical regionalism is the architecture that wishes to provide support for the relationship between people and country or between population group and region. It looks for images, working methods, concepts and materials that provide occupiers and users, owners and administrators with alternatives for the standardisation and normalisation that are the consequence of a division of influence, which is seen as unjust, over the use of legal and financial instruments and means of production in the field of environmental planning and building. In 1984 Tzonis wrote in the magazine Bouw: 'The essence of critical regionalism is not

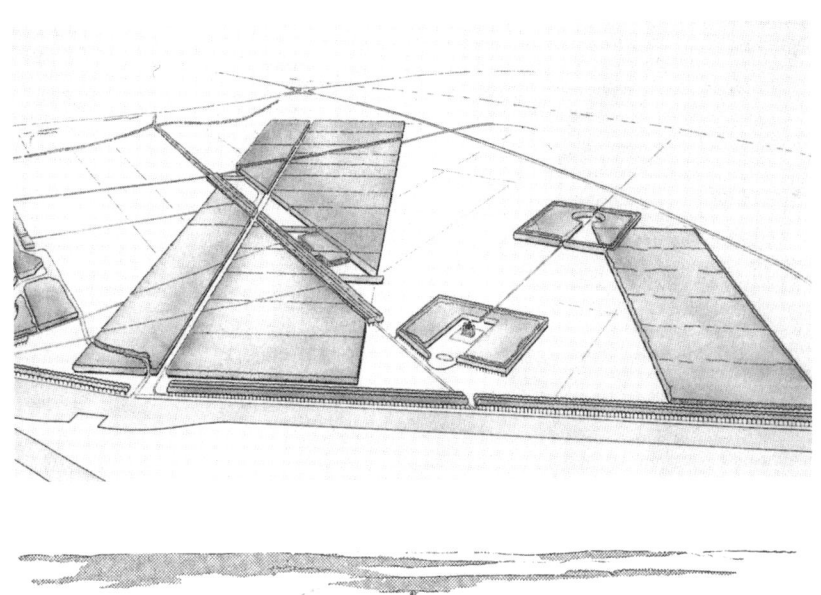

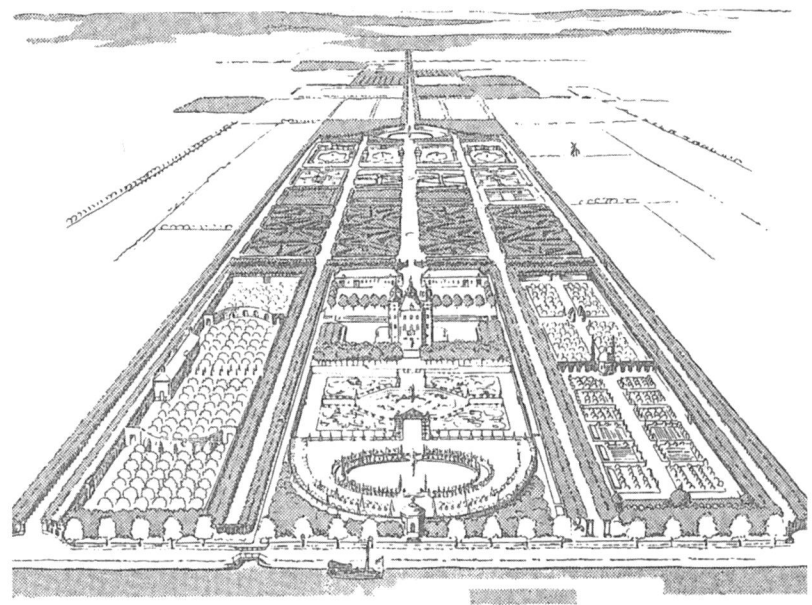

The 'Sorrow of Belgium' forestry plan
This design, entitled 'The Sorrow of Belgium', which was generated by Berdie Olthof and Walter Oerlemans in 1984 for a concept competition for planting new woods in the Netherlands, was an explicit reaction to the cultural historical qualities of the strip landscape south of Utrecht. The plan proposes developing the Amsterdam-Rhine Canal as a contemporary basis for the exploitation of new functions in this gradually urbanising landscape, analogous to the way the Heemstede country estate was constructed on this site in the seventeenth century. At that time this country estate was the culmination of the agrarian exploitation of the wilderness; in its turn, the forestry plan symbolises the transformation of this now obsolete agrarian pattern into an urban landscape. The relics of the Heemstede house, avenue and lake are superbly integrated into the purposes of the new woods.

the conservation of an architectural dialect, but resistance by means of architecture to the disintegration of a collective social bond. This is one of today's clearest attempts to give back to architecture its critical function and the task of social responsibility.'

In the Netherlands, which in politics seeks consensus and in geography and economy is relatively coherent, it would probably be taking us too far to employ environmental design in general or landscape design in particular as a vehicle for social revolt in the various parts of the country. The differences between the inhabitants of such areas have become too small and our national character is just too moderate. What it is about is the question of whether, and if so how, despite this socio-cultural solidarity that has gradually developed, the components and processes that formed the basis of the diversity of the landscapes of Veenkoloniën, Schouwen and Mergelland can be brought up to date without losing their differentiating effect. Because it is there that the motivation of historical geographers and landscape designers converge, in the fascination for topographical differentiation. Critical regionalism offers landscape design several planning guidelines. To quote Tzonis again: 'The definition of regionalism does not imply a series of common visual characteristics. It is not a style. In fact each region produces a different vocabulary of form. (...) Typical features of this iconographic system are, on the one hand, the systematic violation of classical, formal, so-called academic rules, and on the other the employment of design models including the existing dominant configurations of a particular region. (...) Whereas repetition, uniformity, coherence and the completeness of the formal composition are familiar as the positive qualities of the academic approach, it appears that regionalism looks to the opposite of all these things. It is oriented towards the variant, the unique, the exceptional and, more than anything else, to what is special about a special place.'

What recent examples of critical regionalist architecture in the world, ones that appeal to the imagination, designed by such architects as Botta, Antonakakis, De Carlo and MBM, all have in common is that the choices in form and construction made while creating the design are based on intelligent interpretations of ways of building that were customary on the spot, and that the limitations the architects imposed on themselves with regard to location, access and the exposure of the building or group of buildings were derived from local, topographical idiosyncrasies. The attractive power of good regionalist architecture is that it is reminiscent of something, without directly quoting, copying or restoring. In this architectural manipulation of regionally-specific knowledge and this active reuse of the qualities of a location there are elements that bring this way of working very close to landscape design.

More than this, on further consideration one could call landscape design inherently regionalistic. This profession is by definition oriented towards the contextual aspects of an environmental assignment and always draws inspiration from the characteristics of the area in question. So you could say that the ambition the critical regionalists have set themselves in the course of architectural history should embrace landscape design, and in a certain sense urban design too. Architecture alone cannot be considered capable of carrying a cultural historical echo. For this, the collective memory, where it involves the use and organisation of the land, has to be updated and translated into architectural terms.

Critical regionalist architecture holds up an interesting mirror to landscape architects, who are looking for social relevance and historical awareness. The first lesson we can learn from regionalist work is that the scope of landscape design for a region does not necessarily have to cover the whole region. A concrete plan for arranging the landscape, a park or even a garden can function as the 'core of condensation' for memories, insights and skills typical of a much larger domain or stretch of land. Figurative art is generally entrusted with capturing an area in one go. Think of Us Mem in Leeuwaarden, the somewhat coarse reference to the whole rural economy of Friesland, and of Bartje in Assen, who continues to remind the people of Drente that life is a regional novel. Landscape design has so far produced few such regionalist condensations. Perhaps this sort of significance might be attributed to the design for the Lingebos open-air recreation site on Tielerwaard, reclaimed sandy ground in the form of a stylised river meander in a wooded setting. But there are not many more of this sort of interesting, completed landscape design monuments in this country (in this case it is a monument to the tamed river area).

Another instructive element in regionalist architecture is its dynamic handling of the past. Historical research in itself cannot in this context give a decisive answer to the value to be allotted to architectural or topographical relics. The only deciding factor in the significance of society (regional or otherwise) is the degree to which historical topography is recycled in a design. Historical geography can be of great service to landscape design by analysing and describing the object of its study as the result of a continuing occupation of the physical substrate and not as a timeworn schoolroom picture by Cornelis Jetses. Critical regionalist architecture and its possible landscape design counterpart are not intended to preserve folklore, but to selectively reinterpret landscape antecedents and return them to circulation. In the best of cases, historical geographers and landscape architects collectively seek these antecedents and together decide on the degree to which they may inspire an environmental design.

A third and last consequence of an emphatic orientation towards the genius regionis is the qualification of the landscape designer's creativity as a condition for good planning. Regionalistic receptivity is hardly compatible with the reputation of a brilliant renewer of the profession or a grand creator of new landscapes. Regionalistic architecture benefits more from a genuine interest in the environmental task, almost chameleon-like empathic powers and a high level of selectivity, than from virtuosity and the creative urge. This implies the capacity to seek out what Alexander Tzonis calls a region's iconographic system and reactivate it in a design, and this requires from the designer first of all the will to renew himself instead of his surroundings.

Eric Luiten, landscape-architect and coordinator Landscape architecture of the Amsterdam Academy of Art.

BRABANT: A POSSIBLE CONTINUATION

'Everything that will be, drags along with it that which has been'
(Friedrich Nietzsche)

My grandfather was the organist at the reformed church in Helmond. There in the deep Catholic south the psalm 'Oh Lord, how awesome you are on every side' must have resounded to the lofty tones of his organ. His father, from Friesland, had once crossed the great rivers to work in the flourishing textile industry in Helmond. He was not the only one. At the end of the nineteenth century the textile manufacturers recruited labour on a large scale from the protestant north. Since it was created under the regime of the Batavian Republic two hundred years ago, North Brabant has been a province with an increasingly mobile population. There always was a lively movement of migrants and commuters into and out of the province. The Protestants from Holland who were then looking for work have now been succeeded by today's North Dutch commuters looking for a house in the Brabant countryside. But the people of Brabant are also very mobile. They travel in large numbers everyday to go to work north of the rivers. But they do no more than put up with these long trips, because in fact they are homelovers. Everyone knows the builders who make no bones about getting into their cars in the middle of the night to get to their building site at the top of North Holland on time for work. The people of Brabant are proud of not being part of the Randstad.

Anyone who traverses North Brabant will not be able to avoid the uneasy idea that the province is in danger of drowning in its own success. The industrial sites lie in close succession along the arterial roads. Sometimes they seem to act as one long shop window displaying the widest range of goods: from cars (lots and lots of cars), garden statues and building materials to the complete swimming paradise. Nowhere are the consequences of unbridled suburbanisation so visible as here. There are countless villages that have shapelessly outgrown themselves. Old village centres have been disjointed and blown up into something-for-everyone shopping centres. Whereas on the one hand villages have started to look like towns, on the other the towns absolutely do not want to become towns. Nowhere has space been spilt so clumsily as in Brabant. Rampant building has proliferated most especially in the wind-borne sand landscape of Mid-Brabant. North Brabant also contains areas that have developed in a more balanced way and where the landscape has retained its characteristic qualities, such as the Oostwaard and the Noordwaard, the Land of Altena and the Land of Cuijk. But wherever you look you come across gardens and yards laid out with great devotion, and a jolly sort of untidiness that reveals the slightly anarchistic streak in Brabant people.

North Brabant reminds one of Los Angeles before the Fall.

How did this transpire?

In its present form, North Brabant is largely a product of the last half century. In 1947 the provincial authorities of North Brabant presented their 'Prosperity Plan' in order to tackle the postwar reconstruction with abundant force. The plan was based on the three elements underlying Brabant society: business, church and state. The Prosperity Plan was an attempt to guide the industrialisation and modernisation of North Brabant along the right lines. They found themselves faced with the dilemma of how to modernise the province at high speed without uprooting the new postwar industrial worker. The harmony in which the various ranks and classes of Brabant society had lived together in their villages since time immemorial could not be put at risk. But how could it be prevented? After all, industrialisation and the creation of mass labour everywhere went hand in hand with the rapid growth of the major cities and the depopulation of the countryside. In the background there was the fear of socialism, to which the mass population of the metropolis was very susceptible, as had been proven elsewhere in the Netherlands. Active government interference in welfare and especially environmental planning were essential to averting all these dangers. The heart of the policy was clearly expressed by the then Queen's Commissioner, De Quay: 'As little mobility as

Pandora's Box just after it was opened, Rijksweg 58 [arterial road] in 1960, still only three lanes.

possible among the population: an as gradual as possible transfer from one trade to another and from one home to another. In other words, one should as far as possible leave the people in their own social and local environment'. The route taken by Brabant was found by a simple combination of progress and tradition in a policy recorded as 'village-scale industrialisation'. The starting point for this policy was the harmony between the new working and living environments that would be developed. The dimensions of the ideal living unit were based on the size of the average church parish. Home and place of work had to be at a reasonable cycling distance from each other, about six kilometres. The spread of employment was promoted to make it possible for the workers to stay in their familiar surroundings. This policy, which went under the title of 'moderate deconcentration', was intended to promote employment in several centres of industrialisation, partly in order to curb migration. This enabled such boroughs as Oosterhout, Etten, Bergen op Zoom, Oudenbosch, Rucphen, Zevenbergen, Boxmeer, Cuijk and Uden to expand into reasonably-sized industrial centres between 1950 and 1960. In the sixties this policy of scattered urbanisation was continued in the countryside (though somewhat modified) by introducing a hierarchy of centres. The explosive growth of suburbanisation in the seventies and again in the nineties in fact elaborated on the basic principle laid down in the Prosperity Plan. The finely-meshed road network, the diffuse structure of residential centres and, not to be forgotten, the sandy ground that was so suitable for building on encouraged unhindered building in the countryside more and differently than the rest of the Netherlands. Whereas the workman's daily cycle ride to and from the factory or the agricultural company was once the measure for the manageable organisation of land in Brabant, now the car became the driving force behind rampant growth without measure.

The industrial face of the 'sector'.

However, the most spectacular development took place in agriculture. Whereas shortly after the war the agrarian Netherlands looked down pityingly on the smallholders of Brabant, after fifty years the roles have been reversed. While sandy ground formerly condemned one to poverty, this ground offers the modern agrarian company the ideal substrate, enabling the farmer to react more rapidly and flexibly to market conditions than his fellow farmers on peaty and clay ground. The once so proud arable farmers are now trying to make ends meet by selling the right to spread manure. Other farmers are taking a stand against the 'pink' invasion from Brabant, whereby unexpected feelings sometimes come to the surface, as in the protest in Zeeland 'No Catholic dung on Protestant land'. Under the leadership of the North Brabant Christian Farmers Union, the agricultural sector has emerged as a formidable earner. The development of intensive stock breeding into a knowledge- and capital-intensive production sector is most striking. This sector fully substantiates the slogan 'Netherlands, the distribution land' by putting live pigs onto transport as quickly as possible and exporting them. Unfortunately this urge for distribution means the profit from the processing of the pig into meat products (Parma and Cerrano ham!) is lost to the Netherlands. The explosive growth of intensive stock breeding is very much stimulated by the proximity of the port of Rotterdam, where the cheap concentrate tapioca is imported from third world countries and unloaded. The dominant presence of pig farms has had considerable consequences for the appearance and arrangement of the Brabant countryside. Large parts of Brabant are almost entirely at the service of this sector. The extensive maize fields that have everywhere displaced the waving corn of yesteryear act as a supplier of roughage. The grassland (well beyond the boundaries of the province) serves mainly as somewhere to spread the enormous amounts of manure.

The ever expanding pig farming sector has now, with a hard bump, come up against its own limits. A bump that left many stunned and which will rumble on for some time.

However, there is the threat of an even greater disaster towards which we are unnoticeably but irrevocably heading. It is the slowly ticking time bomb of the nitrates and phosphates sinking into the deep ground water. Brabant draws its drinking water from the ground. On the surface it is now only the most nitrogen-loving plant species that are able to retain their niche in the landscape. Brabant has become Europe's deep manure house, the Netherlands the fields on which the muck is spread and Thailand where the former infertile heathland now lies.

The prosperity plan was implemented successfully. But with hindsight we can see that it was in at the birth of a development that makes a thorough reorientation unavoidable.

Embarrassment of Riches

The need for the new 'Manifesto: Brabant 2050' springs from the realisation that the province is now faced with choices as radical as in 1947. At that time the question was how Brabant had to be piloted into the modern industrial age with its gaze turned to the future. Now one has to consider the consequences of the dizzying development the province has been through in recent times and wonder what has actually happened to 'Brabant'.

The debate on the loss of Brabant's identity is not new and crops up regularly. I refer only to the debate in Brabantia magazine in the early eighties, on the subject 'what typifies the Brabander'. Feelings ran high between the defenders of what was typical of the area and their critics, who argued that 'Brabant' did not exist, being no more than a construct invented after the event. Whatever the case may be, there is a great deal of interest in Brabant's past among the population. Nowhere in the Netherlands are there so many clubs occupied in one way or another with their own history. Even in the eighties, the North Brabant Federation of Shooting Clubs still counted 196 clubs with a total of about 7000 members. In various university cities Brabant students have united to form their own student associations.

Because I was asked to 'examine the possibility of giving the cultural identity of Brabant a more emphatic form in the environment', it is essential first and foremost to ask the question what the identity of Brabant actually is and where one has to look for it. The renewed interest in things typical of the area, which the initiators of Manifesto: Brabant 2050 appear to share, may have various causes.

The first may be that people are simply cursed with an ingrained conservatism and see every change as an attack on their familiar surroundings. Paradoxically enough it is mainly the modern city-dweller who prefers to see his dynamic everyday life played out against an unchanging backcloth. But in Brabant a great deal has changed in a very short time. This can only mean that the high tempo of change has reinforced the feeling of unease. We have to realise that the development of Brabant over the last few decades can be compared to that of the tiger economies in South-East Asia, such as Korea and Malaysia.

Another cause has to do with the tendency to project the identity onto the past. Everything used to be better. This attitude blinds one to the fact that the present again and again produces new bearers of identity. While in the sixties people thought that old cars were much more attractive and that all the new models looked alike, the same people now look back on the then detested Daf-Variomatic with tenderness. What is more serious is that this attitude can lead to such a disdain for what is produced now, that no more demands are made of it. The cultural commitment slackens. People forget that future cultural history has to be made now. But this does not alter the widespread unease about the appearance of present-day Brabant. Is it not possible that many Brabanders are chiefly annoyed by the loveless way the environmental changes have taken place and by the poor quality of much of what has been built and done over recent decades? For example, the modernisation of agriculture, with its large-scale land consolidation and autonomous processes, has had a powerful homogenising effect on the landscape. The once so characteristic images of the historical landscapes of Brabant soon faded without being replaced by new and attractive man-made landscapes (with the exception, honesty forces us to say, of the Oostwaard and the Noordwaard near the Brabant Biesbosch). During this operation the public nature of the landscape, which it had possessed since time immemorial, was largely lost. Thousands of kilometres of unmetalled roads, church paths and other rights of way disappeared, making the land inaccessible to city-dwellers (and villagers!). The Brabant countryside is under lock and key.

Lastly there is the trend towards globalisation that sparks off a search for local identity and the rise of a new regionalism. A search for the real heart behind the nettle cheese, beer gruel, brawn and scrapple. The more globalisation and European unification undermine the independence and individual character of the nation state, the more regions crop up to form the focus of a new sort of nationalism, or so it seems. Lombardy, Tuscany, Brittany, Bavaria, Catalonia, Friesland... and Brabant? The ideology of regionalism is leavened with the desire for a harmonious, small-scale society. However disputable this romanticised image is, regionalism is based on an essential need that should not be ignored. Counter to most people's increased radius of action and the shrinking of the world to a 'global village' (car, aeroplane, fax, mobile phone, Internet), there is a growing need for security which one might put under the heading of the 'great homecoming'. It is the other side of the same coin.

Brabant and Otherland

Anyone looking at the history of Brabant after the Second World War (and there Brabant is no different from the rest of the Netherlands) will be able to interpret it as a struggle between the universal forces that push for equalisation and the counter-forces that by contrast seek after or maintain local differences. The forces of equalisation are undeniably on the winning side. But where can the counter-forces be found?

The globalisation of economy and society, which is largely responsible for the levelling of existing differences itself summons up counter-forces that introduce new differences or breathe new life into old ones. In this way this trend brings Brabant into contact with other cultures and in a certain sense educates the citizens to become critical consumers. Consumers who will make demands that run counter to the levelling and homogenisation of the quality of everyday life. Instead of the interchangeable mass products distributed worldwide, people want local products. Local specialities like black pudding are increasingly appearing on menus again. The historical names of the various areas like the Baronie van Breda, the Meierij van 's Hertogenbosch, the Kempen and the Land van Cuijk are gradually being rediscovered. They are often age-old names that fell into disuse and were replaced by the matter-of-fact geographic division of North Brabant into West Brabant, Mid-Brabant, etc.

If we seek out bearers of identity we can locate them on various levels.

One's own house (and for many people one's own car) is the epicentre of one's individuality. The forces of equalisation have often penetrated so far that the 'homecoming' has to be taken literally because it now refers only to one's own home. The freedom of individual expression often seems to have been whittled down to this last 'reservation', the interior and the garden. It is there that a substantial portion of family life is spent. The furniture sector, home decoration shops and garden centres have a turnover of billions.

The neighbourhood or village can also be a crystallisation point to which a local identity attaches itself. The choice made by people who are in a position to choose where they live often depends very much on the particular atmosphere or individual character and not only on measurable quantities such

'Brabant' as an export product. The commercial reincarnation of Duke Jan I.

as the distance to work or the presence of amenities. These are identities that are recognised and shared by groups of people.

A city or town, or a region, perhaps even the province as a whole can in a certain sense also be experienced as an entity. Visual impressions, tactile experiences and even smell can evoke this feeling of being at or coming home. But social bonds and the sense of sharing a way of life with others are probably even more important.

One's 'individuality' or own identity is an amalgam of diverse phenomena with different diffusion areas, and will therefore differ from place to place (and from person to person!). It is tempting to put together a geography of identity-bearers. I shall limit myself to a number of examples.

The Mid-Brabant wind-borne sand deposits are of course a unique topographical entity, but the defining identity-bearers are certainly not. This type of landscape is so widespread that the well-known landscape designer Nico de Jonge always said that it 'continued as far as Moscow'. Shrovetide is often associated with Brabant, but not exclusively. It is celebrated with gusto in Limburg too. It is at most a difference from the Netherlands north of the rivers (a distinction which is unfortunately starting to fade). It is true that the AAA menu in Bergen-op-Zoom (Anchovies fresh from the Markiezaat, followed by Asparagus swaying in the salty wind from the sea, which have a clearly distinctive taste, topped off with local Aardbeien [strawberries]) enjoys a certain renown among gourmets, but further from the city it is hardly known. It is one of Bergen-op-Zoom's identity-bearers, not Brabant's. The annual Balloon Fiesta in Breda in South-East Brabant will be similarly little known. The reverse can also occur. The Acht van Chaam is a local cycling competition that is known nationwide. In parts of Brabant, the Peel and the Peelrand, intensive stock breeding has really taken off, but it is neither exclusive to Brabant nor characteristic of the agrarian sector in other parts of the province. There are of course elements which are unique in the country. Mid-Brabant is the Netherlands' only real industrial region in the sense that life there is permeated by the industrial culture of manufacturing. The annual fair in Tilburg attracts a million visitors from all over the Netherlands. We can distinguish old and new identity-bearers. The numerous monumental monastic complexes and the roadside chapels of Our Lady and crucifixes scattered all over the province are among the signs that seem to have been set up to outface the crumbling of Roman Catholic life in Brabant. Stud farms have a long tradition of producing champion jumpers and riders, as well as entering coach-and-four competitions. On the other hand there are features that typify the new Brabant. North Brabant is characterised by a high concentration of recreational and amusement parks such as the Efteling, the Land van Ooit and Autotron.

The inhabitants of each individual place will invoke a particular set of identity-bearers and objective features as 'theirs'. This will include Dutch things and some associated with Brabant, as well as those linked to, for example, the Land van Cuijk or a particular village. In short, an endless collection of different characteristic features, a sort of library of Babel of self-constructed regions. What makes pronouncements on Brabant identity so restrictive, apart from its drawing an entirely arbitrary line between 'Brabant' and 'Otherland', is that it does an injustice to the richly varied reality behind the notion.

Mixing desk

It therefore makes no sense to postulate a mysterious Brabant identity, track it down, isolate and unravel it in order then to take up the elixir of identity so discovered and produce it in series, hoping that the 'real Brabant' will then rise again. Perhaps by simply solving as well as possible all the tasks that administrators and designers are so fond of, the 'caressable and tangible things from which the cultural identity can be derived' will reappear of themselves. We could then restrict ourselves to lovingly working on the details of the plans. Identity could then be replaced by environmental quality. This is of course a gross overestimation of the significance of the new with regard to the existing environmental reality. It also disregards the issue of whether identity is a question of 'creating' or 'growing'. We have already established that in any case it is not something one can just impose on an area. As a designer or

---

Top-Down   𝔅rabantia
"Let there be light, and there was light"
the designer/administrator as the creator of the Brabant world
> if there is an excess of this:
   it degenerates into an empty marketing concept, Brabant as complete fiction, analogous to city-marketing concepts
> if there is not enough:
   a lack of cultural commitment and de facto submission to the forces of equalisation

Bottom-Up   Brab@Nt
"you are what you eat"
A contented person is the architect without architecture
> if there is an excess of this:
   complete fragmentation into individual expression, a denial of the collective side of environmental organisation
> if there is not enough:
   rigidity, little flexibility

administrator you have to be able to achieve a fine balance between commitment from above and allowing characteristic elements to arise from below to which this wish for individuality can attach itself. The 'mixing desk' below illustrates the consequences if one of the two extremes predominates:

We have formulated this summary for Brabant, as if for a regional plan. However, this sort of approach can be applied to any design brief regardless of scale. But this approach still lacks something. It is too one-dimensional. It is as if this identity would allow itself to be pinned down to a single scale. Moreover, by focusing attention exclusively on the new, what already exists is easily overlooked. The approach to an environmental strategy for a future Brabant demands broader foundations.

Middle game

The pronounced focus of attention on the existing situation need not result in a timid or conservational approach to environmental issues in Brabant. It is mainly a question of recognising the treacliness of what exists and the momentum of developments previously set in motion. We want to take a route which may be unusual for designers so as, for once, not to display professional optimism and pretend that anything is still possible. The designer does not have a magic wand with which he can at a stroke solve every problem by means of well-placed interventions. Some Pandora's Boxes are very hard to close again, such as the addiction to mobility on which the whole environmental organisation of North Brabant is based! If we consider that environmental planning should be taking a different direction, we have to realise that the desired changes must take place very gradually and probably only in part. No quick successes can be scored. Even though it is beyond dispute that the profound changes Brabant has to undergo have to be carried out as a democratic project. This takes time and a great deal of energy but then the new Brabant will either be created by all parties together or not at all.

We can compare the situation of the environmental organisation of Brabant with a game of chess after about thirty moves. The position has largely been established. Some pieces have already vanished from the board. Some of the ways it could continue are favourable, others impossible. We can only think a few moves ahead (and certainly not as far as 2050!). A successful approach to environmental issues depends on the understanding that the disentangling of the complex environmental knot that Brabant has become over the last fifty years can only be done in the form of an evolution. Revolutionary innovations are very rare in the slow world of environmental planning. This will probably be made clear by several examples from the transport sector, which is so closely

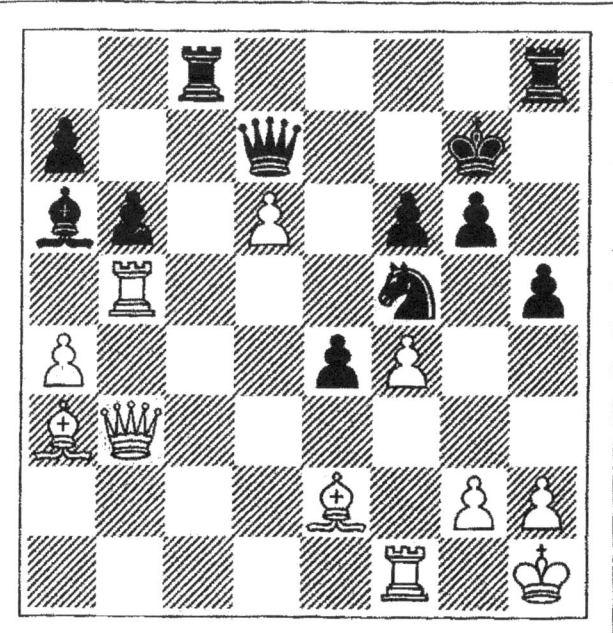

The middle game: the position determines the possible next moves.

linked to environmental planning. Ever since my childhood, splendid artist's impressions have promised me the arrival of futuristic vehicles powered by electricity or a hydrogen engine, which combine the advantages of the individualistic system of cars with the advantages of public transport by linking together to form long trains. In one way or another these ingenious schemes on paper refuse to become reality. But concepts like the smart highway that are associated with existing vehicle technology and road construction do stand a chance of being introduced by way of small-scale innovations. Likewise the high-speed train, because this system builds on the existing steel-on-steel transport technique and may even be able to use existing tracks, a great advantage over the technically superior hovertrain with its linear induction motor, because the latter demands a completely new infrastructure. The reintroduction of old lines of development which were halted for no special reason is in most cases also hard or impossible. Attempts to breathe new life into the airship and steam engine prove this. These technologies lack the necessary fifty years of trial and error development. They have therefore fallen so far behind competing technologies that the gap can no longer be bridged.

Bricolage versus utopism
When setting a new course we should not become absorbed in the past. The romantic idea that everything was better in the past will only produce regressive planning and inevitably leads to what the English call 'down-tide

action'. The past has to be treated as a learning process for the future. Equally, we should not lapse one-sidedly into reflections on a distantly beckoning future. This creates the danger of plans remote from present problems: 'up-tide action'. We actually use the exploration of the future to set the compass, not to mark out the route itself. Apart from these two obstacles there is a third one has to avoid. Too resolute an orientation towards the present, without being able to learn from the past, and robbed of any orientation to the future, may lead the step-by-step approach to become bogged down in narrow-minded pragmatism. The art is to set out a line of advance with a certain cultural self-awareness without constantly consulting the past and without blueprints for the future.

The right approach to solving Brabant's environmental issues may lie in the drafting of a number of simple but effective rules to achieve a gradual improvement in the situation: Brabant step-by-step. The approach we support is based on a positive confidence in the feasibility of making something of the topography, very gradually, but without lapsing into utopianism. We exchange utopism for bricolage.
Brabant step-by-step is the adventure we enter into together while not being able (or perhaps willing) to forecast where it will take us.

Brabant step-by-step

The success of Brabant's race to catch up with the rest of the Netherlands is certainly due in part to the great freedom given to many forms of private initiative there. The fact that this coin has the previously mentioned reverse side should not tempt us into the urge to make rules, which would choke this initiative and the dynamic nature of the province. It comes down to setting out lines for the future that are so simple as to make the goals clear and so that the inventiveness of Brabant society is so stimulated that the solutions emerge from it as a matter of course. The simplification of regulations is also in line with part of the 'Brabant identity' which has until now remained underexposed, the fact that rules are there to be got round, or put more positively, to be played with. In addition to this, the set of rules must also be composed anew in such a way that they set in motion social processes that can produce interesting forms of environmental expression and at the same time bring the permanent nature of society closer. In short, designers and administrators will have to put on a strong show of triple alliance (Rini van Bragt, Van der Smissen and Jaspers will certainly come to the aid of their provincial administrators!).

To this end it is essential that the government recovers its traditional profile and the main basis for the legitimisation of environmental planning. Defining and vigorous when it comes to the 'load-bearing' construction, restrained and

Ignoring the evolutionary nature of technological developments condemns this sort of projection as outdated futurism: it tells more about the time when it was drawn up than about the future.

no more than facilitating when it comes to use and purpose. With regard to this last point, Brabant needs no lessons (though in several respects the reins could even be slackened somewhat), but when it comes to defining the main features a much more vigorous input is essential. Strict subsidiarity is a necessary condition (each problem has to be tackled on the appropriate scale). These considerations lead to rules that can be divided into five groups. They are summarised in the diagram below. In all five cases several 'candidates' are put forward. This list is by no means complete, but only aims, by means of examples, to provide an insight into the operation and range of application of the rules.

Regulation means the sort of simple rule that stimulates citizens, businesses and society's midfield, in short every section of society, to come up with solutions with a socially-desirable orientation. Strangely enough it seems that it is precisely these simple measures that are suited to tackling very complex problems. The toughest problems are definitely those linked to the inevitable turn our society has to make in the direction of greater sustainability. Current environmental policy focuses in detail on all manner of precisely defined objectives and targets in a tangle of sub-problems and therefore comes across as muddled and cavilling. If we make a distinction between the main issue and side issues it turns out that future policy should hinge on our handling of three 'core stocks': biodiversity, energy and space. There has for some time been talk of levies on every form of energy use. By analogy I would like to argue forcefully for the introduction of a system of levies on the wasteful use of space. In the situation in Brabant this is an absolute precondition for the long-term increase in quality. Whereas international agreements are essential for energy taxes, the state and the province have more elbow room when it comes to space as a core stock. Any system of regulatory levies should be based on separate forms of land use. It may result in a number of maps of the province coloured in with a simple three-part key. Exempted areas where the function in question is desired, prohibited areas where a particular function must absolutely be resisted, and taxable areas where toleration of the function goes with the payment of a tax levied by unit of land area. This revenue goes into a provincial

	FUNCTIE	CANDIDATES	SUBSIDIARITY			
			(i)national	provincial	regional	local
Regulation	addressing main problems	regulatory levies on: •energy •space	✔	✔		
Principles of order	putting the landscape in order	per sub-catchment area: •forestation of infiltration areas •wetting of seepage areas		✔		
Interventions	guidance/ protection	•purchase protection areas •cycling/walking network			✔	
Attention by topic	use of environmental change	•pig farming •water extraction •housing construction		✔		
Design rules	measured variation	>margins >long lines			✔	✔

fund to finance poor but useful projects such as landscape restoration or the EHS [Overall Ecological Structure]. This could then be combined with the introduction of annual (and partly negotiable) space allocations such as have already been successfully used for ten years in San Francisco to combat excessive suburbanisation. In short, a package that makes it possible to sail closer to the wind in environmental planning and stimulates devising and implementing space-saving measures.

In order to put the Brabant landscape back in order again it may be advisable to agree on several principles of organisation and to stick to them for a long period. On sandy soil it is obvious that such principles are to be based on hydrology. The nicest thing would be to allot a different land-use function to each sub-catchment area, so that they are not hydrologically at cross purposes. For those sub-catchment areas allotted to nature, this would mean that the upper, middle and lower reaches of the river would be done full justice as cohesive systems. In the situation in Brabant, this will unfortunately not be feasible because too many things would have to be overturned to achieve it. In the long term it is probably feasible to gradually initiate land consolidation in each sub-catchment area, so that infiltration areas can be purchased (using money from the tax fund and from the water extraction companies) and afforested, the upper reaches of the streams can be dammed and the seepage areas made moist again. The intermediate areas will then be suitable for sustainable agricultural use. This sort of agreement will gradually and almost inoffensively lead to a new organisation of the landscape, with exciting exceptions in the form of enclaves in numerous places. At the same time the approach to the partial use of the new woods as a backcloth to Brabant's suburbia should not be too childish.

The interventions involve several inherently governmental tasks in the field of protecting weak functions. In this complicated set of rules, protection takes the form of a 'prohibition area' for certain functions. The government does have a clear task when it comes to the management of such entities. The creation and maintenance of networks also falls into this category. In addition to a substantial increase in semi-public land (by the application of the aforementioned principles of organisation and the implementation of the EHS), the main issue here is the opening up of the Brabant landscape by the construction of a cohesive and dense network of cycling and walking routes.

The province would do well to devote thematic attention to a number of small, carefully chosen social developments whose substantial implications mean they can function as locomotives in the process of environmental change. These adopted themes would have to be supported, coached and subsidised very actively and on all levels of scale. This provides tools to improve environmental quality over a large area in the foreseeable future, if the level of ambition is set high from the very beginning. One thinks of the cleaning-up of pig farming that is going on at the moment. The task is to give it a new and, hydrologically speaking, inherently 'safe' place in the landscape. The undoubtedly much larger and economically almost self-sufficient businesses (roughage production, breeding, fattening and slaughtering being combined for sanitary reasons) will have to be planned as new components of the landscape. A limited architectural competition should be organised for designs for the most attractive new ammonia-proof sty, etc. The drinking water companies' large-scale switch from ground water extraction to bank infiltration is also a process that can fulfil this sort of pivotal function and in which new landscape qualities can be produced with a certain cultural commitment. It is also quite possible to handle urbanisation in this way. In addition to attractive urban projects intended to keep hold of urban clients, it would also be wise to introduce planned suburban projects within reach of regional public transport in the urban regions, offering an alternative to the endless semi-detached wasteland. Since the villages have largely lost their amenities, it is not clear why the newcomers always have to be stuck onto the existing foci. Brabant has a fine tradition of new settlements that has continued until very recently. Villages like Stevensbeek (1937) and Landhorst (1946) on the fringes of the Peel area are highly successful examples of this. Why not establish new villages for the people who choose this pleasant form of living? Well-considered locations in the landscape will then have to be found in the levy areas for these ultra-low densities.

Lastly, the rules of design. Their main function is to regulate the degree of variation on the various levels of scale. Here is an example from Brabant's rural area. Despite the levies, building will undoubtedly be done at low density – but only in certain parts of the province. There is of course nothing wrong with the agreeable freedom of the little private paradises. But there is something deficient about the way they are currently regulated. At first sight, the coalition between the builder-occupier's desire for individual expression and the architects selected for their originality and artistic outlook seems to be a source of rich differentiation in form, colour and use of materials or, in short, a high density of visual impressions. Unfortunately, this overload of visual impulses rather tends to snuff itself out with meaninglessness. Any prosperity there may be only aggravates the problem because only individual objects are subjected to the miraculous game of 'good taste'. The fact that this does not provide the 'safety net' that 'style' or a 'code' offered less-talented fellow designers until the early years of the last century can be seen everywhere in Brabant. It is the problem of a surfeit of variation at the wrong level. This may be the most

An alternative to the semi-detached wasteland. In Haverleij the houses are clustered and the surrender of part of the private garden is compensated by turning the resulting terrain into a 'country estate'.

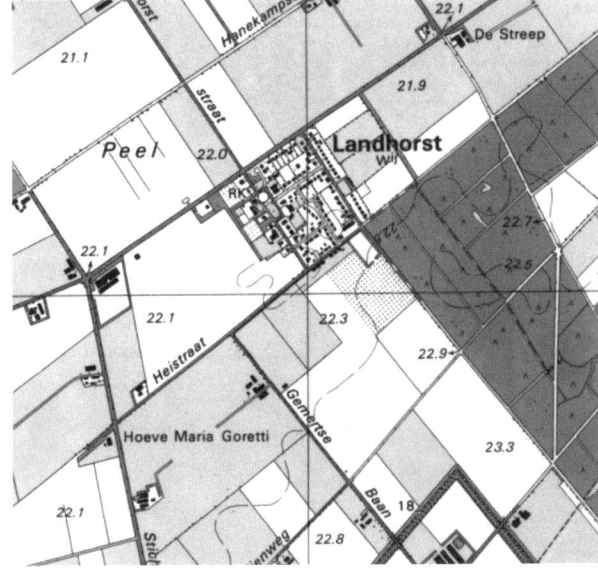

Landhorst (1946), the most recent offspring of the living tradition of creating villages in Brabant.

elusive problem in urban planning and landscape design. If every location tries to stand out the result is visual noise. In his 'Essays over variatie' [Essays on Variation], Taeke de Jong demonstrates how important it is to keep the right balance when it comes to environmental variation. A balance that keeps its ear close to the ground. It is striking that on this subject we find the same paradox almost literally in the words of an architect – Aldo Van Eyck – and an ecologist – Chris van Leeuwen: 'We used always to do the same, with a different result every time, now we always do something different and always get the same result.' Perhaps we should now regulate precisely those elements not subject to prosperity, such as the transitions between private and public domains. As we have seen, it is architecture that provides the most intense example of this. The art is to direct without allowing the freedom of architectural expression to get lost in cavilling. The level at which regulation takes place determines

Rules of design: a fine encounter between one of Brabant's long lines and the boundary of a private plot.

everything. The best way may well be greater linkage at a lower level (building lines, materials used, etc.) and greater freedom at the object level. In the extreme case this may mean allowing no more than two sorts of brick but otherwise imposing little other than technical requirements. At one step up in scale the edge of the plot is the transition between private and public. Here and there in Brabant there are good examples of the way simple agreements on the finish of the boundaries (hedges, walls, clear profiles, etc.) enable highly varied buildings still to belong roughly to the same family.

Experiments in silico

This was of course just a sample of a collection of rules. The nice thing is that this sort of rule tends to rearrange the normal spatial programme. For example, proper guidance on the subject of 'drinking water production' will turn out to yield a substantial proportion of the EHS, which could hardly be achieved on its own. Sometimes, this sort of typology also brings up entirely new programme components, such as new villages. But in the end it is all about the set of rules collectively bringing about the desired result. How can you know now whether you are on the right track? This naturally requires the necessary design research. Modern techniques can help us in this respect. The type of research in which patterns of evolution are exposed by testing the viability of various self-replicating algorithms by simulating millions of generations (Levy, 1992) can also be used in planning. It is possible to ask the Technical University of Eindhoven to simulate conceivable images of the future environmental order in Brabant by means of various sets of rules. We can see whether particular images appeal to us. We can reverse our reasoning, change a few rules or examine adaptations of the rules whose introduction is considered socially impracticable and then do a new simulation, and so on. This is SIM Brabant, whereby the environmental reality can be simulated in silico for those who are wary of allowing their business to develop immediately in vitro. Nice for the people who like to know in advance what the future is going to look like.

Dirk Sijmons, assisted by Hans Venema
An essay commissioned by the Province of North Brabant as part of the 'Brabant 2050' Manifesto. It was published in October 1997 in the foundation document 'Brabant ongemonteerd' [Brabant Unassembled], a collection of all prior recommendations.

The national territorial identity as a piece of embroidery (Artist unknown, photo Jan Wychers)

THE NETHERLANDS – A KUNSTWERK ONCE AGAIN!*

* Translator's note: Kunstwerk = 1) a work of art; 2) construction work

PREAMBLE: THE NETHERLANDS, BETWEEN 'GRAND DESIGN' AND 'GRAND DESSERT'

Osaka 1972: the design of the Dutch pavilion at the World Fair. In compliance with the one percent rule, the artist Wim T. Schippers puts forward the proposal, as simple as it is far-reaching, of designing it as a French pavilion. All the over-familiar emblems of France, from the beret and posters of Notre Dame to a clay model of the Mont Saint-Michel, would be displayed in the pathetic way typical of Schippers. To cap it all, the French flag would also be raised over the pavilion.[1] The Dutch organising committee reacted as if bitten by an adder. Schippers did something that was absolutely inconceivable for a world fair: he mocked national identity. At the same time he touched upon the last remaining Dutch taboo: one does not talk about the Dutch national identity.

When the State Planning Department asked us to write a scenario entitled 'The Netherlands as a Grand Design', I was struck by the unintentional irony of the task. Do 'The Netherlands' and 'Grand Design' mix? *Bien étonnés de se trouver ensemble!* In the world of environmental design flirting with true or supposed French adroitness is very popular. The 'Grandes Projets' carried out by generations of French presidents and the 'Train au Grand Vitesse' (TGV) display a supposed vigour which we sometimes envy. This flirting implies the same tension with regard to our national identity as in Schippers' provocation. The Netherlands are, after all, not a 'Grand Design', never will be, and, even if it were possible, we should not even want it to be! A notion that is so closely linked to centralism is simply irreconcilable with our national identity.

So the question is, how can we characterise the Netherlands? The languages and cultures of our neighbouring countries offer various possibilities. In contrast to the ambitious, cohesive scheme assumed in the 'grand design', one could put forward the culinary *pièce de résistance*, the *'grand dessert'*. This is on the basis of an architecture without urban planning and without landscape design. This metaphor for a collection of sumptuous delicacies without any mutual cohesion might refer to a Netherlands where virtually all new buildings would end up in the Architectural Yearbook but where at the same time there

One connecting block is nothing, a single electric wire futile, a loose fitting doesn't amount to much, 40 watts does not give much light, but everything times eighty makes a fine chandelier.

is a total lack of collectivity. The German *Gesamtkunstwerk* misses the bullseye too: it is on a completely different scale and much too pretentious for our inhabited megastructure.[2] A more precise characterisation of the nature of the environmental reality of the Netherlands must therefore be derived from our own language. Because, after all, our country does have its own identity: there is an historically established territory, there are shared myths and a collective memory, a shared public culture (a mass culture), shared legal rights and duties and a shared economy. Together they assist in creating something like a national identity.[3]

All these characteristics can be linked together by the Netherlands' special geographical situation as land won back from nature: the historical territory which it has in part created itself, the myths regarding the struggle against water, and so on. Conversely, our unshakable belief in environmental and then mainly infrastructural solutions for all manner of social problems (from social training centres for antisocial families to an overall ecological structure for our distressed natural environment) may well be the expression of our national identity. Environmental order and national identity are apparently related. This process of mutual influence is one of history's slowly turning wheels. Changes are measured in centuries and decades rather than years. One can also distinguish several general environmental characteristics in the developed culture whose keywords are tolerance, consensus and egalitarianism. What is 'typically Dutch' is expressed in terms of space. In the first place one thinks of its highly developed environmental planning, which in the city manifests itself

Institutional design: motorway and how it fits into the landscape.

in the form of social housing and the urban planning of building complexes. In the countryside we find it in the new polders and also in land consolidation and new woods, which both produce wood and provide recreation. Then there is the palpable presence of water management and in the case of major roads the attention paid to attractive routing, fitting into the landscape, the choice of furniture and the signposting. In short, miscellaneous forms of more or less anonymous and institutional environmental design, with a graphic counterpart in postage stamps and banknotes.

For this reason the Netherlands is neither Grand Design nor Grand Dessert, but rather a Kunstwerk. The double meaning of this word as examined in the 1995 Nai exhibition is in exactly the right place in this scenario. After all, the Netherlands' most appealing projects include civil engineering works and all manner of utilities. The concern for the design of the environment has led to a very high 'standard quality' with few exceptions above or below it. This sort of work, in its function, genesis and execution, is also far removed from the prestigious Grandes Projets. It is precisely the concept of the kunstwerk, with its double meaning, that covers the neutral, subservient but meticulous design which in England is called the Fine Dutch Tradition. So it is not the culture with a capital C, but rather the activities patiently carried out with a sort of regulated traditional approach and which form the environmental cement of our society.

Institutional design: the arrangement of land.

The application of the scenario

In this scenario there is therefore little point in dozing off into an 'architect's wet dream', filled with revolutionary plans. We have no use for the sort of muscular centralism in which prestige projects are set up by decree. It is better to make the scenario correspond to the specific nature of the Dutch culture of consultation, in which successful plans come into being as a result of a search for consensus and often after endless attempts to bring about vertical policy coordination between the layers of administration.

However, even this modest approach to the scenario is currently a thorny problem. New plans are immediately greeted with the greatest suspicion. In the country where the word 'landscape' was invented, the landscape created by man is often mistakenly taken for natural! This country, almost entirely created by human hands, appears strangely enough to have lost its confidence in its ability to form its topography. Perhaps this confidence was deposited on the rubbish dump of history together with the 'ability to shape society'.

The chief purpose of the 'Netherlands as Kunstwerk' scenario is to increase confidence and faith in the country's own capacities. It is precisely the characteristics of the Netherlands that should form the basis of this. If we want better results, finer projects or whatever else, the only the only way we can go is that of raising the level of the debate in the 'everlasting news feature' as the culture of discussion in our country appears to the critical outsider. If that works, it will turn out that the culture of consultation so typical of our country does not so much put a spanner in the works as yield added value to the planning process.

Institutional design: polders.

THE NETHERLANDS IN 2030

The history of the future

The first decades of the twenty-first century are characterised by a pronounced upsurge of interest in environmental planning and the shapability of society. The Netherlands has rediscovered the pleasure of tinkering with its own land, the largest inhabited megastructure. There is lively debate. The proponents and opponents of each project naturally nag each other constantly, often in 'nimby' arguments, but there is an ever-increasing focus on 'how' it is executed and on the level of ambition. The opinion is broadly shared that we only advance by controversy and disputes on matters of taste must be carried on correctly.[4] The culture sections of the serious newspapers are the platform on which the academic and technical aspects of 'kunstwerk Netherlands' are judged on their merits. The common intention of solving problems at a high architectonic level is recognised as one of the binding elements of national identity. This insight is consequently deployed politically and ideologically as one of the binding elements of an increasingly multiform society. This revaluation arises out of the pursuit of federalism encouraged by Brussels. The emphasis on national and regional identity can also be seen elsewhere in Europe. It also seems that, with the decreed end of science,[5] society's energy has shifted to other areas of collective endeavour. Where this has repercussions on architecture and environmental planning, it leads to major differences. Paris, for example, has become increasingly 'Paris-like' as a result of an unceasing flow of presidential *Grandes Projets*.[6] By the same token, the Netherlands is becoming increasingly 'Netherlands-like' because the designers' attention to every possible change is

The initiation of a new urban icon: the pylon of the new bridge of Ben van Berkel as the king between other known Rotterdam buildings.

stirred up by public debate and penetrates ever deeper. 'Dutch Design' permeates into the smallest capillaries of the spatial environment and the large-scale work is also lovingly embraced.

The government follows the social trend. Whereas the first Architecture Paper (1991) concentrated mainly on buildings, with a short look at micro-urban planning, its successor (1997) brought the cultural component of urban planning, the design of the landscape and major infrastructure into the realm of the policy. In about 2010 the somewhat artificial division between architectural policy and environmental planning will be removed. In professional circles it is agreed that this linkage will be of benefit to both fields: architectural policy will be freed from its false territory of aesthetics and environmental planning will get the essential cultural impulse.

The Fifth Environmental Planning Paper deals with a reorientation of environmental policy. It opts for a clearer distinction between the State Planning Department's planning and policy tasks. By making good use of the divisions of the Ministry of Agriculture, Nature Conservation and Fishing, a Planning Office for Land Policy (POB) has been created, uniting environmental research and monitoring.

For this reason the Sixth Extra Environmental Planning Paper (ZESNEX) presents a broad policy for land use. The starting point is the environmental approach, but the paper makes the link to ecological policy, social policy and (this is new) time policy. The main thing of importance is the recognition of the social and collective importance of gradients between rest and activity, between night and day. The 24-hour economy is strongly resisted. The vulnerability of the social arrangement for Sundays has also been understood in secular circles. Local measures prevent the darkness of night from being forced out of its last reservations. Where environmental and time policy meet, parts of

Institutional design: urban development.

the Overall Ecological Structure (EHS) and old infrastructural systems are designated and developed as 'deceleration areas'. Planning finally concerns itself with the programme with the lowest dynamics.

The importance of the publication of the book 'Zen and the Art of Environmental Planning' in 2017 should not be underestimated. It offers modest but elegant solutions to environmental planning at the highest level ('the shortest way between two points is the finest way between two points'). The title is a paraphrase of the abbreviation of the Seventh Paper, ZENO. The most striking element in this paper is possibly the break with the detailed concern shown by state environmental policy and the introduction of models for indefinite urbanisation. Not that the government is launching into continuing urbanisation, but it does want to develop occupation strategies in the urban Randstad-Zandstad area that do justice to the wish both for condensation and the relaxed atmosphere of the outskirts. It also makes suggestions for the most desirable configuration of other functions (agriculture, nature, amenities for the urban metabolism, etc.). The results of these growth models have been tested by calculating endless generation changes. The results are used for the introduction of a system of regulatory levies in environmental planning.

The broadening of the policy reaches its provisional peak in the Eighth Paper on Economy, Risk Management & Land Use Policy which, because of its multiple nature, is issued under the coordinating aegis of the Scientific Council for Government Policy. This paper develops the full integration of ecological issues into environmental planning. Whereas it started as an ad hoc search for all manner of ecological adaptations to environmental projects, asking the right questions turned out to result in a substantial enrichment of sustainable solutions. The process of radical conversion that is intended to lead to a

Front: proper regulation, the 'Noud de Vreeze side' of the Dutch tradition.

Back: the necessary freedom of action, the 'Carel Weber side' of the Dutch tradition, which at the same time embraces both sides.

healthier relationship between ecology and economy is seen as one of the greatest challenges faced by 'Kunstwerk Netherlands'. It is a new task that must and can be solved collectively and which is not to be avoided. This commonsense approach makes the problem manageable and removes its ponderous connotations of planetary doom and the decline of humanity.

In an overview of this period, a remarkable change takes place in the professional views of environmental designers. Whereas the great emphasis on the cultural component of architecture led chiefly to the 'yearbook syndrome', it is now all about the architectural component of culture. Between 1990 and 2030 there was a huge diversity of styles, with the periods all overlapping each other. Postmodernism was embraced for only a short time and by 2005 the infatuation has passed. It is primarily from the world of environmental planning that we hear the dry observation that fragmentation and peripheral conditions do indeed provide a picture of reality, but do not therefore have to be elevated into standards for every design solution. It is no wonder that comment comes from that direction, because it is mainly in these fields that the forcing of analytical material to form solutions leads to great disasters. The Cyberarch in which architectural objects are gracefully bent with the help of the computer is not a genuine style and in the end turns out to comprise as many different movements as architecture itself has. The most expressive examples of this new design technique, the blossoming of the 'Rotterdam School', can be dated to around 2015. There is no lack of reaction to the purely formal nature of the two movements. As a result of its craving for individual expression, architecture itself begins to become a problem. In about 2010 the first traces begin to appear of an architecture that is once again taking account of society. This change is in its turn the consequence of decreasing individualism and a reorientation towards moral values in and of society.

As one of the last all-embracing disciplines, architecture embodies this development. An architecture, incidentally, which once again puts itself at the service of urban planning without losing face. In its turn, the latter increasingly accepts a landscape programme as a basis. Everyone involved, architects, urban planners, landscape designers and even ecologists recognise the cultural stratification of the object to be worked on: the Dutch Urban Landscape. The standard quality of the design is raised even further. Exceptional projects that stand out above this (high) average derive their power from programmatic experiments rather than the poetry of the subjects chosen. It is after all still the Netherlands.

General characteristics

This leads us to an image of 2030, in which a blend of naturalness and self-conscious pride is expressed in new projects, from window sill to local plan and from road sign to dam. The major projects do however easily adjust to the topographic map. There is a perceptible contextual approach on all scales.

The extent to which the Netherlands has changed is demonstrated by the different view of environmental problems which was previously thoughtlessly dismissed under the motto 'not in my back yard'. In 2030 the Netherlands is beyond shame. The ambivalent attitude with which many large projects used to be approached has been shaken off. No more half-hearted solutions for assignments whose social necessity is endorsed but whose design suffers from compromises with its opponents. In this way every design ultimately becomes the result of measures to combat negative effects. The social debate has gone beyond the level where everything humans do is bad and has to be hidden or toned down. The attitude to what already exists and to the making of new things has also changed. The past is approached in a more adult way. This is apparent from the position taken by the Department of Monuments, which not only fights for the conservation of the heritage but also indicates those parts of it that may be relegated to oblivion or where a ruinous scene is appropriate. At the same time landscape conservancy has grown out of its role as a 'second line of defence' in nature conservancy. Landscape conservancy demands a place of its own on the new map of the Netherlands.

To many people's surprise, the Netherlands turns out not to be an over-regulated and overdesigned country. On every scale there is a clear distinction between that which is formally laid down and that which is left free. At the highest level, alongside tightly directed infrastructural networks, space has also been reserved for indeterminacy: the so-called 'wilderness reserves'. It is the new wilderness without a programme that offers man and nature freedom and provides a counterweight to the hectic, diary-dominated existence. On the scale of the home, unambiguous building line regulations are formulated and enforced. At the same time the freedom is given to adapt and develop the 'backs' according to individual insight.

In the same way the introduction of the Overall Ecological Structure leads to innovations that can be seen as a cross between the Dutch and Danish models. The state government only provides general indications with regard to new functional land areas and essential linkages in the overall structure. The actual filling in is done from below upwards, whereby initiatives by citizens' groups and associations are financed but only marginally tested by the state and provincial authorities. It is precisely here that tinkering with the Netherlands shows up the patchwork of central and non-central initiatives, professional and dilettante initiatives and all environmental and architectural views.

Institutional design: ecological infrastructure.

Following a programme or generating one?

A cultural policy scenario such as 'Netherlands, kunstwerk again' does not in principle have a specific programme. Projects that were already on the programme are simply carried out with greater consideration and elegance. Yet it can be assumed that the changes of mentality described will ultimately make a difference to the map of the country.

One thing which will lead to this is the design research that will reach great heights in the 'Netherlands, kunstwerk again' scenario. Design is employed as the most advanced instrument of research into society's future. This resource can be refined by entering into dialogue with academics in all fields. It will be to the benefit of the depth and plausibility of the exploration. Because its possible and desirable developments are sought across a broad spectrum, this research may open up unexpected perspectives with consequences for the programme.

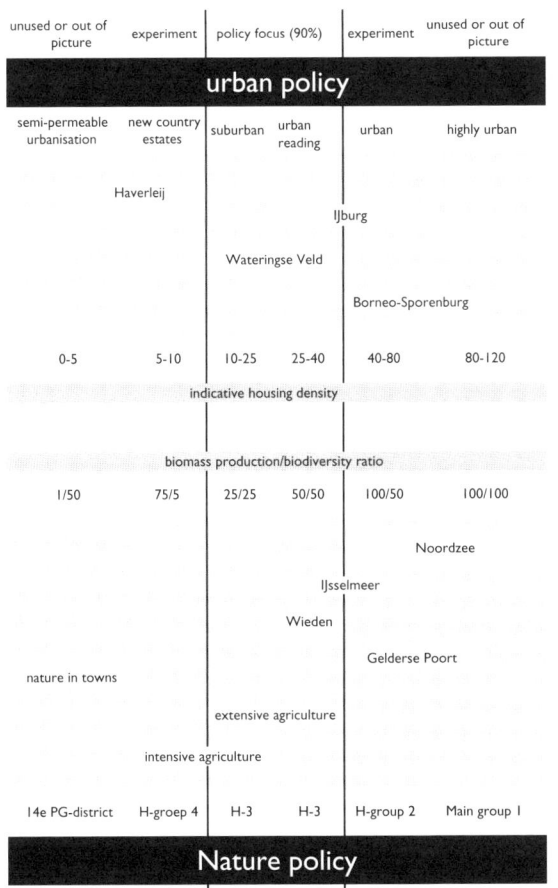

Space for experimentation in Nature Policy and Urban Policy.

Old forms of collective activity.

Institutional design: recreation.

New forms of collective activity.

In the second place the broadening and deepening of design culture, in combination with refined environmental regulation, will undoubtedly act as a great stimulus to seeking and finding elegant and innovative solutions for the problems that arise.

The design professions will enter new domains and gain or regain them as design tasks. In this way the scope of solutions for urban development and natural development will certainly expand into uncultivated or underexposed domains. This terra incognita is charted in the accompanying diagram. In addition to this, a lack of space will lead to an ever-increasing optimisation of land use. The regulations which curb wasteful use of space elicit exceptional combinations of functions and multi-functional solutions.

Working with and taking advantage of natural processes, as can be seen in landscape design and water management, turns out to yield equally elegant and challenging innovations. Natural engineering turns out to be land engineering (and civil engineering!) for advanced students.

The nature of shifts and innovations will give the map a new appearance and, more importantly, will to an extent turn out to be capable of generating their own programme. New solutions create new possibilities and these then create their own demand.

Examples

How will a scenario like this develop? What are its consequences for its everyday surroundings? A first category of examples shows that the increased attention paid to environmental design reveals all manner of new tasks for designers. The second category is more spectacular and involves the new programme generated by the broadening and deepening of the design culture. In this respect it is striking that in the consensus-seeking Netherlands these examples are brought in both from 'above', directed by a resolute and self-assured government, and from 'below', at the instigation of a group of citizens, organisations and companies. Virtually all examples are a mixture of the two.

From above, from outside

In 2002, by way of a compromise, an elegant quadruple decision was taken, after all, to combine the tempestuous growth of Schiphol with its location in the Randstad. The fifth runway will not be built. A second airport will be built on a new island in the North Sea off Katwijk, reducing the problem of noise to a minimum. The new terminal will be linked to Schiphol by a branch of the Schiphol Line. This will also make it possible to close the navy airfield at Valkenburg, enabling Leiden at long last to regain the Valkenhage district and make it unnecessary to build in the Groene Hart. Thirdly, it has been agreed to

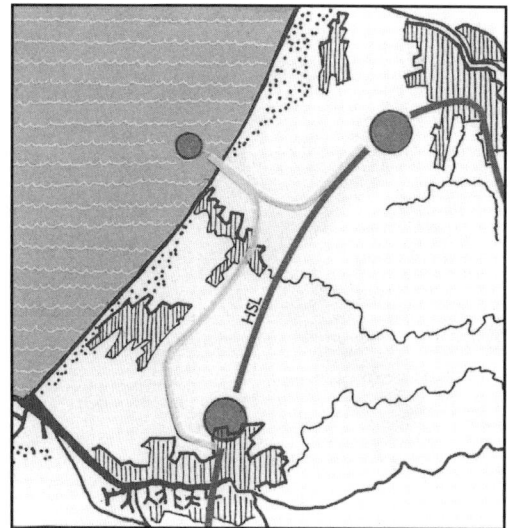
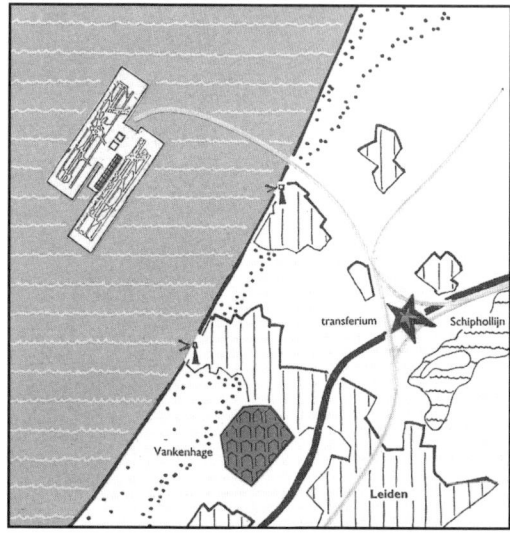
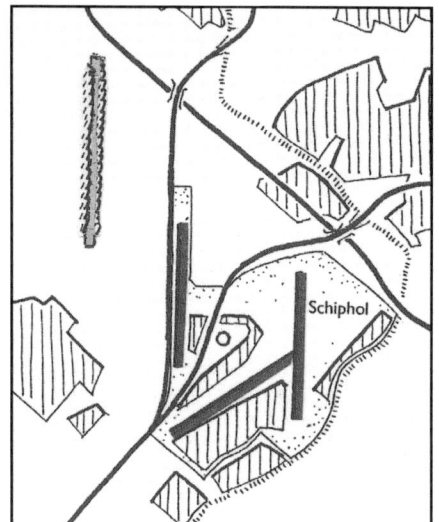

The airport system: Schiphol-Noordzee-Rotterdam, linked by sprinter and high-speed trains. Drawing.

The second national airport and the transfer point.

The relief of the Bosch Plan: the national competition rowing course.

close the Buitenveldert runway, which produced the most noise. When it has been lengthened, Zestienhoven will, because of the similar orientation of the runways in the new airport system, be able to function as a 'storm runway', thereby taking over the function of the 'Thunder Runway'. The Paris-Amsterdam high-speed train stops at both Zestienhoven and Schiphol and continues to guarantee rapid transfers. Lastly, a success for social consultation is the initiative by the Van Eesteren, Fluks and Van Lohuizen Foundation. At last there is the possibility of saving the most handsomely sized space in the Amsterdam Woods, Van Eesteren and Mulder's masterpiece, from the broadening and lengthening of the rowing course. A new, four-thousand metre long rowing course is to be gracefully located in the Haarlemmermeer, perfectly accessed by the southern tangent, on the land already compulsorily purchased for the fifth runway.

• The sea level is rising faster than expected. This provides the stimulus to switch to more dynamic coastal protection and an integrated approach to the whole North Sea coast. From the fore-delta to Noorderhaaks a pre-shore defence is to be built to break mounting waves. This will be done partly using

Reaction to the rise in sea-level 1: dynamic coastal defences.

islands (including New Schiphol) in the sedimentation areas. In the erosion areas supertankers will be sunk one on top of another, great interest having been shown in them in the Integrated Coastal Plan because it appears that twelve percent of the total biomass of the North Sea lives on shipwrecks. This forward defence also makes it possible, despite the rise in level, to move the actual sea-defence line back to the Young Dune Line in places. Wind-scattered dunes, new wet dune valleys and the local formation of tidal gullies are within reach.

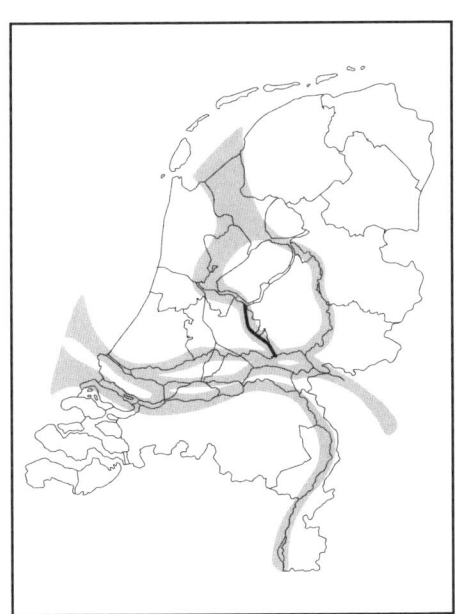

Reaction to the rise in sea-level 2: a new river outlet.

• The most radical intervention in reaction to the rise in sea-level casts its shadow in front of it. Land is being reserved for the construction of a new river drain[7] along two courses in the valley of the Gelder. Urban expansion and all forms of capital intensive function are being kept away. A green river comes into being, inspired by the old course of the Grift in the Gelder valley. Since it only involves the drainage of high water, the second course cuts into the western edge of the Veluwe massif. An extensive seepage area unique in Netherlands would thereby automatically come into being, within which ground water and river water would encounter each other in the best ecological conditions. The reserves attract the combination of forms of wild-country recreation and fugitive biotopes that are so characteristic of this sort of situation.

• Swedish research demonstrates the health risks of the electromagnetic radiation from high-tension cables. This leads to a substantial expansion of the right in rem zone round the 380 Kv cables and the gradual recabling of all routes with low voltages. Two organisations immediately see the extraordinary potential of the release of a continuous network of unbuilt bands in our densely populated country: the Long-Distance Walking Association and the World Wildlife Fund. Together they claim this land. The state government takes advantage of this by putting forward the hectares that were never completed for the connecting zones in the Overall Ecological Structure. The Industrial Archaeology Association is able to save several outstanding portals from demolition.

The new wilderness on old roads: deceleration.

• The government and the farmers, in close collaboration, succeed in organising new production landscapes for several modern production sectors (bulbs, greenhouses and intensive cattle-breeding). It appears that under the new, optimum production conditions on the scale of the landscape, ecological problems can be tackled which seemed insoluble at company level (in addition, they are of course a visual treat for the people living and working there).

• The old motorway network with its characteristic centre-to-centre connections forms the basis for a secondary network whose capacity is considerably increased, mainly by technical devices. The new European link: Paris-Brussels-Rotterdam-Utrecht-Zwolle-Groningen-Hamburg, with only five or six turn-offs (a turn-off for The Hague is still under discussion) is causing quite a stir. A typology for the road furniture (such as standard noise-screens) is being designed and adapted for the old and new networks. The bricking up of the motorway network in locations with a view is a thing of the past. The view will be restored. Where noise-screens are still necessary in

exceptional urban situations, experiments are carried out with combined functions. Techikahara's Walvis shopping centre alongside the A20 in Rotterdam and the tomato greenhouses on the A73 are good examples of this.
• The third generation of urban renewal (garden districts, the expansions of the seventies and eighties) provides a mixed picture of condensation (encouraged by the regulatory levies) which is used well by combining functions, and of thinning out, as a result of homes being merged.
• The local authorities have learnt from the unfounded panic of the nineties to accept immigration as a permanent phenomenon. More than this, in the Netherlands immigration is a condition for boosting its competitive position on the world market. Part of the migration takes the form of a 'bridgehead within the fort of Europe': a branch of the 'native country' that operates as an intermediary in trade. A sizeable Korean settlement has grown up in the Haarlemmermeer, for example. There is also a spectacular takeover of a large part of Maasvlakte III by the Singapore Port Authority. A Little Singapore has been built on the Maasvlakte. Because many of the investments were made using capital that fled Hong Kong, Rotterdammers are wont to call it 'Rotkong'.

From below, from inside outward

• Ruigoord is purchased by an association of residents and users and remains an island in the new Africa Dock. In this way this small part of the Netherlands has gone full cycle: island-(poldered)-island in a sea of sand-(redigging)-island. The encircling dyke has turned out dreadfully high, however.
• There will be new housing corporations offering suitably large houses for large families (the so-called 'seven-breadwinners') in the city, with business spaces, storage and garages. This new type also appears to be a success outside ethnic minority circles.
• The 'compact city' policy survives due to the creative use of the extension potential of newly built houses ('backs') whereby the 'storage problem' and establishment of businesses at home can also be solved in the urban context and the competition with suburbia becomes fairer. In the major cities a broadened architectural policy is a harsh necessity because there is a need for residential environments within their boundaries that can compete with exceptional locations (at the seaside, on lakes, etc.).
• After several exasperating slip-ups (Mendini!) The consumer electronics and household apparatus divisions of Philips are saved by the rediscovery of 'Dutch Design'. The international market reacts with enthusiasm to this new simple styling.

Institutional design: the Forestry Department's woods.

• Local farmers' corporations are set up that hold onto other segments of the consumer market by market differentiation. A range of regional specialities becomes increasingly successful. The optimisation of the conditions for this new cultivation in cooperative groups leads to the development of new agrarian landscapes.
• Monuments have undergone a liberating emancipation. They are at last allowed to be ordinary buildings. And the Department of Monuments is no longer the preserve of super-specialists. A number of volunteer groups are at work on exceptionally labour-intensive projects, such as the repair of the Amsterdam ramparts and the relaying of the former Zuiderzee dykes in basalt, which takes place entirely under private management.
• Ethnicity and philosophy of life are expressed primarily by countless new buildings: prayer, meditation and discussion centres, schools and collective dwellings, and also buildings for alternative forms of work. The mosques that appeared everywhere at the beginning of the twenty-first century, have partly lost their function and have been taken over by new immigrant groups. In the meantime, those who preserve monuments and the guardians of building style

Institutional design: postage stamps.

have reconciled themselves to the fact that these groups have other means of architectural expression at their disposal. The monument is no longer seen as an architectural idea frozen forever, but as a support to which new meanings can continually be attached. This religious stratification of architectural layers on and around church buildings yields interesting images.

- In Friesland the ecology movement takes the wind out of the provincial authorities' sails by developing a mega-location of wind turbines in collaboration with the Triodos Bank at a location it sees as favourable.
- Several companies themselves initiate innovative research that also leads to experiments being carried out. At the Arnhem-Nijmegen intersection, for example, we find the latest generation of logistical company warehouses (about three hectares of useful business land) built so that greenhouse cultivation companies can be established on the roof.
- In consultation with municipal engineering departments, the links between the motorway network and the urban networks are also tackled as a challenging public-private assignment. These in-fills in the road network turn out to be perfect location sites, but are also an area for experimentation on traffic systems and the design of public space.
- The smallest conceivable party on the market, the private home-builder, has become a significant factor. Three converging developments have led to a 'housing boom'. The accessible design software combined with the associated digital building catalogue established by the NDB and the Architecture Shops have made it much easier for the individual to design and build. The Dutch have always been fixated on owning their own house and in many people's case this expression of individualism and cocooning expands into building it too – one only has to look at the IKEA building stores that have opened everywhere. One of the factors determining this are the radically changed building regulations, which apart from their strict rules (which differ greatly from one local authority to another) also increase the freedoms and very much stimulate the aspiration to build.
- Parts of the 'Groene Sterren' [Green Stars – top green belt areas], which rising administrative expenses have made unaffordable, are released for housing construction and semi-public open areas, for which the most interested candidates are Dutch people of Turkish origin who have succeeded in business. They were in fact for decades the only group that gave any substance to the possibility of collectivity on these sites designed for now obsolete forms of open-air recreation.
- The street scene is also particularly striking. Restoring and keeping roadworthy old top-of-the-range models from the twenty-tens and even from the twentieth century has been elevated into a true folk art.

• Even so, once every two months even these showpieces have to stay in the garage. A monstrous alliance between the 'Joop den Uylstichting' and the ecology movement instituted and won a referendum on the reintroduction of car-free Sundays.

The role of government regulation & planning concepts

Society's call for elegant solutions will ultimately have repercussions on the instruments available for use in environmental planning. There is after all a strong direct relationship between types of regulation and types of habitation. The link is so close that one might even call it the spatial expression of a set of instruments. The new division of tasks between the government and the free market also necessitates a reform of the planning system. The government must once again concentrate on its inalienable tasks. This reform is seized upon to clear out counter-productive over-regulation on the one hand and a search for more effective means of regulating environmental processes on the other.

It appears that notions of regulation are themselves increasingly part of the culture of design. Gradually, by building up and cutting down, there forms a clear division of tasks between the various relevant levels of scale. The role of the European authorities is becoming ever clearer, while the 'good old' provinces, with such extended powers as a landscape plan, themselves occupy a strong position. The local authorities are developing an overall planning pattern – the structural view – in which the administration pronounces on the

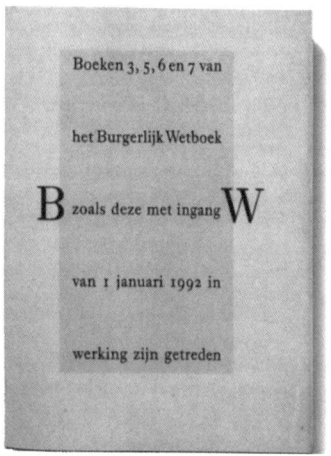
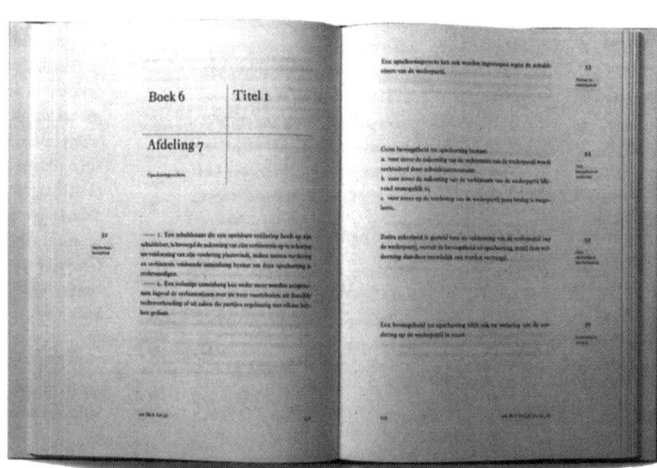

Institutional design: typography on official printed matter.

most important processes of spatial change throughout its territory. The structural plan, land-use plan and urban plan are grafted onto this.

All in all, one can say there is a sharply defined and meticulously observed subsidiarity. Spatial problems are addressed to the administrative level most involved with them, which is as close as possible to the citizen. The government relies on simple but rigid and enforcable rules that facilitate the national, regional and local infrastructural systems while also leaving space for a wide variety of bottom-up developments. This is not a question of a remote lack of engagement. The government and semi-governmental bodies like water boards are increasingly aware of their responsibility in commissioning work. The last remaining cores of institutional design play a major part in the professionalisation of the way government hands out commissions.

Citizens have a responsibility and are given space for the organisation of their own living environment. To urban planners and landscape designers this means there is a greater distinction between what one wants to see formally determined by plans and where natural and social processes should be left to take their own course.

The introduction of a system of regulatory levies intended to put a brake on the wasteful use of space as described in the last chapter is entirely in keeping with this. There are local authorities in whose planning permission system they have set an annual ceiling on granting land and changes of use and ballot projects on this basis. In these districts, in-fill plans are usually exempted from property and property transfer tax. Both measures have a highly stimulating effect on the inventiveness of certain sections of society and elicit much innovation.

Designers

The demands made of designers are constantly on the increase. The institutions evolve in accordance with this. The final requirements of designers' courses are no longer automatically equivalent to the initial requirements of the register of architects. Postgraduate courses with a substantial practical content are common for all design professions. And one of these is the ESNA, the Erna van Sambeekinstituut voor Neutrale Architectuur, where an attitude of service is considered of paramount importance. Life-long 'membership' of the register is also being abolished. A system of constant in-service training is taking shape, inspired by the medical world; the exchange of experiences and protocols regarding how one should act in certain situations (such as consultation between colleagues) ensures prolongation of registration.

Communication between the different scales and between the design professions is eased by the development by the Technical University of Delft of

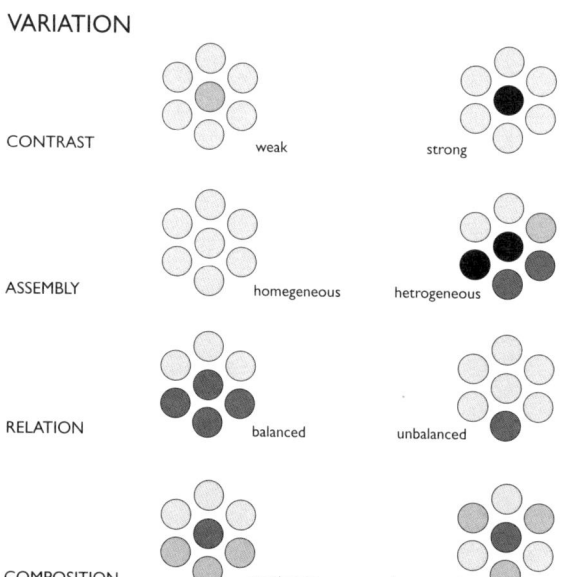

VARIATION

CONTRAST — weak, strong

ASSEMBLY — homegeneous, hetrogeneous

RELATION — balanced, unbalanced

COMPOSITION — continuous, fragmented

Notation of nature and measure of variation, Variation Agreements.

so-called variation agreements, in which the (desired or recorded) measure and nature of environmental variation on differing ranges of scale (R = 0.3; 3; 30; 300 and 3000 metres) are given.[8] Urban development and landscape structure plans use this new notation technique in combination with function zoning to advance desired developments without patronizing the architectural process. Too much or too little variation on the wrong scale is thereby regulated without lapsing into the nitpicking of 'visual quality plans'.

Tests by the building regulation inspectors are carried out partly on the basis of this system of notation and are otherwise steered by local authorities by means of the aforementioned instrument of structural inspection. In several districts building regulation inspection (or the lack of it!) is even employed as a deliberate means of design by way of such indications.[9]

The flywheel effect of the enthusiasm for working on a dynamic and collective kunstwerk will also have an infectious effect on the cultural torchbearers in other disciplines. The late twentieth-century puzzle of why the majority of this elite took an extremely conservative stand with regard to environmental changes, is now being forgotten. It is not only the market but also organised citizens that play an important part. In order to get new solutions off the ground, increasing use is being made of environmental laboratories and 1:1 prototypes of solutions that are still regarded with hesitation by the market. The financial risk is borne by several organisations very reminiscent of the 'Society for Public Welfare'. Many areas in the Netherlands have their Regional Plan Associations in which the ambitions of the inhabitants and the intentions of the various authorities are gathered together and, perhaps equally important, whereby sponsor funds from local business are tapped.[10] In this way 'Kunstwerk Netherlands' has become one big board game.

FROM NOW UNTIL LATER

Hypotheses

In this scenario we do not control whether the flame of the belief in progress will remain alight. If society is gripped by a dispiriting fin de siècle feeling, the hypothesis that the Netherlands may once more enjoy the pleasure of tinkering with and embellishing the land is of course wildly optimistic.

Another macro-trend that is equally hard to influence is how and in what depth social participation in decision-making processes and involvement in politics will develop. In this scenario we go so far as to assume a development towards a form of social participation in the design of changes to the environment, based on inquisitiveness and not suspicion. It is true that in the last chapter it was said that the rediscovery of the shapability of topography can also be used politically, but in fact the reality will be that – if one turns away from politics and administration – on the basis of this scenario, this cannot be sufficiently counterbalanced.

A third assumption is the successful integration of minorities into our society. As far as this is concerned, the 'moral panic' that is gradually arising in connection with the formation of ghettos, increasing ethnic tension and the creation of mafias among various ethnic groups provides the worst advice. In order to see a more diverse view these groups have to be involved in and develop an affinity with 'the Netherlands, a kunstwerk again'. In so doing we cannot become bogged down in noncommittal clichés such as 'multicultural society'. There has to be space for authentic additions from various ethnic minority groups. This sort of integration only has a chance of success if we preserve our own ethnic identity, or better, rediscover and develop it.

Driving forces: tail wind

A number of social trends and forces can be distinguished as being positive for this scenario or are catalytic in processes that should create the conditions for 'the Netherlands kunstwerk again'. In the first place, the nicest thing about this scenario is perhaps that a great many social problems do not present a hindrance but in fact act as fuel. In the coming 35 years there remains a set of extremely challenging problems to stimulate our ingenuity. Many can only be solved by means of a collective approach by society. They put restrictions on individualism.

Then there is the role played by history. Nietzsche's wise words, 'everything that will be, drags along with it everything that has been' apply perfectly to our megastructure. Water management problems have led to highly developed infrastructural planning. Since time immemorial environmental solutions have also played a crucial part in our way of managing conflicts. These traditions have – sometimes to excess – brought about confidence in environmental and infrastructural solutions. The Netherlands are so artificial and so hydrologically finely adjusted that social and natural changes will forever make adaptation and modification necessary. The Netherlands are a kunstwerk, whether we like it or not.

The source: the Dutch 'good living' interior.

In this scenario the computerisation of society is also a contributory process because it enables the exchange of ideas in society to be carried out in completely different ways and because it will influence the design process to a degree that cannot be overestimated:
• Developments in presentation, 3D and virtual reality techniques make it possible to rapidly reproduce conceivable realities. The ability to quickly generate alternatives makes another form of decision-making possible.
• Spectacular development can be expected in the family of software in which very long sequences of generation changes in living systems can be simulated 'in silico' instead of 'in vitro'.[11] This can be applied to complex anthropogenic systems that work with a limited set of rules so that alternative strategies of occupation and developing environmental configurations can be examined on their merits.

- In the course of 35 years the already impressive ramification of the Internet can of course expand unimaginably far, which will enable this new communication medium to be used for social debate too (It is already possible to participate in the design process on the Volkswagen Website!).
- Lastly, the new Dutch will be able to make a major enriching and far-reaching contribution to 'Netherlands kunstwerk again' by adding new elements and also by putting their new forms of collectivity into action against the generally accepted forms of individualisation.

Driving force: head wind

There are clear counter-forces that reduce the chances of a scenario in which 'the Netherlands, kunstwerk again' can blossom. The flame of the belief in progress is burning only very weakly. There is not a great deal of confidence in innovative solutions, but most of all there is very low tolerance of their changing effect on the environment. The cultural elite of the Netherlands plays a notably conservative part in this.

Considering the great stratification and tangle of used and discarded networks and the capital intensiveness of land use, it is also extraordinarily hard to devise new solutions and to give them a meaningful place in the environment. What exists is highly viscous in its complexity.

In addition, now the axe has been taken to the roots of the welfare state, environmental planning is seen more and more as the second bastion of our society of consultation and consensus. Energetic representatives of the increasingly international economy view it with suspicion and terms such as 'demobilising arrangement' are used. A random example: the rather tendentious comparison between the agreement on the Betuwelijn in the Netherlands and the tripling of Singapore's GNP, which both took the same amount of time.[12]

The strong tendency towards individualisation (the 'me generation', cocooning, less interest in everything with a hint of collectivity) may work very much against this scenario.

The starting mechanism

This scenario has a surprisingly simple starting mechanism whose three components can more or less be directed by policy. In the first place there is European federalism which in the Netherlands has produced a reaction[13] leading to a revaluation and a reassessment of miscellaneous elements of Dutch society which we consider important to preserve, recycle, reinterpret or develop.[14] One of the elements that is essential to our way of living together is the organisation of space. This is fostered and even deployed politically in this debate. In larger groups in society this leads to a rediscovery of the manipulability of our topography.

The second component that has a tremendous effect is simply the seriousness of a number of problems. We shall mention just two. Even when the wheat of environmental problems is sifted from the chaff, enough remains to show that is a major task to return our environmental order to harmony with the ground and demands that can be made of a sustainable society: mobility, CO2, biodiversity, water management and the rising sea level. A problem of the same order of magnitude (and not unrelated) is the social problem of overpopulation and underdevelopment abroad that will lead to an unceasing flow of immigrants. There are increasing numbers of ecological and economic refugees as well as political ones. Both examples have a powerful impact on our surroundings. On the one hand they have direct environmental effects, plus the fact that environmental resources are sought for the solution. Far-reaching, bold solutions will undoubtedly play a part in this. This too, even though it may be forced, leads to a focus on the shapability of our surroundings.

The spark is provided by the third component: the spreading of the 'architecture virus' to higher levels of scale. The wave of public interest in architecture that arose in the late seventies also affected other design areas in the succeeding decades. The ascending levels of scale gradually become involved in the architectural debate. The national level is ultimately also embraced as a dynamic and never-completed collective kunstwerk. The latter also brings with it a partial settling of the division between technocracy and sociocracy.

The coach driver's magic wand unites 5000 museums, 3000 fantasy castles and 61,000 ice cream machines into 'the Netherlands, the biggest amusement park in Europe'.

All three of the factors sketched here point in the same direction: a recognition of the shapability of the topography. The conversion of this broadly accepted insight into a situation in which the deliberate, conscientious and artistic manipulation of space is the rule rather than the exception is a task for a well-directed cultural policy. This policy will have to reconcile at least three differences:

Starting mechanism for 'the Netherlands as kunstwerk'!

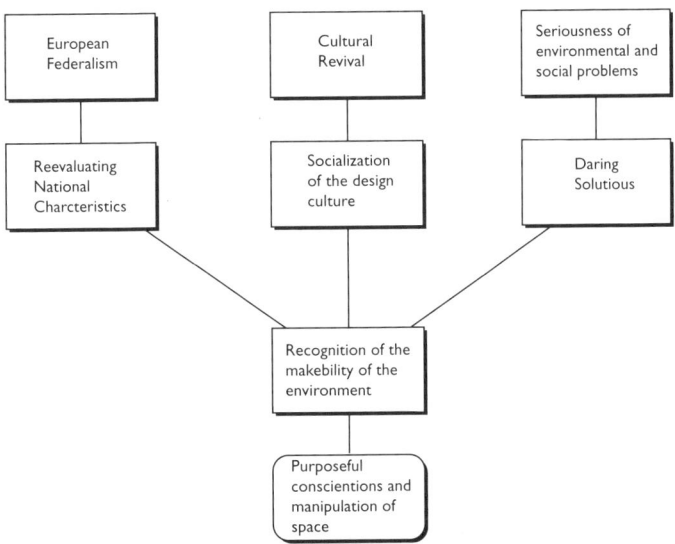

- the difference between the protection of towns, villages and landscapes based on the glorification of history, and the undifferentiated, undirected urge for creation and renewal;
- the difference between the paralysing ecological criteria of chemists, toxicologists, environmental psychologists and eco-hydrologists, and the inner feelings of designers, which hardly come up for discussion;
- the difference between human-inclusive and human-exclusive approaches to nature.

T E S T

Probability and robustness

Only thirty years separate us from the optimistic sixties and in these three decades many of the processes relevant to this scenario have taken place. In this light, when looking forward to the year 2030 it is not impossible that major changes in the population's attitudes may occur. For example, the run-up to an architectural policy already started in 1979, but only bore fruit in 1996. Considering the present increased interest in this sector it is probably not unrealistic to express the ambition of taking cultural self-awareness and the discussion on environmental processes to a higher level and make it clear to far more people that designing at this level is a matter for society as a whole.

Economic development is not a deciding factor in this sort of reorientation. The renewed rise of cultural self-awareness depends rather on a moral reorientation and a broader development in society. If there is further growth in the GNP the environmental expression of the approach taken in this scenario will be able to assume greater luxury and in the case of spreading wealth the adage 'environmental planning is free' can be abandoned.

This scenario draws heavily on the forces of integration in our organisation of administration and government departments, while everything shows that the conglomeration of sector-bound ministers, parliamentary party specialists, special interest organisations and specialist officials has actually dug itself into the almost impregnable fortifications of 'sector interest'.

Other effects

In the description of the scenario, the examples, and in sketching several series of causal links, various mostly environmental effects this development would bring about have been touched upon along the way. Nevertheless, in the case of several other categories it is useful to give a short outline of the effects. These are mainly on employment and the ecology.

With regard to the development of employment we shall limit ourselves to that which is scenario-specific. The nature of this scenario means a general prognosis can scarcely be made. One can expect effects in the building industry, the design service sector and small-scale manufacturing. In the building sector employment will probably not increase in an absolute sense. There will be a relevant shift within the sector however. It is to be expected that the standard of professional practice will rise sharply. There will be a demand for the craftsmanlike diligence that makes a connection between detailing and materialisation on the one hand and the technique of execution on the other. It is probable that in the craftsmanship of the present restorers there lies a core round which will crystallise an improvement in quality. In the service sector we can expect a shift from environmental advice to design. A contribution to this is made by the balance, forced by regulation, between the number of design hours put into the project and the number of hours spent on determining the effects, by means of ecological effect reporting (at present, this ratio is sometimes 1:15). In addition, it is not inconceivable that 'Dutch Design' is an important export product, and also brings about export-oriented employment in small and large industrial companies. It is also very probable that, emerging from cooperation on individual solutions, exceptional mergers between branches of industry which we currently consider separate will be able to count on eager demand from the world market. One might think of the tremendous potential which a fundamental linkage between civil engineering companies, natural development consultants and the dredging sector could have.

The fifth facade as an outlet: the last remaining back-side.

When it comes to ecological effects this scenario will in the long term score well because of its positive recognition of sustainability issues as a part of the puzzle. This will enable the now somewhat isolated and always worrisome ecological aspect to be better integrated into the course of the project. Since considerable involvement from below will be generated in this scenario, in the case of ecological solutions it may be that there are many installations too small and deployed on too low a level of scale. Slurry fermentation at the village level, wind energy at domestic level and CHP coupling at neighbourhood level. This move is a token of local involvement, thereby occasionally has a more metaphorical value and will consequently have a slightly lower ecological performance than installations where the law of the economy of scale is perfectly complied with.

Epilogue: the secret of the Netherlands

While reflecting on a picture of the future like this, you start to wonder whether there might be something more to say at a higher, more abstract, level about the essence of our methods of environmental planning. Is there a thread running through the history of the deliberate handling of the environment that can be used in the future too? There are several twin phenomena and dualities which together may form a sort of prescription for the environmental order of our delta, and which may lift a corner of the veil in which the Netherlands' secret is covered. It is the right petroil lubrication between central direction and local initiative, which encounter each other in the search for consensus in the midfield; the handling of main principles and their substantiation; with strictly regulated fronts and free, flexible backs; the way nonconformism and individualism are always embedded in recognisable institutions and uniformity; the open relations with foreign countries and the constant influence of foreign ideas and foreigners (was the Netherlands actually created by the Dutch?); all culminating in the eternal conflict between the belief in the shapability of society and accepting that attempts to do so will never fully succeed.

Dirk Sijmons
This essay is an adaptation of a study report commissioned by the State Planning Department (Ministry of Housing, Physical Planning and Environment). It was published under the title 'Nederland als Kunstwerk' as discussion-scenario no. 6 for 'Nederland 2030'. RPD, September 1996.

1. After a series of proposals as brilliant as they were impracticable, the artistic contribution ultimately consisted of a metal flag that moved mechanically and which, by means of an ingenious construction, always flew against the direction of the wind, so that the Dutch tricolour flapped contrarily in the sea of 250,000 flags at the world exhibition.

2. Characterisation by the American Joseph Buch in 'Een eeuw Nederlands architectuur' (1993) in which he called the west Netherlands 'the world's first, biggest and most successful megastructure'.

3. These distinguishing features of national identity were listed by Anthony Smith in 'National Identity', Penguin, London, 1991, and quoted from Paul Scheffer's 'Land zonder spiegel; over de politieke cultuur in Nederland' in 'Het nut van Nederland', Uitgeverij Bert Bakker, Amsterdam, 1996.

4. As Benno Premsela said, 'If I criticise the culture of design, it is often because most people take design for granted. It does not make anyone put their own ideas aside. It is precisely resistance to culture that is important to culture itself. Art does summon up this resistance, and always makes you revise your judgements. It breaks down all forms of standardisation'. (Interview in the 1993-95 Yearbook of Dutch Landscape Architecture and Urban Development, Uitgeverij THOTH, Bussum, 1996.

5. Horgan, John: The End of Science, Facing the Limits of Knowledge in the Twilight of the Scientific Age', Addison-Wesley, New York, 1996.
6. H. Michel.

7. If sea-level were to rise by about 1 metre, in the case of a planned high-water drainage of the rivers (16,000 m3 per second) there would be a problem with the drainage of about 4000 m3 per second as a result of the loss of drop. No storage for this amount can be provided in the system and a new outlet would have to be made. D. de Bruin, RWS.

8. The basis of this was laid down in: Taeke De Jong, 'De Baarsjes' visual quality plan (1993), Stadsdeel de Baarsjes, Amsterdam/TU Delft.

9. Rients Dijkstra, Masterplan Leidsche Rijn, Archis 6, 1996.

10. Nothing new, I know. New York had a Regional Plan Association as early as the thirties.

11. Steven Levy, 'Artificial Life; the Quest for a New Creation', Penguin Science, London, 1992.

12. Geelhoed at the congress entitled 'De Zuidvleugel van de Randstad, voldongen feit of fictie', Bleiswijk, 1994.

13. The main aim of this counter-movement is to stop the straightforward handover of national powers to a European government that is still insufficiently rooted and has still not acquired sufficient democratic powers and legitimacy. It will probably not stop European unification but probably will give it a completely different content.

14. Paul Scheffer, 'Land zonder spiegel', from Koen Koch & Paul Scheffer, 'Het nut van Nederland; opstellen over soevereiniteit en identiteit', Uitgeverij Bert Bakker, Amsterdam, 1996.

LITERATURE

Anonymus (1995):
> *De Bronzen Bever; Rijksprijs voor Bouwen en Wonen 1995.* Den Haag: Ministerie van VROM.

Baerselman, F.; F.W.M. Vera (1989):
> *Natuurontwikkeling. Een verkennende studie.* Den Haag: Ministerie van Landbouw en Visserij. [Achtergrondreeks Natuurbeleidsplan; nr. 6]

Bams, C.J.; L. Harkink & J.S.L.J. van Alphen (red) (1997): *Noordzee-atlas voor het Nederlands beleid en beheer.* Amsterdam: Stadsuitgeverij Amsterdam.

Becker, S. (1994):
> *Selbstorganisation Urbaner Structuren.* [Arch+; nr. 121]

Bijhouwer, J.T.P.; J. Vallen & J.W. Zaaijer (1961):
> *Hollands Groene Zone; meer ruimte voor de openluchtrecreatie van een miljoenenbevolking- nadere uitwerking van het ANWB denkbeeld 1960.* Koninklijke Nederlandsche Toeristenbond ANWB.

Bijhouwer, J.T.P. (1942):
> *Nederlandsche tuinen en buitenplaatsen.* Amsterdam: Allert de Lange

Boekholt, P.; D. Jacobs & W. Zegveld (1990):
> *De economische kracht van Nederland; een toepassing van Porters benadering van de concurrentiekracht van landen.* 's-Gravenhage: Stichting Maatschappij en Onderneming.

Boelens, L. (1990):
> *Stedebouw en Planologie; Een onvoltooid project.* Delft: Delftse Universitaire Pers.

Boo, M. de; R. Coops (1988):
> *Voeten in de Aarde.* Zutphen: Terra.

Bouman, O. (1994):
> *Holland op zijn breedst.* [Archis; nr. 4]

Bouwens, B. e.a. (1997):
> *Lijnen door het Brabantse land; 200 jaar verkeersinfrastructuur in Noord-Brabant 1796-1996.* Zwolle: Waanders Uitgevers.

Brand, J.; H. Brand (red) (1986):
> *De Hollandse Waterlinie.* Utrecht: Veen.

Brian, C.K. (1981):
> *The Hunters or the Hunted? An Introduction to African Cave Taphonomy.* Chicago/London: The University of Chicago Press.

Broekhuizen, R. van; L. Klep; H. Oostindie & J.D. van der Ploeg (1997):
> *Atlas van het vernieuwend platteland.* Doetinchem: Misset uitgeverij bv.

Broess, H.; S. Grijzen (red) (1997):
Brabants Manifest. 's-Hertogenbosch: Projectbureau Brabant 2050.

Bruin, D. de; D. Hamhuis; W.M.M. Overmars; L. van Nieuwenhuijze; D.F. Sijmons & F.W.M. Vera (1986):
Ooievaar, de toekomst van het rivierengebied. Arnhem, Gelderse Milieufederatie.

Corner, J.; Photographs: A.S. MacLean (1996):
Taking Measures Across the American Landscape. New Haven / Londen: Yale University Press.

Commissie Boschplan Amsterdam (1931):
Rapport van de commissie voor het Boschplan Amsterdam. Amsterdam: Gemeente Amsterdam.

Dennett, D. C. (1995):
Darwins gevaarlijke idee. Amsterdam: Uitgeverij Bert Bakker.

Devolder, Anne-Mie (2000):
AIR-SOUTHBOUND. De Hoeksche Waard, New Landscape Frontiers. Thoth Publishers

Dijkstra, R. (1996):
Masterplan Leidsche Rijn. [Archis; nr.6]

Dooren, N. van; G. van de Ven (1997):
De nieuwe rivierdijken. Dijkversterking als ontwerpopgave. Rotterdam: NAi Uitgevers.

Eerenbeemt, H.F.J.M. van den (red) (1997):
Geschiedenis van Noord-Brabant. Deel 3 1945-1996 Dynamiek en Expansie. Amsterdam/Meppel: Boom.

Ekkelboom, J. (1997):
Platohout: gekookt en gebakken zachthout, procédé verhoogt duurzaamheid. [Het Houtblad; nr. 9]

Ekkers, P.; H. Mastop; A. Dekker & J. Raggers (1990):
Regionaal ontwerp en beleid; plananalyse stad en land op de helling. 's-Gravenhage: Eo Wijers Stichting.

Elerie, J.N.H.; P.P.P. Huigen (red) (1997):
Stadslandschap in ontwerp; Visies op Assen in een nieuw stadsgewest. Groningen: REGIO PRoject.

Feddes, F. (1995):
When do we switch to plan B. [Architectuur Lokaal; nr. 4]

Feddes, Y.C.; F. L. Halenbeek (1988):
Een scherpe grens, ontwerpstudie naar de ruimtelijke kwaliteit van verzwaarde rivierdijken. Utrecht: SBB, afd. Landschapsarchitectuur.

Gleason, D.K (1990):
Over Miami. Louisiana State University Press.

Goewie, E.A. (1993):
Ecologische landbouw: een duurzaam perspectief? Wageningen: Landbouwuniversiteit.

Harms, W.B.; P.J.A.M. Smeets (1988):
Dissipatieve structuren: theorie en implicatie voor de landschapsecologie. Arnhem: WLO-Landschap

Harsema, H.; S. Cusveller; E. Luiten e.a. (1996):
Landschapsarchitectuur en stedebouw in Nederland 93-95. Bussum: Uitgeverij Thoth.

Helmer, W.; W. Overmars; G. Litjens (1990):
Rivierenpark Gelderse Poort. Laag Keppel: Stroming, bureau voor natuur- en landschapsontwikkeling b.v.

Hooftman, E. (1991):
Who is afraid of the new Landscape? [Landscape Design]

Hoog, H. de (1990):
Verstedelijking in landschappen. [De Architect; nr. 4]

Horgan, J. (1997)
Het einde van de wetenschap. Over de grenzen van onze kennis. Amsterdam, Ambo.

IWACO BV vestiging Noord (1995):
Natuurdoeltypen Midden-Groningen. Groningen: Ministerie van LNV, directie noord, NBLF.

Jong, T. de (1993):
Beeldkwaliteitsplan 'de Baarsjes'. Amsterdam / Delft: Stadsdeel de Baarsjes / Technische Universiteit.

Joosten, H. en R. During (1992):
Referentiebeelden en duurzaamheid. [WLO-Landschap; nr. 4]

Kleefmann, F. (1984):
Planning als zoekinstrument; ruimtelijke planning als instrument bij het richtingzoeken. 's-Gravenhage: VUGA-Uitgeverij. [Planologische verkenningen; nr. 5]

Kloos, M. (ed) (1996):
Amsterdam in detail. Amsterdam: Arcam & Architectura & Natura Press. [ARCAM pocket series; nr. 10]

Koch, K.; P. Scheffer (red) (1996):
Het nut van Nederland; opstellen over soevereiniteit en identiteit. Amsterdam: Bert Bakker.

Koningsveld, H. (1987):
Planning en (on)zekerheid. Lelystad In: Verslag van het symposium Polderlandschap als cultuuruiting. Flevoberichten no 293 Rijksdienst voor de IJsselmeerpolders.

Kuhnert, N.; P. Oswalt (1991):
Das abenteuer der Modernität. [Arch+; nr. 106]

Levy, S. (1992):
Artificial Life; the Quest for a New Creation. Londen: Penguin Science.

Lippard, L. R. (1966):
Pop Art: Fleng! Wham! een boos kunstkindje slaat terug. Den Haag: Uitgeverij W. Gaade.

Luiten, E. (1988):
Het analoge landschap. Cultuurverleden en cultuurverschiet als ontwerpuitdaging. [Contour; nr. 3-4]

Meeus, J.; J. Bosch (1992):
Genius Regionis and other metaphors. Den Haag: Stichting Conferentie Artivisual Landscapes.

Meijer, H. (1908):
Ons Eigen Land (vier delen). Arnhem: De Algemeene Nederlandsche Wielrijders Bond.

Ministerie van Cultuur, Recreatie en Maatschappelijk werk (1977):
Structuurvisie Natuur- en Landschapsbehoud. 's Gravenhage.

Ministerie van Landbouw, Natuurbeheer en Visserij (1991):
Visie Landschap. 's-Gravenhage: SDU Uitgeverij.

Mulder, W; D. Schuiling (1994):
De vijfde gevel; de aantasting van het stedelijk daklandschap. Amsterdam: Amsterdamse raad voor de monumentenzorg.

Neutelings, W.J. (1990):
Willem-Jan Neutelings, architect. Rotterdam: 010-uitgevers

Nieuwenhuijze L. van; N. Hazendonk N. (1991):
Toekomstverkenning Veenweidegebieden. Utrecht: H+N+S / Directie Bos- en Landschapsbouw.
[Bouwen aan een levend landschap, Directie Bos- en Landschapsbouw; nr. 23]

Nieuwenhuijze L. van (2000):
Waterrijk Deltametropool, Stichting Deltametropool, Delft

d' Oliviera, M. (1990):
Alles op zijn plaats; Het moderne interieur in de fotografie 1935-1965. Haarlem: Stichting voor fotografie projekten en Kunst. / Joh. Enschede & Zn.

Philips, R. (1983):
Puur natuur op tafel. Utrecht/Antwerpen: Uitgeverij Het Spectrum.

Prigogine I.; I. Stengers (1988):
Orde uit chaos; 'de nieuwe dialoog tussen de mens en de natuur'. Amsterdam: Bert Bakker.

Projecteam Zonering (D.F. Sijmons (red)) (1990):
Multiplex; 'een bouwsteen voor zonering van de landelijke ruimte'. Den Haag: Rijksplanologische Dienst.

Provincie Noord Brabant (1947):
Prae-adviezen inzake een Welvaartsplan voor de Provincie Noord-Brabant. 's-Hertogenbosch: Provincie Noord Brabant.

Projectgroep bruisend water (1997):
Bruisend water, verslag fase 1 'Analyse van de toekomst'. Den Haag: Provincie Zuid-Holland.

Projectgroep Waterhuishouding Leidsche Rijn (1997):
Nieuwe stad, schoon water. Het watersysteem van Leidsche Rijn. Hoofdrapport. Utrecht: Projectbureau Leidsche Rijn.

Reijnders, L.; R. Beckers; L. Jansen; H. Tieleman (1994):
De Groene Doorbraak. Amsterdam: Wetenschappelijk Bureau Groen Links.

Rijksplanologische Dienst (1996):
Nederland 2030. Tussenbalans; Verkenning Ruimtelijke Perspectieven. Den Haag: Ministerie van VROM.

Rijkswaterstaat (1994):
Waterstaatkaart van Nederland, schaal 1: 50.000, vijfde editie, Utrecht west blad 31. Delft: Rijkswaterstaat.

Severy, M. (red) (1976):
Grote godsdiensten. National Geographic Society en De Haan.

Sijmons, D.F. (1990):
Regional Planning as a Strategy. [Landscape and Urban Planning; nr 18].

Sijmons, D.F. (1992):
Het casco-concept; Een benaderingswijze voor de landschapsplanning. Utrecht: H+N+S. [Bouwen aan een levend landschap, Informatie- en kennis-centrum/NBLF; nr. 24]

Sijmons, D.F. (1993):
Nieuwe avonturen tegemoet. [WLO-Landschap (10) 1993; nr. 2].

Sijmons, D.F.; N. van Dooren, (1995):
Groene Hart? Groene Metropool!. Den Haag: NIROV. [Stedebouw & Volkshuisvesting; nr 9/10]

Sijmons, D.F. (1995):
Randverschijnselen in het land van Cuijk. [Architectuur Lokaal, platform voor Lokaal Architectuurbeleid nr. 10, dec-95).

Sijmons, D. F. (1997):
In IJburg valt voor mens en natuur veel te beleven. [NRC Handelsblad]

Sijmons, D.F. (1997):
Geen brilduiker zal zich door IJburgplannen laten verjagen. [Trouw]

Sijmons, D. F. (1997):
Rotterdam Vakantieland. Uit: Arnold Reijndorp, Vincent Kompier en Luit de Haas (red); *Leefstijlen; wonen in de 21e eeuw.* Rotterdam: NAi Uitgevers.

Sijmons, D.F.; Y. Feddes & L.Tummers (1996):
Wonen in de natuur. [Noorderbreedte; nr. 6a Stadslandschap]

Sijtsma, F.J.; D. Strijker; G.J. Rotmensen & A. van den Berg (1996):
Effect-analyse Ecologische Hoofdstructuur 1995. Samenvatting. Groningen: Stichting Ruimtelijke Economie.

Smeets, P. (1996):
Koeien en Koersen. Wageningen: LEI-DLO / SC-DLO.

Steenbergen, C.M. (1990):
De landschapsarchitectuur van de Hollandse metropool. Utrecht: Stichting LOCUS. [Catalogus van het tweede LOCUS seminar]

Sweeting, A. W. (1996):
Reading houses and building books; Andrew Jackson Downing and the architecture of popular antebellum literate, 1835-1855. Hanover: University Press of New England.

Tzonis A.; L. Lefaivre (1981):
Het raster en het pad. [Wonen TA / BK]

Tzonis A.; L. Lefaivre (1983):
De terugkeer van het regionalisme. [Bouw 9; nr. 5]

Tzonis A.; L. Lefaivre (1983):
Het naoorlogse regionalisme en de toekomst van kritisch regionalisme. [Bouw 13; nr. 6]

Vroom, M.J. (1992):
Buitenruimten. Bussum: Uitgevrij Thoth

Vroom, M.J. (red) (1993):
Locus Seminar; Vormgeven aan natuurontwikkeling. Rotterdam: Stichting Locus.

Werkgroep klimaatverandering en bodemdaling (1997):
Klimaatverandering en bodemdaling: gevolgen voor de waterhuishouding van Nederland. Den Haag: Projectteam vierde Nota waterhuishouding.

West 8 (1989):
De periferie als centrum. Utrecht: Ministerie van LNV, IKC-NBLF. [Studiereeks Bouwen aan een levend Landschap; nr. 16]

Wetenschappelijke Raad voor het Regeringsbeleid (1992):
Grond voor keuzen; vier perspectieven voor de landelijke gebieden in de Europese Gemeenschap. 's-Gravenhage: Sdu uitgeverij. [Rapporten aan de Regering; nr. 42]

Wit, C.T. de (1987):
Landbouw en milieu in de Europese Gemeenschap; goed en slecht bedeelde regio's. [Spil]

Wit, C.T. de (1985):
Scheiding of verweving van functies. [Bedrijfsontwikkeling; nr. 3]

Woud, A. van der (1987):
De geschiedenis van de toekomst. Den Haag: SDU. [Catalogus van de tentoonstelling 'Nederland Nu Als Ontwerp' deel 1]

Zeeuw, D. de & W.G. Albrecht (1990):
Duurzaam samengaan van landbouw, natuur en milieu. Amsterdam: Werkgroep 'Duurzaam samengaan van Landbouw, Natuur en Milieu'.

ILLUSTRATION ACKNOWLEDGMENTS

COVER

Part of the collection of landscape slides made on commission to the Academie van Bouwkunst Amsterdam (1973)

INSIDE COVER

H+N+S (1995): *Fun on the Waal. A study of the possibilities of recreational joint use on the Waal.* Commissioned by RWS, Dir. Oost Nederland Inset: photo by H+N+S

Landscape planning from A to Z

PAGE 8

www.huistenbosch.co.jp

The programme guide

PAGE 14

High-speed train above locks, photo H+N+S. Part of a landscape clock made by Frans Halenbeek (1990)

PAGE 19

Bruin, D. de; D. Hamhuis; W.M.M. Overmars; L. van Nieuwenhuijze; D.F. Sijmons & F. Vera (1986): *Plan of the Ooievaar* Entry for the 1st Eo Wijers competition for Nederland Rivierenland

PAGE 20

Map from '*Zelfportret van het kunstwerk, een kartografisch betoog*'. H+N+S / Heidemij Advies (1996): commissioned by the State Planning Department

An Amsterdam delicacy

PAGES 23, 24, 25, 26

Photo: H+N+S

PAGE 24

Gemeentearchief Amsterdam.

PAGE 26

H+N+S (1992): *Model plan for the Vechtplassen area. An alliance between drinking water extraction, nature and recreation.* Hilversum: Zuiveringschap Amstel- en Gooiland.

PAGE 27

(1997): *What comes out of the tap is good, but for how long?* (Consumer Guide)

The return of the Water Management Map

PAGE 31

Rijkswaterstaat (1994): *Water management map of the Netherlands, scale 1:50.000, fifth edition, Utrecht west, sheet 31.* Delft: Rijkswaterstaat

PAGE 32

Nieuwenhuijze L. van and Hazendonk N. (1991): *Exploration of the future of the Veenweide* [peat meadow] *areas.* Utrecht: H+N+S / Directie Bos- en Landschapsbouw. (Bouwen aan een levend landschap, Directie Bos- en Landschapsbouw; no. 23)

PAGE 36

H+N+S

PAGE 37

Ministry of Housing, Regional Development and the Environment (1995): *The Bronze Beaver; State Prize for Building and Homes, 1995.* The Hague: Ministry of Housing, Regional Development and the Environment

PAGE 38

Leidsche Rhine Water Management Project Group (1997): *'Nieuwe stad, schoon water. Het watersysteem van Leidsche Rhine'.* Main report. Utrecht: Leidsche Rhine Project Agency

PAGE 40

H+N+S / IWACO (1996): *The Colour of Water. Vision of the future of the 'Green-Blue Streamer'.* The Hague: Province of South Holland

PAGE 41

H+N+S: Waterrijk Deltametropool. Een toekomstverkenning van de waterhuishouding in de Deltametropool (2000)

The Skill and the Art of Engineering

PAGE 45

Feddes, Y.C.; Halenbeek F.L. (1988): *A distinct boundary, design study into the environmental qualities of strengthened river dykes,* Utrecht: SBB Landscape Design Dept

PAGE 46

photo: H+N+S

PAGE 47

DHV Milieu & Infrastructuur / H+N+S (1995): *Improvements to the main Waal dyke between Afferden and Dreumel. Initial note.* Amersfoort / Utrecht

PAGE 48

H+N+S (1996): *Windpolder.* Utrecht

PAGE 49

H+N+S (1996): *Windpolder.* Utrecht

PAGE 50

H+N+S (1996): *Windpolder.* Utrecht

PAGE 51

H+N+S (1995): *Over scherven van geluk; een rapport over de versnippering van de natuur in Nederland.* Utrecht

PAGE 53

Resource Analysis / H+N+S / Oranjewoud (1997): *Ontwikkelingsplan Wijkermeerpolder e.o.,* Werkgroep Wijkermeerpolder

PAGE 54

H+N+S (1996): *Breda; Zaartpark, Molenleij, Turfvaart. 3 Projecten aan de zuidelijke rondweg van Breda.* Utrecht

Worked out and done with?

PAGE 56

Boekholt, P.; D. Jacobs & W. Zegveld (1990): *De economische kracht van Nederland; een toepassing van Porters benadering van de concurrentiekracht van landen.* 's-Gravenhage: Stichting Maatschappij en Onderneming

PAGE 57

Citroën Nederland BV (1994): *à la Ferme* (post card)

PAGE 59

H+N+S

PAGE 61

Rijkswaterstaat, Meetkundige Dienst: *Water Management Map of the Netherlands,* scale: 1:50.000. Delft: Rijkswaterstaat

PAGE 67

H+N+S (1991): *Waterland, planning in onzekerheid.* Unpublished, part of a series of discussions about the role of design in preparing policy, commissioned by the Province of North-Holland

PAGE 68

Smeets, P. (et al.) (1996): *Koeien en Koersen.* Wageningen: LEI-DLO & SC-DLO

PAGE 70

H+N+S

PAGE 71

Corner, J.; Photographs: A. S. Maclean (1996): *Taking Measures Across the American Landscape.* New Haven/London: Yale University Press

PAGE 71

Boo, M. de; R. Coops, (1988): *Voeten in de aarde.* Zutphen: Terra

PAGE 72

Province of North-Holland

PAGE 72

H+N+S (1991): *Zijpe, een nieuw productielandschap.* Unpublished, part of a series of discussions about the role of design in preparing policy, commissioned by the Province of North-Holland

PAGE 73

H+N+S (1992): *Duurzame tuinbouw in Over-Betuwe. Voorbeeldplan vierde nota ruimtelijke ordening.* Arnhem: Landbouwschap (Gewestelijke Raad voor Gelderland)

PAGE 73

H+N+S (1992): *Duurzame tuinbouw in Over-Betuwe; Voorbeeldplan vierde nota ruimtelijke ordening.* Arnhem: Landbouwschap (Gewestelijke Raad voor Gelderland)

PAGE 75

photo: Kyowa Hakko Kogyo Co, Ltd (1980) *Scientific American*

PAGE 75

MIT(1981): *Scientific American*

PAGE 76

Philips, R. (1983): *Puur natuur op tafel* Utrecht/Antwerp: Uitgeverij Het Spectrum

PAGE 77

Poule den Dungen chicken label

PAGE 78

H+N+S (1997): *Het zwerfnetwerk; recreatie- en mobiliteitsplan WCL De Graafschap,* Province of Gelderland

PAGE 79

H+N+S

PAGE 80

Ekkelboom, J. (1997): *Platohout: gekookt en gebakken zachthout, procedé verhoogt de duurzaamheid.* (Het Houtblad: no. 9)

PAGE 81

photo: H+N+S

PAGE 82

After: Bams, C.J.; L. Harkink & J.S.L.J. van Alphen (eds.) (1997): *Noordzee-atlas voor het Nederlands beleid en beheer.* Amsterdam: Stadsuitgeverij Amsterdam

PAGE 84

photo: H+N+S

New adventures in prospect

PAGE 89

Brand, J. ; H. Brand (ed.) (1986): *De Hollandse Waterlinie.* Utrecht: Veen

PAGE 90

DHV Water / H+N+S (1991): *Raamplan Beerze-Reusel; een gebiedsgerichte benadering.* Eindrapport. Utrecht: Province of North-Brabant

PAGE 91

IWACO BV vestiging Noord (1995): *Natuurdoeltypen Midden-Groningen.* Groningen: Ministerie van LNV, directie noord, NBLF

PAGE 92

Brian, C.K. (1981): *The Hunters or the Hunted? An Introduction to African Cave Taphonomy.* Chicago/ London: The University of Chicago Press

PAGE 94

photo: Kevin Lamarque / Persbureau Reuters

PAGE 95

Prigogine I.; I. Stengers (1988): *Orde uit chaos; 'de nieuwe dialoog tussen de mens en de natuur'.* Amsterdam: Bert Bakker

PAGE 96

Kaaij, Th. van de; F.J. Los (1995) Advies Waterkwaliteit drie ontwerpplannen "IJburg". Delft, Delft Hyraulics Lab.

PAGE 97

H+N+S / Stichting voor Toegepaste Landschapsecologie / Buro van den Boogert (1991): *Ontgrondingen: een bijdrage aan natuurontwikkeling.* Utrecht / Nijmegen / Berlicum

Green Heart? Green Metropolis!

PAGE 101

Bijhouwer, J.T.P.; J. Vallen & J.W. Zaaijer (1961): *Hollands Groene Zone; meer ruimte voor de openluchtrecreatie van een miljoenen- bevolking - nadere uitwerking van het ANWB denkbeeld 1960.* Koninklijke Nederlandsche Toeristenbond ANWB

PAGE 103

Becker, S. (1994): *Selbstorganisation Urbaner Strukturen.* (ARCH+, no. 121)

PAGE 106

Helmer, W.; W. Overmars; G. Litjens (1990): R*ivierenpark Gelderse Poort.* Laag Keppel: Stroming, bureau voor natuur- en landschapsontwikkeling b.v.

PAGE 106

H+N+S (1995): *Groen Hart? Groene Metropool! Recreatie en Natuur in de Randstad van morgen.* The Hague / Zeist: ANWB / WNF

PAGE 107

H+N+S/de Nijl Architecten (1995): *Overholland!* Entry for the Eo Wijers competition, Utrecht/Delft

Blue surprise

PAGE 110

H+N+S

PAGE 113

H+N+S

PAGE 115

H+N+S

Suburbia

PAGE 117

Sweeting, A.W. (1996): *Reading houses and building books; Andrew Jackson Downing and the architecture of popular antebellum literate,* 1835-1855. Hanover: University Press of New England

PAGE 119

Pieter de Hoogh (1658): *The Country House.* Amsterdam: Rijksmuseum

PAGE 120

(1996): *Various articles and advertisements* (Kavel & Huis)

PAGE 123

Sijmons, D. F.; Y. Feddes & L. Tummers (1996): *Wonen in de natuur.* (Noorder- breedte no. 6a: Stadslandschap)

PAGE 126

H+N+S

Plans

PAGE 128, 129

H+N+S (1996): *Breda; Zaartpark, Molenleij, Turfvaart. 3 Projecten aan de zuidelijke rondweg van Breda.* Utrecht

PAGE 130, 131

H+N+S (1997): *Het zwerfnetwerk; recreatie- en mobiliteitsplan WCL De Graafschap.* Province of Gelderland

PAGE 132, 133

background photo: Ton Broekhuis H+N+S (1996): *Wonen & De Wolden* limited competition for Keunig-congres

PAGE 134, 135

model: Joke Witkamp, photo: Martin Kerkhof. Sjoerd Soeters Architecten / H+N+S Landschapsarchitecten / Grontmij Noord-Brabant (1996): *Ontwerp structuurvisie Haverleij.* Amsterdam / Utrecht / Eindhoven

PAGE 136, 137

H+N+S (1996): *Container terminal for Alphen aan den Rijn. Schetsontwerpen voor de landschappelijke verankering.* Utrecht

PAGE 138, 139

DHV Milieu & Infrastructuur / H+N+S (1995): *Verbetering Waalbandijk Afferden-Dreumel;* Startnotitie. Amersfoort / Utrecht

PAGE 140, 141

H+N+S / Tauw Mabeg (1997): *Waterland Neeltje Jans,* unpublished, commissioned by Waterland Neeltje Jans and RWS directie Zeeland

PAGE 142, 143

H+N+S / Stichting voor Toegepaste Landschapsecologie / Buro van den Boogert (1991): *Ontgrondingen: een bijdrage aan natuurontwikkeling.* Utrecht / Nijmegen / Berlicum

PAGE 144, 145

H+N+S

Rotterdam: holiday zone

PAGE 146

Gleason, D.K (1990): *Over Miami.* Louisiana State University Press

PAGE 149

Photo: Martin Parr / Magnum / ABC (1998): *The Myazaki indoor beach*

PAGE 150

Collage: Richard Hamilton (1956) Just *What Is It That Makes Today's Homes So Different, So Appealing?* In: Lippard, L. R. (1966): Pop Art. Fleng! Wham! een boos kunstkindje slaat terug. The Hague: Uitgeverij W. Gaade

PAGE 151

Severy, M. (ed.) 1976): *Grote godsdiensten.* National Geographic Society and De Haan

PAGE 152, 153

H+N+S.

PAGE 154

Computer image: Controle Image.Design: H+N+S / Tauw Mabeg (1997): *Waterland Neeltje Jans.* Unpublished, commissioned by Waterland Neeltje Jans and RWS directie Zeeland

Designing with landscape antecedents

PAGE 156

Vroom, M. J. (1992): *Buitenruimten.* Bussum: UitgeverijThoth

PAGE 159

Nederlands Bosbouwtijdschrift (volume 57) Koninklijke Nederlandse Bosbouwvereniging. Bijhouwer, J.T.P. (1942): Nederlandse tuinen en buitenplaatsen. Amsterdam: Allert de Lange

Brabant: a possible continuation

PAGE 164

Bouwens, B. et al. (1997): *Lijnen door het Brabantse Land; 200 jaar verkeersinfrastructuur in Noord-Brabant 1796-1996.* Zwolle: Waanders Uitgevers

PAGE 165

Photo: H. Venema

PAGE 169

Hertog Jan Bier

PAGE 173

H+N+S

PAGE 175

drawing: Eldorica (detail) by Jurriaan Andriessen. In: Reijnders, L.; R. Beckers; L. Jansen; H. Tieleman (1994): *De Groene Doorbraak.* Amsterdam: Wetenschappelijk bureau Groen Links

PAGE 179

photo: Martin Kerkhof. Sjoerd Soeters Architecten / H+N+S Landschapsarchitecten / Grontmij Noord-Brabant (1996): *Ontwerp structuurvisie Haverleij.* Amsterdam / Utrecht / Eindhoven

PAGE 180

Emmen: Topografische Dienst

Netherlands: a kunstwerk again!

PAGE 182

Anonymus, 1961: Borduurwerkje Nederland. Foto: Jan Wychers (Het Moderne Sprookjes-theater)

PAGE 184

vestibule lamp, designed by Rody Graumans, *ITEMS*

PAGE 185

A50 turn-off Wolvega/Steenwijk, designed by RWS. Photo: H+N+S

PAGE 186

farm road in Noord-Oostpolder, designed by SBB/RIJP, photo: H+N+S

PAGE 187

polder road in Zuidelijk Flevoland, photo: H+N+S

PAGE 188

Schaakspel Rotterdam, municipal library, photo: Bas Czerwinski (NRC)

PAGE 189

Cycle path in Zeewolde, designed by RIJP/TKA. Photo: H+N+S

PAGE 190

Keizersgracht, Amsterdam. photo: H+N+S

PAGE 190

Inner area, Prinsengracht-Kerkstraat. photo: H+N+S

PAGE 192

Tunnel for toads, Bloemendaal, designed by Natuurmonumenten. photo: H+N+S

PAGE 193

H+N+S

PAGE 194

Recreational route, Veluwe, designed by SBB. photo: Rijksdienst Nationaal Plan

PAGE 194

Spaarnwoude, designed by dRO Amsterdam
photo: H+N+S

PAGE 194

Picnic in the Flevopark. photo: H+N+S

PAGE 196

H+N+S

PAGE 196

H+N+S

PAGE 196

H+N+S

PAGE 197

H+N+S

PAGE 197

H+N+S

PAGE 198

H+N+S

PAGE 200

Horsterwold Flevoland, designed by Jaap Nip. photo H+N+S

PAGE 200

Postage stamps, designed by Ger Dekkers, 1981

PAGE 202

Nieuw Burgerlijk Wetboek 1992, designed by Walter Nikkels. *ITEMS*

PAGE 204

design by Taeke de Jong drawing: H+N+S

PAGE 206
Model home, Slotermeer, photo: Jan Versnel, in: d'Oliviera, M. (1990): *Alles op zijn plaats; Het moderne interieur in de fotografie. 1935-1965.* Haarlem: Stichting voor Fotografische Projekten en Kunst / Joh. Enschede en Zn

PAGE 208
Flyer for Zomerzwerfkaart

PAGE 209
H+N+S

PAGE 211
Roof garden, photo: Dick Schuiling. 1994 Mulder, W.; D. Schuiling: *De vijfde gevel; de aantasting van het stedelijk daklandschap.* Amsterdam: Amsterdamse raad voor de Monumentenzorg

Every effort has been made to contact the photographic copyright holders. Any we have been unable to reach or to whom inadequate acknowledgement has been made are invited to contact H+N+S, Utrecht.

LIST OF PROJECTS

The following projects (H+N+S, or otherwise) are mentioned or illustrated in this book:

1991:
Ontgrondingen: een bijdrage aan natuurontwikkeling.
Commissioned by: Provincie Noord-Brabant, afdeling Ontgrondingen.
In association with: Stichting voor Toegepaste Landschapsecologie / Buro van den Boogert, Nijmegen / Berlicum.

1991:
Raamplan Beerze-Reusel, een gebiedsgerichte benadering.
Commissioned by: Provincie Noord-Brabant, 's-Hertogenbosch.
In association with: DHV Water, Amersfoort.

1991:
Zijpe, een nieuw productielandschap.
Commissioned by: Provincie Noord-Holland.

1992:
Duurzame tuinbouw in Over-Betuwe; Voorbeeldplan vierde nota ruimtelijke ordening.
Commissioned by: Landbouwschap (Gewestelijke Raad voor Gelderland), Arnhem.

1992:
Voorbeeldplan Vechtplassengebied. Een bondgenootschap tussen drinkwaterwinning, natuur en recreatie.
Commissioned by: Zuiveringschap Amstel- en Gooiland, Hilversum.

1992:
Zaartpark-waterpark.
Commissioned by: gemeente Breda.

1994:
- *Handreiking; Inventarisatie en waardering LNC-aspecten. Een methode voor beschrijving en betekenistoekenning van de LNC-aspecten in de planvorming van de dijkversterking.*
- *Handreiking; Ruimtelijk ontwerpen. Dijkversterking als ontwerpopgave.*
- *Handreiking; Visie-ontwikkeling. Keuzen en afbakening van het werkterrein van de dijkversterking.*
Commissioned by: Technische Adviescommissie voor de Waterkeringen, Projectgroep D10, Delft.

1994:
Het cultuurlandschap; Een terreinverkenning over landschapsarchitectuur en cultuurbeleid.
Commissioned by: Ministerie van WVC Directie Kunsten, Den Haag.

1994:
Werklandschappen; Ontwikkelingsmogelijkheden van groene bedrijventerreinen in de regio Rotterdam.
Commissioned by: Ontwikkelingsbedrijf Rotterdam.
In samenwerking: met Heidemij Advies.

1995:
Groen Hart? Groene Metropool! Recreatie en Natuur in de Randstad van morgen. Den Haag.
Commissioned by: ANWB / WNF, Den Haag / Zeist.

1995:
Markering Molenleij.
Commissioned by: gemeente Breda.

1995:
Over scherven en geluk; een rapport over de versnippering van de natuur in Nederland.
Commissioned by: Ministerie van LNV.

1995:
Verbetering Waalbandijk Afferden-Dreumel. Startnotitie.
Commissioned by: Polderdistrict Groot Maas en Waal, Druten.
In association with: DHV Milieu & Infrastructuur, Amersfoort.

1995:
Waalvertier. Een studie naar de mogelijkheden voor recreatief medegebruik op en langs de Waal.
Commissioned by: Rijkswaterstaat, Directie Oost-Nederland.

1996:
Containerterminal Alphen aan den Rijn. Schetsontwerpen voor de landschappelijke verankering.
Commissioned by: GOederen VErvoer RAndstad (GOVERA).

1996:
De kleur van water; Toekomstvisie 'Groen-Blauwe Slinger'.
Commissioned by: Provincie Zuid-Holland, Den Haag.
In association with: IWACO.

1996:
Grootschalige windenergie. Beleidsmatige en ruimtelijke mogelijkheden.
Commissioned by: Novem, Nederlandse Onderneming voor Energie en Milieu.
In association with: Haskoning / Adviesbureau E-Connection.

1996:
Knooppunt Turfvaart.
Commissioned by: gemeente Breda.

1996:
Nederland als Kunstwerk! Een scenario.
Commissioned by: Rijksplanologische Dienst, Den Haag.
With contributions by: Ole Bouman, Noël van Dooren, Eric Luiten, Wietze Patijn, Arnold Reijndorp, Paul Scheffer & Ed Taverne.

1996:
Ontwerp structuurvisie Haverleij.
Commissioned by: Gemeente 's Hertogenbosch, Heymans Projectontwikkeling en Bouwfonds Woningbouw b.v.
In association with: Sjoerd Soeters. Architecten / Grontmij Noord-Brabant, Amsterdam / Eindhoven.

1996:
Windpolder.
Provincie Friesland, Leeuwarden.

1996:
Ontwerp voor IJburg, nota van uitgangspunten.
Commissioned by: Gemeente Amsterdam.
met: Frits Palmboom, Jaap van den Bout en Klaas van der Lee.

1996:
Zelfportret van het kunstwerk, een kartografisch betoog. Verkenning naar de mogelijkheden van een kwaliteitskaart van Nederland.
Commissioned by: Rijksplanologische Dienst, Utrecht / Arnhem.

1997:
Inrichting terrein Waterland op de Neeltje Jans.
Commissioned by: WNJ en RWS, directie Zeeland.

Projects

1997:

Het zwerfnetwerk, recreatie- en mobiliteitsplan WCL De Graafschap.
Commissioned by: provincie Gelderland.

1997:

Ontwikkelingsplan Wijkermeerpolder e.o.
Commissioned by: Werkgroep Wijkermeerpolder.
In association with: Resource Analysis en Oranjewoud

1998:

Vier toekomstscenario's voor het IJsselmeergebied, Noordzeekanaal en Amsterdam-Rijnkanaal. Achtergronddocument ten behoeve van project Instrumentarium waterhuishouding in het Natte Hart (in bewerking).
Commissioned by: RWS RIZA, Lelystad
In association with: Rik Herngreen.

1999

Blue surprise, the future of the Hoeksche Waard, commissioned by the Foundation Architecture International Rotterdam (AIR) with contributions of: ATO, Wageningen and was first published in: Annemie de Volder: *De Hoeksche Waard. New Landscape Frontiers.* Toth Publishers, 2000.

2000

Waterrijk Deltametropool, commissioned by the Deltametropool Foundation.

These plans form a selection of the production of H+N+S Landscape Architects in the period 1991-2000.

The following landscape architects are working or were working (*) at H+N+S:

Paul van Beek(*), Patrick McCabe(*), Katja van Dalen, Nikol Dietz, Noël van Dooren(*), Yttje Feddes, Laetitia van Horn(*), Dick Hamhuis(*), Angela Hinz, JanDirk Hoekstra, Harma Horlings, Frank de Josselin de Jong, Wiebe Oosterhof(*), Lotte Paans(*), Ruut van Paridon, Liesbeth Rijnja, Jutta Raith, Paul Roncken(*), Renée Santema(*), Pieter Schengenga, Dirk Sijmons, Joof Tummers(*), Livina Tummers(*).

COLOPHON

=LANDSCAPE offers a selection of plans, lectures, essays and articles of the production of H+N+S Landscape Architects. =*Landscape* is a revised version of = *Landschap* published in 1998

Editor:
Dirk Sijmons
In collaboration with:
Hans Venema
Foreword:
Eelco Hooftman
Contributors:
Noël van Dooren, Yttje Feddes, Dick Hamhuis, Eric Luiten, Lodewijk van Nieuwenhuijze, Berdie Olthof, Dirk Sijmons & Hans Venema.
Translation:
Gregory Ball, except 'An Amsterdam Delicacy' translated by Jane Zuyl-Moores and 'Blue Surprise translated by Ulrica Vrijman.
Illustration editing by:
Harma Horlings and Liesbeth Rijnja
Graphic Design:
Thijs van Delden (†)
Printed in the Netherlands:
Drukkerij Mart.Spruijt bv
© 2002 H+N+S Landscape Architects, The Netherlands

ISBN 90 76863 02 4

Architectura & Natura Press
Leliegracht 22, 1015 DG Amsterdam
The Netherlands
Distributed outside the Netherlands by
Idea Books
Nieuwe Herengracht 11, 1011 RK Amsterdam
The Netherlands

This publication was made possible, in part, by the Netherlands Architecture Fund

Landscape is one of the few Dutch words that has found its way into other languages. We find it so natural that the topography of our country has been shaped by its inhabitants that we tend to forget it. Once they are outside the built-up area, many people seem to think they are in a purely natural zone. What is more serious is the fact that the debate on the future of the Dutch man-made landscape often goes no further than stock pronouncements on the conservation of our valuable heritage. We hear little or nothing about the transformations our present landscape is undergoing. We seem to have lost faith in our own abilities. But even today, if you look closely at your surroundings, you will find that attractive, living man-made landscapes are still being created. New assignments ranging from drinking water extraction to cultivation under glass, from suburbanisation to wind turbines, provide points on the programme for the design of the landscape of the 21st century. The plans in this book offer a foretaste of this. In this publication, **H+N+S** Landscape Architects intends to call attention to the cultural policy task of regaining the pleasure of creating our landscape: the Netherlands as a work of art once again!